Contents

Speaking of Jane Roberts

Remembering the Author of the Seth Material

Susan M. Watkins

Moment Point Press
Portsmouth, New Hampshire

For information please address Moment Point Press, Inc.

Moment Point Press, Inc
P.O. Box 4549
Portsmouth, NH 03802-4549
www.momentpoint.com

Cover design by Metaglyph
Typeset in Goudy
MG

Portions of "The Flood, and What Washed Up There" originally appeared in the *Observer*, Dundee, New York.

The Strange Case of the Chestnut Beads appeared in somewhat different form as "Where Did Sue Watkins Really Come From?" in *Reality Change* magazine.

Library of Congress Cataloging-in-Publication Data

Watkins, Susan M., 1945–
Speaking of Jane Roberts : remembering the author of the Seth material/Susan M. Watkins.
p.cm.
Includes bibliographical references and index.
ISBN 0-9661327-7-7 (alk. paper)
1. Roberts, Jane, 1929–84 2. Psychics—New York—Biography
I. Title

BF1027. R62 W37 2001
133. 9'1'092—dc21
[B] 00-061283
Printed in the United States of America

10 9 8 7 6 5 4 3 2 1

In Memory of Tim Hilts

Also by Susan M. Watkins

Conversations with Seth

Dreaming Myself, Dreaming a Town

Garden Madness

Acknowledgments

Though writers ultimately fashion their work in isolation, they are never really alone. Mary Dillman works tirelessly in the Jane Roberts archives at Yale University in New Haven, Connecticut, and on my behalf researched and copied lengthy batches of material, which Robert F. Butts very kindly gave me permission to use as I wished.

I am grateful to everyone who sent me dreams and memories of Jane Roberts. Your candid responses let me know that my own recollections might have value in the world at large.

Susan Thornton and Barbara Coultry have commiserated with me about the writing process for many years. They have never failed to supply me with empathy and approval, and for this I am in their debt. Editor Susan Ray plied her considerable organizational skills to a manuscript that originally meandered all over the place, as memories will. And my cousin Mike Young has always helped me see with wiser eyes through many a glass darkly.

Death is Following

Death is following.
I hear his step upon the stair.
And birth is waiting,
And behind this death and birth
A million doors
Which will open and close,
Through which my image must pass.

There is always one following,
And one waiting, and none forgotten.
For the end shall overshadow the beginning,
And the shadow of the rock is the rock.
This moment is Forever, poised upon our dream.
I am born a million years and know no tomb.

Jane Roberts
November 17, 1954

INTRODUCTION

Memories, Memoirs And Something in the Middle

Memories are unruly creatures, and memoirs tend to be their bastard offspring. You decide to write about the past and suddenly all those scenes you thought were waiting there, inviolate, scatter at your touch into a thousand images that blend and merge into associations you never would have noticed or had to face at all, if not for this demented attempt to make them conform into some sort of narrative accounting.

You might even have imagined when you began this endeavor that it would be an easy task because both you and the object of your retrospection were inveterate journal-keepers, but you would be wrong. You soon discover that what journals provide is not proof of your memories but another set of memories—trespassers skittering in from other rooms entirely, complicating every scene, every conversation in your head with endless variations until what you end up with is a gelatinous hybrid whose form, you realize with some despair, will never stop recombining, even after your story is done and you have long since left it behind.

The idea for this memoir came to me in a clear, golden moment in 1994 while I was sitting at my desk reading a beat-up old copy of Jacques Vallee's *Dimensions: A Casebook of Alien Contact.*[1] The book is a collection of remarkable, sometimes frightening experiences recounted throughout history and compiled by Vallee as anecdotal evidence for encounters with UFOs or aliens. I'm not especially drawn to abduction literature, as it's come to be known, but I'd spotted the book in a garage sale not ten minutes after telling my rummage trail partner about seeing a UFO, in 1960, when I was fifteen, in the daylight skies over Webbs Mills, New York, the tiny hamlet south of Elmira where I'd grown up. And there was the book at our very next stop, exactly the kind of coincidence that Jane Roberts and I, and her ESP class,[2] had so loved dissecting; for that, and a dime, who could resist?

What struck me more than the book's UFO stories, however, was the common thread weaving among them of breathtaking alterations in consciousness associated with the experiences—sensations of leaving the body, of flying through the air or being "carried along by the wind," and receiving "startling and novel insights into the nature of reality" that reverberated thereafter with profound, life-changing effects. I identified with these descriptions for a lot of reasons, including my own vivid flying dreams and other odd adventures, but more than that, they reminded me strongly of Jane's description of her initial "psychic" experience in 1963 that resulted in *The Physical Universe As Idea Construction* . . . that sensation of flying through space while an avalanche of "radical new ideas" about the nature of reality burst into her head, seemingly out of nowhere . . .

> . . . as if the physical world were really tissue-paper thin, hiding infinite dimensions of reality, and I was suddenly flung through the tissue paper with a huge ripping sound . . . My body sat at the table, my hands furiously scribbling down the words and ideas that flashed through my head. Yet I seemed to be somewhere else, at the same time, traveling through things . . . I felt as if knowledge was being implanted in the very cells of my body so I couldn't forget it—a gut knowing, a biological spirituality . . .

I'd read these paragraphs (excerpted in *The Seth Material*[3]) a dozen times or more (they are among the most beautiful of Jane's writing) and they'd never failed to thrill me—a small vicarious hint of what her original experience had felt like, possibly. And on that fall day as I sat there reading Vallee's book, Jane's words kept coming back to me, like a background narration of the evocative similarities between her experiences and those of Vallee's subjects—and the profound differences in how those experiences had been interpreted.

I thought to myself: How graced Jane was, in her genius, therefore. Graced in the way she used the combined force of her intellect and intuitions to discover new definitions for extraordinary experience. How graced and remarkable, how courageous and stubborn—for in an odd quirk of culture, abduction by aliens is more acceptable (and in a way easier to explain) than forging, through the matrix of a trance personality, an utterly original complex of ideas in which each of us, out of our beliefs and intent, literally constructs the reality we know.

Too bad, I thought, that readers of the Seth books didn't know more about Jane the person, in that regard—for however you might categorize the Seth personality, it was Jane whose abilities gave it voice.

At this point, with no particular urgency, I felt an impulse to read the *Idea Construction* passages again, see what other details might compare. I got up from my desk and went over to the shelf where I keep Jane's books and reached for my old copy of *The Seth Material* that Jane had autographed so long ago.

I put my hand on the book's brittle spine.

Immediately, as if in reaction to my touch, a bright yellow . . . *orb* ballooned up out of the space directly above the book's position on the shelf. In sheer milliseconds, less than the time it took me to register what I was seeing, it expanded like a burnished soap bubble in the air in front of my face, glowing brighter and brighter until suddenly, abruptly . . . it vanished. For the briefest moment, the space where it had been seemed to quiver with a life of its own. Then it was gone.

I looked around, blinking. What was *that*? I still held Vallee's book in my hand.

A yellow-colored orb appearing out of the top of Jane's book, eh? Just as I was reading about—thinking about—strange orbs in the sky? About Jane's *Idea Construction* experience? About the UFO I'd seen years before?

"It has a connection," Seth had told me in class about that object, "with an event in what you think of as your future, and some of your future comprehension had to do with the way in which you perceived that particular event in your past . . . In a way, it was a sign sent from a future self into the past."

Hmmm, I mused, how interesting I should think of that just now—though it applies, sort of . . . And then the obvious burst out of the invisible world and smacked me (as it so often does) on the head: Why not write a memoir of Jane Roberts?[4]

What an idea, I thought—what a terrific idea! Yes, it certainly was. And I was appalled.

Dear friend or not, great book idea or not, a Jane memoir carried with it uncomfortable feelings from *Conversations with Seth* days that creatively I'd doomed myself forever to hang on the coattails of someone else's work, an edge that had existed to some extent between Jane and me while she was alive. On the other hand I felt a duty, albeit an impassioned one, to impart, or preserve, something of the complex person that she had been, and to lock horns on her behalf with the odious perception of her as a passive "channel," and thus not only stand up for Jane, but for the rumply and difficult blend of characteristics that comprise us all. Furthermore, I'd always wanted to explore the concept of counterparts as it theoretically applies to Jane and me, and thus demonstrate something of its practicable mechanics. Between us, it seemed to me, lay a rich vein ripe for mining about the nature of personality and the nuances of individual purpose in coming into this world to begin with.

Originally presented in *The "Unknown" Reality*,[5] the counterpart idea holds that each of us is neurologically and psychically connected to others who are living in roughly the same given time period and exploring related areas of interest or life-themes; counterparts spring, as it were, from the same entity, or source-self, thus gaining experience from many simultaneous viewpoints. Among many other intriguing examples of this type of relationship suggested at the time were Jane and Rob (unsurprisingly), and Jane and me. This made instant sense to both of us when it first came up in 1974, but she and I talked about it in personal terms only one or two times—it was an oddly awkward subject between us, partly because we were a little embarrassed by it, in the way we were somewhat embarrassed by the notion of reincarnation: just a bit too pat, too New-Agey, to be studied with serious exploratory intent. And for me to dwell on it too much always seemed like self-aggrandizement, something on the order of claiming an insider position with Jane that simply didn't exist. Yet a working example of counterparts could provide a key to discoveries about the psyche in general, as Jane's *Oversoul Seven* novels demonstrate in fictional form.

Well, nothing like going for broke, as they say. Problem was, I started out thinking I could do all this simply by arranging memories from fans and friends into a literary pastiche that would do the job for me. I wasn't sure my memories of her were good enough—maybe not even trustworthy enough. By 1994, Jane had been dead for ten years, and memories warp and woof with every moment that passes, or so I told myself. The fact is, I was afraid of my own recollections. Maybe they were a bit *too* trustworthy.

Others, as I suspected, were not as intimidated. With minimal effort and a few advertisements, I collected stacks of material in just a few months, including funny moments, odd conversations, advice she'd given that had meant everything to the recipients, pages and pages of dreams about her both before and after her death in 1984, transcriptions of tape-recorded comments and interviews, on and on and on—even an entire journal kept by mutual friend Debbie Harris, who'd moved to Elmira in 1980 specifically to meet Jane and visited her almost daily in the last months Jane spent in the hospital. Ultimately, the "Jane material" filled two large tomato boxes and several thick file folders.[6] Oh boy, I thought, this will be a cinch.

But it wasn't. Far from it. As I read through the pages of anecdotes, I began to suspect that something was radically wrong with this strategy. It took me a while to admit to myself what it was, but there was no escaping it: By themselves, the pieces were terrific—funny, moving, insightful, exactly what I'd hoped to gather—but taken all together, what I had before me was The Book of Saint Jane, with pink frosting on top. With a few exceptions, everyone loved her dearly, dreamed of her epically, and rhapsodized about her in words of such fantastic goodness and light that even her hell-raisin' irreverence went curiously flat. I'd loved Jane too, and some of my own dreams about her have been pretty epic, and without question she was a good and compassionate person, but left as is, the sum of these memories added up to a sugary fanzine that would have gagged Jane herself (and no doubt many of her readers).

So I reluctantly acknowledged that I'd have to open up my own memory banks and make some sort of balance here—or earthiness, anyway; something. The realization caused me considerable distress, not the least of which was the fear of saying something I shouldn't, of hurting the feelings of her husband, Rob Butts, of inadvertently creating a perceived smoking gun where none existed—after all, I would certainly hate to have anyone use the spontaneous remarks and moods of *my* life as an excuse to attach significances I hadn't intended. Moreover, I knew that I'd have to reveal some humiliating details about myself and talk about less than flattering moments in all our lives. My memories of Jane are mixed and difficult, much like the memories of a mother and daughter who could never quite come to terms with who they were, either to one another or to themselves. And like the memories of a parent long gone, they can, if one is not careful, blend too well with the need for approval or last-word getting by the living.

Still, as Gore Vidal observes in his own memoirs, "Even an idling memory is apt to get right what matters most." And all of it mattered; every word, every moment in that matrix of time and place, as it always does and as we never quite understand until it has moved irrevocably beyond us and can be visited no more except in memory, and dreams.

All in all, therefore, writing this memoir has been an unquiet reflection. My recollections are the innocent voice of my past as they speak through the present; yet the present cannot help but alter my perceptions and create focuses that did not exist. I must, therefore, be careful and wise, and yet remain naive. Wanting more from Jane than I was able to have back then for whatever reasons, I must acknowledge the more difficult aspects between us as well as the joys, which were many, and imagine that Jane would appreciate the ironies in the fact that I'm the one reading through her papers now and striving, with all our many memories put together, not to count coup upon the quick or the dead.

1

Nobody Ever Asks Me This

It's a gorgeous fall day in October, 1994. I'm sitting with my friend Debbie Harris at a sidewalk café in the village of Watkins Glen, New York, drinking cappuccino. The air is bright and crisp, a chilly breeze coming off Seneca Lake a few blocks away. Groups of late-season tourists are walking around the downtown streets. Ironically, as it turns out, the idea of putting together a memoir of Jane Roberts, using the collected memories and dreams of others, has just come to me that morning. In fact I'm so full of the idea I feel as though I'm about to explode. Already I've talked Debbie into contributing her journal notes from the weeks she visited Jane in the hospital. This will be a snap, I think to myself. Easy as pie.

At that exact moment, as if on cue, a woman steps out of a passing trio and comes over to our table. She's maybe in her late thirties, pretty, slender, dark blonde hair, and she's staring directly at me with a wide-eyed, eager expression.

Somewhere in my head, an alarm bell switches to "on."

She asks me if I'm Sue Watkins. If she mentions her own name, I don't remember it. As soon as I reluctantly admit to being the personage in question, she leans over and whispers, "Do you know Abraham?"

I think . . . Abraham? Abraham . . .

—Lincoln?

—the Old Testament guy?

—her dog's name and it's missing?

—a town bigwig?

—a rock-and-roll tune?

None of this makes any sense. So I take the bait and ask, who's Abraham? And now her voice turns heavy with significance.

"Abraham is the name of a group of entities who speak through some people over near Ithaca," she tells me. "And what we'd all really like to know is, where has Seth gone now that Jane is dead?"

Silently, I think . . . Oh, crap. Memoir, schmemoir. For-get it.

Looking back on this incident, I realize that the woman's question was innocent enough . . . I suppose. But sitting at the café table that afternoon, my three dollar cappuccino not to mention my new book idea going cold, I wasn't so generous with my response.

I say to her—somewhat nastily, I'm afraid—"You know, nobody ever asks me where the hell *Jane's* gone now that Jane is dead." And the woman just stares at me, so I add, with sudden sarcastic inspiration, "Where did Picasso's paintings go after he died? Ever think of that?"

She steps back a pace, glances toward her friends, who are window-shopping up the street. I lean across the table, half rising from my chair. "I'm serious," I say, almost snarling. "That question was serious. Where do you think Picasso's paintings went when he died? Huh? Where?"

With that, something in the woman's demeanor closes down; her face turns to slate, and immediately, I'm a bit ashamed of myself . . . just a bit. "I wasn't aware that he had any unfinished ones," she says. Her voice is as cool as the Seneca Lake shore breeze.

"What I'm getting at is that Seth was a masterwork of art—Jane's art," I say. "*She* made the artwork possible."

"But Seth has to be somewhere!" the woman insists. "He should be speaking through someone else by now!"

"Oh, come on," I snort, disgusted anew. "Jane wasn't just a piece of meat that Seth animated for his own nefarious purposes! If that were the case, why not just use a piece of meat—less irksome! No arguing! Doesn't require sleep!"

"Well, these entities will tell us where Seth is," she informs me in a snide tone, one plenty equal to my own snide tone. With obvious disappointment—Sue Watkins has turned out to be a close-minded shithead—she turns away and joins her friends and all walk on up the block without looking back.

"That was quite a scene," Debbie says, also not looking at me.

"Was I too nasty?"

Debbie hesitates, decides to tell a fib. "No, I don't think so," she says. "No, you weren't bad at all. Not really. Nah."

Later, thinking about it, I did feel guilty for my tone (though not for my words). The woman was only looking to find her own way, as everyone must. And really, how odd, that during the entire disaster of a conversation, an image kept coming to me of Jane's physical position as it often was in ESP class: sitting in a chair, holding a glass of wine and (more often) a cigarette, being pressed by earnest people filled with the possibility of Seth's appearance and whatever wondrous secrets he might unveil. I ought to know. I'd done the same, often enough.

Part of me was infuriated by the whole café scene. Part of me had enjoyed it. Despite our mutual rancor over the results, on some level that woman and I had sought out the encounter for our own reasons. At least we were . . . well, trying . . . to exchange something original, and ultimately inexplicable, about the nature of the universe. Maybe.[1] Besides, she hadn't come out of nowhere, with no connection to the moment. We'd responded on some level to one another before either of us said a word, and in a way, we'd each voiced the other's worst expectations about the so-called "psychic" arena. A smooth and crafty response from the universe—from the mirror of our selves.

Jane often said, "I speak for the Seth in all of you." She was right.

* * *

I FIRST ENCOUNTERED JANE ROBERTS in December of 1963, though I didn't know it at the time. I was nineteen, a freshman at Syracuse University, already bored with my courses and unsure of an increasingly tenuous world; instead of studying for finals I picked up a Rod Serling science fiction anthology and quickly found myself absorbed in the tale of *The Chestnut Beads*. It was a story I never forgot, and a story that its author—Jane Roberts—and I would later discover contained the prescient seeds of a future connection between us. The first time we actually met was in 1967, at a raucous New Year's Eve party she and Rob threw in their small second-floor apartment in my home town of Elmira, New York. I was there with my gay friend Dan Stimmerman, who'd been pressing me for weeks to come over to Jane's place with him and meet this woman who spoke, as he put it, for the spirit of a dead person. (Initially I'd refused, thinking, "Yeah, right. Yuk.") By then, Jane had been speaking for Seth for almost exactly four years and had published *How to Develop Your ESP Power*, which I didn't even know existed.

Jane and I said nothing of import that evening, though I remember her clearly—she yelled jokes, told hilarious stories, smoked like a factory, drank large quantities of cheap red wine, and kept a clear bead on everybody's remarks, including her own, a feat I found especially impressive.

Small and dark-haired, dressed in black turtleneck and jeans, she reveled in doing and saying exactly what she goddamned felt like in front of this unruly crowd, much to the apparent delight of her dapper-looking artist husband. She tried pulling me into the various conversations, to no avail, which wasn't her fault. I was twenty-two, fat, single, secretly pregnant, miserable. At midnight, Dan kissed me chastely on the lips and made a funny announcement about us being sisters. The next day, I crammed my possessions in my car and left my parents' home for Martha's Vineyard—alone, to a place I'd never been, with no plans, no idea what I was going to do when I got there, knowing only that I had to leave, audaciously banking on my writing skills and my journalism education to somehow see me through.

I wasn't gone all that long. I returned to Elmira in the fall of 1968, my secret intact—not even my parents knew that I'd had a baby and given him up for adoption. To this day I have never fully understood why I left the Vineyard, a magical place where a life had opened for me on the *Gazette*, working for world-renowned editor Henry Beetle Hough. I only knew that I felt a huge, undeniable urgency to get back home, as if there were something of immense importance that I had to do, and this was my last chance to do it.

I took a teaching assistant job at Cornell that I quickly learned to hate, and at Dan's insistence I asked Jane if I could join the ESP class she had been holding for a couple of years. There, and in the Friday night get-togethers at Jane and Rob's apartment, where ideas about the nature of reality would roar like the wind, where Seth would come through and enter the conversations as easily as the ghost of a wise old uncle might step through the kitchen door—there, Jane and I made our uneasy friendship and Rob suggested that I write a book about her ESP class and the fabric of the universe ripped open with a loud and boisterous racket and Jane and Rob and all the others who passed through their living room began debating the idea that each of us, literally, from birth to death and beyond, creates, on purpose, the reality that we know.

The last time I saw Jane Roberts was September 2, 1984, at St. Joseph's Hospital in Elmira. I had only visited her a few times in the last year and a half of her life that she spent there. Everyone around me, it seemed—parents, relatives, friends—was vanishing through the doorways of hospitals in those years. Rob came out of the room when I knocked. Jane had stopped eating, Rob told me, and no intravenous feeding was being given. "You'd better prepare yourself," he said, and I suppose I must have. Jane lay naked and uncovered on her bed, curled up on her side in a fetal position, luminescent skin on bones. She looked as weightless and translucent as an abandoned insect shell caught on tree bark.

I went over and rubbed her head and said hello. "Oh, you don't have to bother touchin' me," Jane said, but I thought that she enjoyed it. She was so thin—all bones and dark eyes. I hadn't known that it was possible to be that thin, and still be alive.

That last day, as the first, we said nothing of great import; our visit was brief. When I got up to leave, I rubbed her head again and said, "Good-bye, Jane." I hadn't meant to say it like that, but the fact of her pending death was right there, simply and plainly before us, hanging unavoidably in the warm hospital air. In a strange way, it was like the first time we'd met, all those years ago, but in reverse: each time, one of us had held another, secret life deep inside us, about to be born.

Still, she roused up into her old feisty self. "Well, hell, Sue, you don't have to say good-bye like *that*," she sputtered.

I didn't dare look at her, then, or Rob either. Half-turned away, the edge of my vision illuminated by the soft glow of her pearly skin, luminous as the light of dreams, I said, "Oh, I just mean I'll see you again, don't worry." And I thought, what am I saying? But I knew what I was saying, and so did Jane. And so there was nothing more to say, and I left. She died three days later, on September 5, taking that journey we all must take, alone, no plans, no idea what we'll find when we get there, banking on whatever beliefs or hope about such things as we may amass in our lifetimes to somehow see us through.

2

A Life of the Mind

Dorothy Jane Roberts was born on May 8, 1929, in Saratoga Springs, New York, the only child of Delmar and Marie Burdo Roberts, into circumstances reminiscent of a Charles Dickens novel. Her parents divorced when she was an infant and soon afterwards her mother became bedridden with rheumatoid arthritis, the same condition to which Jane would eventually succumb. ("I'd never seen her walk," Jane later remembered.) Raised in the Catholic Church, Jane was sent to an orphanage run by nuns while her mother was hospitalized with the disease. Jane lived there for nearly two years. The nuns enforced strict rules of behavior, including a ban on showering nude: the girls were required to soap up and rinse over a cotton "shower slip," forbidden to touch their own bodies even to wash. "Of course," Jane would add in telling this tale, "all of us would sneak a peek down our shirtfronts whenever we could."

Then she was sent home to care for her embittered, invalid mother. They were supported by welfare and assisted by a succession of housekeepers, but the main burden of Marie's care fell on young Jane's shoulders. Thus her early life was one of cooking, cleaning, doing laundry, getting up in the night to put more coal on the stove, bringing her mother the bedpan, and enduring a never-ending stream of appalling psychological abuse. "She blamed her physical situation on the breakup of her marriage," Jane later wrote, "and, I guess, on my birth." In a 1973 interview in the Elmira *Star Gazette*, she states:

> My mother was a strong, domineering woman, probably scared to death of the position she found herself in. She was psychotic, attempting suicide several times and scaring the devil out of me as a kid with threats . . . One day [she] would say that she loved me, and the next day she'd scream that she was sorry I'd ever been born—that I'd ruined her life . . . [She] would often stuff her

> mouth with cotton and hold her breath, pretending that she was dead, to scare me when I was small. Sometimes she'd tell me she really could walk and during the night she was going to get up, turn on the gas jets, and kill us both. I would be absolutely terrified . . .
>
> And yet . . . she encouraged my writing and would tell me that I was a good kid and she didn't know why she acted that way . . . but then she'd do it again.

"Early on," Rob has said about her upbringing, "Jane began a pattern of repressing her impulses by refusing to retaliate against her abusive mother." Nonetheless, in the midst of everything, and from an early age, Jane wrote poetry—"at home, in school, anywhere, everywhere, and at any time," Jane once said. "It was when I was sitting on the back porch writing poetry . . . [that] I used to feel incredibly safe . . . and I also felt that [the neighborhood] was filled with the magic voice of nature. When I wrote poetry, the universe seemed to talk to me. Sometimes I talked back, and on rare occasions we spoke at once." (Her poetry had been considered heretical by the orphanage nuns, who confiscated and burned it.) Even at the age of five, she knew she was going to be a writer. Or, as she'd loftily tell people, "I am one already."

And while her childhood was difficult, her neighborhood was filled with vitality and unique characters. "I had no models for the socially accepted conventional female role, which was certainly a blessing," Jane recalls in *The God of Jane*. "There were women galore and few men in my early background . . . The women I knew *did* things." Moreover, Saratoga was a center of the creative arts, and Jane managed to get inside the circle. "When I was really young," Jane later told an interviewer, "I'd take my poetry to Yaddo, and knock at the back door and ask if there was a poet there who would read my stuff because it was really good. They'd take it but I'd never hear from them . . . One time a staff member gave me a piece of cake and told me to go away." When she was a teenager, a well-known writer of the day, Caroline Slade, took Jane to parties at Yaddo where such notables as Louis Untermeyer and Adrienne Rich were in attendance. "I asked Untermeyer to read some of my poetry—which I had with me, naturally—and he said he was too busy." But Jane was undeterred. From an early age, her work was her central focus. "People would tell me that I would forget all this stuff about poetry and writing when I grew up and got married and had kids," she said. "But I'd tell them they were wrong. Even then, I knew that I didn't want to have children, that I wanted to devote my life to my work—and that for me was the most important thing in the world."[1]

In her senior year in high school, Jane won honorable mention in a poetry contest sponsored by *Scholastic Magazine*, and as a result was awarded a scholarship to Skidmore College in Saratoga. Expelled at the end of her junior year for attending an all-night party at a professor's house ("All I did was sit up drinking wine and reading poetry—at least that's all *I* did"), Jane placed her mother in a nursing home and took off on a motorcycle with her friend Walter Zeh, to visit her father in California. She and Walt returned to Saratoga several months later, married ("We didn't dare show our faces in town otherwise") and Jane took a variety of jobs, including one as Society Editor for the Saratoga newspaper and another as a supervisor in a radio factory.

Then in 1953, while "cutting up, dancing and raisin' hell at a party," she met Robert F. Butts, an artist who was working on the Mike Hammer comic strip with someone Jane knew and had shown up at the party as a lark. Jane was twenty-four and married; Rob was a thirty-four-year-old bachelor.

"I took one look at him and that was it," Jane told me years later. "Not long after that—I mean, we hadn't even kissed or touched or anything—I told him, 'I'm leaving town and I'm leaving either with you or without you, so make up your mind.' And Robbie felt the same, and he did the honorable thing, you know, and talked with Walt, and told him that we were leaving, and you know, Walt was relieved . . . he never said a thing." Jane's first marriage had been entirely platonic—she was a virgin when she met Rob, she would admit much later in an ESP class "secrets" session. She and Rob drove to Marathon, Florida, to file for Jane's divorce, and were married on December 27, 1954.

"We were deeply in love," Jane said. "But besides that, we both knew we wanted to devote our whole lives to our work—he to painting and me to writing—no matter where it led or whether or not we were successful."

In a remarkable correspondence between Rob and Walt Zeh after Jane's death in 1984, Walt provides, in a gracious, thoughtful style very much like Rob's own, some fascinating details of Jane's early life and their relationship. Walt, who had also lived as a child in a Saratoga orphanage, met Jane in 1947 at a picnic. "Of a sudden, as it were, I was being introduced to a beautiful woman with the bluest eyes and blackest hair that I had ever seen," Walt remembers:

> She seemed to be possessed of an inner vibrancy and soon we were discussing the merits of certain works of literature with which we were both familiar. . . . [I]t was not long before I became a constant visitor to her home, where I was not unwelcome because I was a pianist and able to entertain Marie with music, which she admired.
>
> Marie Burdo Roberts . . . was, by testimony of those who had known her in earlier years, a beautiful, glamorous, and extremely compelling personality. It

was not difficult to see where Jane had gotten her looks and intelligence . . . [Marie] was very articulate, obviously well-read (her bedridden condition gave her lots of time to read) and always very demanding. . . . She was "Queen." Jane usually, while I was there, had to ask me to leave the house when bedpan and bed-making roles were required . . . Directly to the rear of the "bedroom" was the kitchen, where Jane prepared all of her own and her mother's meals. Now, you must recall that she had been doing this for an unknown number of years before I arrived on the scene, so the extent of Jane's activities (and captivities) can be appreciated.

Marie was twenty-six years old when she became afflicted with rheumatoid arthritis, and went to bed for the last time because of it. In the years that followed, she became "comfortable" with the syndrome of dependency, having a young daughter who, from the earliest years of capability, was able to wait on her, give her the bedpan, and look after her other bodily needs. You can imagine what life must have been like for Jane, having physically to look out for her mother's body, cater to her needs for food (they did not have any help when I first went to Jane's home), and later to assist her when Marie, to give her credit, decided to take on a doctor's answering service, which as many crippled people do, she learned to handle with her badly swollen wrists and almost insensate fingers. I can see her picking up those telephones on the bed yet—an amazing study in personal determination—no doubt the basis for Jane's inner drive.

When I became a regular visitor to Jane's home on Middle Avenue, I met a number of young priests from [the] parish where Jane attended mass whom I came to feel were interested more in Jane than in her mother's condition. It may be a bit unfair to them, but I could not shake the feeling that it was Jane's good looks and vivacious personality which attracted them. Some of them had money and were later to bestow gifts upon them, such as a typewriter, a bed, and others, which could have been defined as the outreach of the church to those in need, but which I felt had sexual overtones . . .[2]

In the six years during which Jane and I were together, she never, as far as I could determine, was aware of the impact that good looks and intelligence have on men. All of which brings me to another aspect of Jane's early life in Saratoga Springs, during her high school days and her three years at Skidmore.

She was thought to be "far out," interested in difficult and remote subjects (philosophy, spirituality, etc.) and at the same time disconnected from reality, even by some of her closest friends. What this was, of course, was an inwardness which acted as insulation from a very difficult and demanding childhood, the degree of which is seldom surpassed in the experience of most people. When you are in college, and a monitor comes to the door of the class (she and I were in several of the same classes) and states that Jane Roberts is wanted at home immediately by her mother, what does one do? She had no alternative but to do just that, and as you can imagine, it was to give her mother the bedpan. . . . In short, Jane lived, and breathed, her mother's bedridden existence, and I was witness to nearly three years of it before Jane finally decided at the age of 21, in 1950, that she had had enough, and we rode off together in the fall of that year to Santa Monica and new events. I sensed that Jane's mind was somewhat tortured by the thought that she had left an invalid mother at home. How any young person could go on for years in such a morbid atmosphere, and still keep her sanity, is beyond me. It is no wonder that Jane eventually revolted . . .

As our relationship deepened, there were those of my friends who warned me that, from a psychological point of view, I was taking on a burden with her for which I would ultimately pay a big price. However, I felt I knew what I was doing—I did value her love and friendship; we did have a lot in common (music, poetry, and literature in general), and I resented the inference that I too was becoming a bit unusual in pursuing the relationship. Some of my friends implied that Jane would never shake off the paradox of dependency on her mother and her desire to be free of the dross of her early life. You see . . . [there was] jealousy on the part of those who wished that they had special talents, and envy of the accomplishments of others. Of one thing I am certain—there was a large coterie of people in Saratoga Springs, at Skidmore College, of the faculty at Skidmore, who saw in Jane a manifestation of what they themselves would like to be, but lacked the talent, sensitivity, and perception to make it into reality. For that reason, she was rebuked, reviled, ridiculed, and misunderstood. . . .

When she was tried by the Honor Board of Skidmore College for an alleged breach of "Social Discipline," for spending a night at the home of sculptor Robert Davidson (now deceased) with some resident senior students, she was picked from the group for punishment. Her scholarship was withdrawn, and the other girls, all of them members of wealthy families and seniors, got off "scot-free," a most serious breach of the fairness doctrine, something today which the college could not get away with. The fact was that the college authorities . . . felt she was ungovernable, and removed her as a threat to themselves. Never was there a greater perversion of justice.

Looking at a transcript of Jane's grades from Skidmore for February of 1949, though, it would seem that her interests were not all that academically inclined anyway. "I did well in subjects I liked, poorly in those I disliked" she notes in *The God of Jane*, "and very nearly flunked biology twice. I couldn't, wouldn't, dissect the frog." In that, one can't help being cheered by Jane's mediocre grades, especially the D⁻ she received in Psych 201. Contemplating the Jane I knew sitting in a psych class listening to all that presumptuous theorizing—well, obviously she didn't pay too much attention, or discarded it. A portent of the future?

And as Mr. Reeves, her American Lit professor points out in his evaluation of her (accompanied by a C), Jane did indeed rely heavily upon her critical sense, and maybe too heavily at that (as he suggests), at least where it was directed toward herself.[3]

"[As to] Jane's and my life together as a married couple," Walt writes, "She and I were both seeking and on our long trips together, we traveled separately as spirits. What had begun as both a romance and a sense of the need to escape an unhappy childhood together became an endless odyssey, on the motorcycle and later by car to distant points in the country. The long trip had come to an end, for us, and when you [Rob] stepped into the picture, you did all of us a great service. You freed her, and me, from something which both of us would have come to hate. You freed her talents for development into the reality that became her artistic mode. It has never ceased to impress me, the multifold ways of destiny as it writes upon our conscious life . . ."[4]

After Jane and Rob were married, they lived for a while in Tenafly, New Jersey, commuting to New York City, where Rob found office work in the comic book field while the two of them tried unsuccessfully to peddle some ideas for their own syndicated strip. "In spite of whatever intuitive knowledge our larger selves had when we were married," Rob later wrote of these early years, "we simply had to survive from day to day. We had no [regular] jobs, very little money, no luxurious feelings of security. We had [Jane's] beloved sheltie Mischa, and a beat-up 1947 Cadillac convertible, with a back seat and a trunk big enough to hold much of what we owned, including a few clothes, books and art work and notes, and my drawing table, lamp, and some art supplies." It was during this time that Jane became pregnant but didn't realize it until after she had spontaneously miscarried. Not long after that, a chance meeting—chance in the usual terms—would send Jane and Rob back to Rob's hometown of Sayre, Pennsylvania. "One fine day in New York City," Rob recalls, "I walked into the office of a company that produced labels and advertising designs for clothing. The owners . . . had moved its manufacturing facility to Sayre, and were looking for an artist who was willing to settle in a small town, way up there in the sticks in northern Pennsylvania . . .

"The position offered us an unexpected sense of belonging and security that we badly needed at the start of our marriage. My parents were delighted that I was back home. So was I . . ."[5] And so was Jane, it would seem. In an October 15, 1958 letter to Blanche Price, her French Novel teacher from Skidmore days, Jane wrote:

Rob and I . . . just wonderful. Our apartment, our work, and our love is our life . . . He designs labels in a local plant four hours a day (in the art department), and the other four he paints, writes, or sometimes when we need more cash, does commercial work. Yours truly, with an old bicycle and three baskets, wearing slacks, oodles of sweaters and bright lipstick, sells Avon products three hours a day or so and between us, financially, we manage pretty well.

This includes rent on our three rooms (five rooms now—Rob made me two rooms out of the attic. They are cardboard rooms with cardboard walls but well insulated and covered with paintings), our daily supply of food, cigarettes, magazines, books, etc.

In 1956, Jane emerged into the science-fiction field with the sale of "The Red Wagon," a story about a child's fading awareness of past lives, to *Fantasy and Science Fiction* magazine. In the next few years, she would publish dozens of stories in *F&SF* and the "men's magazines" of the day, as well as three novels—including *The Chestnut Beads* and its sequel, *The Bundu*. "They were more science fantasy; her imagination could take off," Rob says of those stories. "She wasn't too interested in the nuts and bolts idea of spaceships, you know, and aliens and things like that. But she was laying the groundwork for her lifetime's work all the time, intuitively . . . without much conscious understanding of what she was doing. But it was all a great preparation . . . [Her stories] all had that germ or basic idea of the possibilities or potentials of human consciousness. [6]

"I remember being a little surprised at her subject matter for 'The Red Wagon,' Rob noted, "for it's not contradictory to [say] that even though she was so interested in reincarnation as a theory, we seldom talked about it."[7] *The Rebellers*, which like *The Chestnut Beads* and *Bundu* is about social destruction and psychic redemption, was published by Ace in 1963. In it, the main male character ("A hero type that I took right from Robbie") makes this speech:

At one time, the race depended upon quantity for survival. Now it is destroying itself. We believe that man's unique characteristics, imagination, psychic understanding, sympathy, and so forth are being undermined. Even if the race survives physically, it won't be the same race. We won't be bright enough to recognize our fall from grace, either . . .

"At the time, all this was pretty real to me," Jane remarked about her science fiction in a 1977 radio interview for KPFA, Berkeley, California. "I really did think that the world would be destroyed, and I grew up with that idea . . . But I think a lot of science-fiction writers are really psychic as all hell and pick all this stuff up and just write it as fiction. I mean, I'm sure I did . . . The reincarnational thing is in a lot of stories, and . . . you can hide from your own knowledge, put it off in a corner without having to really . . . look at it.[8]

"But [intellectually] . . . I didn't believe that we survived death once, much less over and over again."

On the other hand, "you can't escape dealing with human consciousness," as Rob would observe. They'd moved to Elmira in 1960 so Rob could work part-time in a local greeting card company and Jane at an art gallery. They found a one-bedroom second-floor apartment at 458 West Water Street, with big wraparound bay windows looking out toward the Chemung River, a block away. They were determined to pick up their lives and devotion to their work where they'd left off in Sayre. But the publication of *Rebellers* shattered Jane's enthusiasm for the science-fiction genre. It was an Ace double paperback, cheaply done, combined with another novel in tandem reverse. "When I laid eyes on that, I burst into tears," Jane said later. "All these people were congratulating me, and all I could think of was what a crappy job [the published book] was." In *The Seth Material*, she writes, "The year 1963 . . . [was] a poor one for us . . . Rob had severe back trouble, and hardly felt well enough to paint when he came home from work. I was having difficulties settling on another book idea. Our old pet dog, Mischa, had died. Perhaps these circumstances made me more aware than usual of our human vulnerability . . . Perhaps, all unknowing, I had reached a crisis and my psychic abilities awoke as the result of inner need."

And so it was that on the evening of September 9, 1963, Jane sat down at her table to work on her poetry. Rob was painting in the back room he used as a studio. "It was very domestic, very normal, very unpsychedelic," Jane explains in *The Seth Material*. "I took out my pen and paper and settled down with my ninth or tenth cup of coffee for the day, and my cigarettes. Willie, our cat, dozed on the blue rug . . .

> What happened next was like a "trip" without drugs . . . Between one normal minute and the next, a fantastic avalanche of radical, new ideas burst into my head with tremendous force, as if my skull were some sort of receiving station, turned up to unbearable volume. Not only ideas came pouring through . . . but sensations, intensified and pulsating.
>
> It was as if the physical world were really tissue-paper thin, hiding infinite dimensions of reality, and I was suddenly flung through the tissue paper with a huge ripping sound. My body sat at the table, my hands furiously scribbling

down the words that flashed through my head. Yet I seemed to be somewhere else, at the same time, traveling through things . . . I felt as if knowledge was being implanted in the very cells of my body so that I couldn't forget it—a gut knowing, a biological spirituality.

At the same time I remembered having a dream the night before, which I had forgotten, in which this same sort of experience had occurred. And I knew the two were connected.

When I came to, I found myself scrawling what was obviously meant as the title of that odd batch of notes: *The Physical Universe As Idea Construction*. Later, the Seth material would develop these ideas, but I didn't know that at the time. In one of the early sessions Seth said that this had been his first attempt to contact me. I only know that if I'd begun speaking for Seth that night, I would have been terrified.[9]

As Rob recalled:

I was in the back studio painting, and Jane was in the living room making poetry notes . . . or I thought she was. But it was awfully quiet out there . . . I realized this after a while 'cause she used to play the radio while she worked. So I went out there and she said, "Boy you'll never believe the adventure I just had!"

And she had fifteen or twenty pages of manuscript [lying] on the table in front of her which she had written in this altered state of consciousness, when she didn't even know enough to even call it that . . . So she said to me, "Look at this!" And she said, "My first insight is that when you look at something, you create it." And I said, "What are you talking about?" And I didn't laugh, you know, and it was so unusual to us both . . .

This is back in 1963. You couldn't go down to the store and pick up a bunch of books on ESP, say, or related subjects. There were some technical journals available that you could subscribe to, but we didn't know anything about those. The whole thing was brand new to us. And yet instantly it struck cords with us, see, and what we had been doing all these past years, almost automatically, fell into place.[10]

Shortly after this episode, Jane suddenly began recalling her dreams ("It was like discovering a second life") and recorded two distinctly precognitive dreams, the first she'd ever had. Their curiosity aroused, Jane and Rob managed to find one paperback on ESP in the local supermarket, but it didn't satisfy their questions—or even begin to relate to Jane's *Idea Construction* experience.

So Rob suggested, "Why don't you write a do-it-yourself book on ESP?" (Fifteen years later, Rob would suggest to me, "Why don't you write a book on Jane's ESP class?") Somewhat against her better judgment, Jane wrote up a proposal and chapter headings for such a book and to her amazement, it was accepted by Fred Fell Books of New York. "Rob and I were delighted, but somewhat appalled, too," Jane writes in *The Seth Material*. "We'd never been to a medium. We'd never had a telepathic experience in our lives, never even seen a Ouija board. On the other hand, I thought, what have I got to lose? So we began . . ."[11]

Borrowing a Ouija board that their landlord had stashed away in the attic, they began their experiments. They sat in a fully-lighted room, both of Jane's hands on the pointer, one of Rob's hands free to write down whatever they might get. Much to their surprise and embarrassment, the pointer quickly began spelling out messages, claiming to come from a man named Frank Watts who'd lived in Elmira and died in the 1940s. "I thought it was a riot," Jane wrote, "two adults watching the pointer go scurrying across the board, and we didn't take it too seriously. For one thing, of course, neither of us particularly believed in life after death—certainly not conscious life, capable of communicating. Later on, we did learn that a man with the communicator's name was known to have lived in Elmira, and died in the 1940s—that took me back a bit. But we were much more interested in finding out what made the pointer move than in the messages it gave."[12]

To their continuing surprise and discomfort, the messages began to take on a definite *tone*. Frank Watts began spelling out information about past lives where the three of them had known one another, and giving more and more elaborate replies to Rob's questions . . .

> *(Can you see everything where you are now?)*
> MOST, NOT ALL. IF I SAW ALL I WOULDN'T BE INTERESTED IN COMMUNICATION.
> *(What is your form while you communicate with us?)*
> THOUGHT WAVES, TIME CURRENTS.
> *(What would be your favorite topic or subject of communication with us?)*
> PSYCHIC TRUTHS, DIMENSIONS OF KNOWLEDGE.
> *(Does a person know immediately when he dies?)*
> NOT ALWAYS.
> *(Why not?)*
> TIME TO GET BEARINGS. CONSIOSNESS [*SIC*] CONTINUES. CONFUSING.
> *(How long does it take for a person to realize his death, usually?)*
> GRADUAL REALIZATION, BY STAGES OF WITHDRAWAL AND ARRIVAL.[13]

Even now, reading these first sessions somehow imparts the feeling of the entire, huge body of material that was to follow, as if you are holding in your hand a seed, quivering, ready to burst free. Everything that Seth would later expound upon is right there, in these simple passages; but once let loose, it never again fits inside those first words . . .

Certainly it was all interesting enough to keep Jane and Rob going, but what began to make Jane uncomfortable was her realization that she knew the answers to Rob's questions before the board spelled them out. Not trusting that method, she insisted they keep plugging away with the pointer.

"Then on December 8, 1963, we sat at the board again, wondering [as usual] whether or not it would work," Jane writes, "[and] suddenly the pointer began to move so fast that we could hardly keep up with it . . . Now the answers became longer and their character seemed to change. The atmosphere of the room was somehow different.

> "Do you have a message for us?" Rob asked.
>
> "CONSCIOUSNESS IS LIKE A FLOWER WITH MANY PETALS," replied the pointer.
>
> From the first few messages, Frank [Watts] had insisted upon the validity of reincarnation, so Rob said, "What do you think of your various reincarnations?"
>
> "THEY ARE WHAT I AM, BUT I WILL BE MORE. PUN: THE WHOLE IS THE SUM OF ITS HEARTS."
>
> "Is all of this Jane's subconscious talking?" Rob asked.
>
> "SUBCONSCIOUS IS A CORRIDOR. WHAT DIFFERENCE DOES IT MAKE WHICH DOOR YOU TRAVEL THROUGH?"
>
> "Maybe it's *your* subconscious," I said to Rob, but he was already asking another question.
>
> "Frank [Watts], can we refer back to you on any specific question in the future?"
>
> "YES. I PREFER NOT TO BE CALLED FRANK [WATTS]. THAT PERSONALITY WAS RATHER COLORLESS . . .
>
> "YOU MAY CALL ME WHATEVER YOU CHOOSE. I CALL MYSELF SETH. IT FITS THE ME OF ME, THE PERSONALITY MORE CLEARLY APPROXIMATING THE WHOLE SELF I AM OR AM TRYING TO BE . . ."[14]

By the next session, Jane was hearing the words in her head loud and clear, and the impulse to speak them grew stronger, "and I became more determined to fight it," Jane writes. "Yet I was terribly curious—The pointer began to spell out the answer to Rob's question . . . The pointer paused. I felt as if I were standing, shivering, on the top of a high diving board, trying to make myself jump while all kinds of people were waiting impatiently behind me. Actually it was the words that pushed at me—they seemed to rush through my mind. In some crazy fashion I felt as if they'd back up, piles of nouns and verbs in my head until they closed everything else off if I didn't speak them. And without really knowing how or why, I opened up my mouth and let them out."[15]

And thus, from one moment to the next, Jane's life had changed utterly, and her life's work truly began. From then on, in developing her gifts and following the implications of them and the material she produced, she left behind the comforts of virtually every institution of accepted thought there is: religion; conventional science; the literary world she once yearned to win over; the conventions of her time, especially where women's roles were concerned; and in the end, Jane even—or perhaps especially—eschewed the traditional spiritualist and mediumistic ideas that only served to embarrass her. In her journal, on May 1, 1978, she writes:

> A woman in a letter I received yesterday writes: Surely you've been given the power to contact Seth for more than writing books—and goes on to mention other psychics, Garrett, Ford, etc. who contacted "the dead" for the living. The woman had written before wanting to contact her husband, and I told her to get on with life, and to let her husband carry on in HIS reality.
>
> But I think: this minute anyhow: that I am lonely; except for Rob, my work or Seth's is so often misunderstood; used for ends that to me are unfortunate; as if somehow despite all Seth says or I say—we are just a slightly more exotic species of the psychic master and his holy sister . . .
>
> And to those people how selfish—how incomprehensible are the actions of anyone whose goals are those of art; in whatever form; for they feel scandalized that a person could . . . search for the unknowable, which may or may not have practical benefits or that may not be bent to THEIR ends.
>
> I know I'm exaggerating yet—doing something for itself; for the love of beauty—seems almost incomprehensible [to some] . . . and have I to some extent fallen into that trap?[16]

Out of this determined search for new answers to the new questions she was raising, Jane developed her theory of "aspect psychology," centered on the idea that each of us, the individual "focus self," springs from a multidimensional "source self," with other portions, or aspects (including, of course counterparts), operating simultaneously in various dimensions, each drawing from the experience of the rest.[17] This theory, which nicely answers the "spirit guide" question, and which contains a mountain of speculative possibilities in itself, in fact sprang from *The Education of*

Oversoul Seven, a novel that came to Jane in much the same way as *The Physical Universe As Idea Construction* manuscript.

And yet, even as she produced these innovative concepts of personality and consciousness, she was holding herself back, clamping down hard so as not to go "too far"—a fear, and a response pattern, she'd used from an early age. She was intensely worried about "leading people down the Primrose Path" (her words), of creating false gods, of attracting worship of any kind, even while she recognized the beauty—the wild, untamable, utterly original nature—of her own ideas.

Indeed, the vicissitudes and dilemmas of Jane's personality were as enigmatic as any of the material she produced. She was simultaneously ahead of her time and oddly quaint (she dreamed in 1981 that households of the future would be connected through a network of home computers, but was mildly scandalized by my suggestion that she buy herself an electric typewriter), and to the surprise of those expecting an otherworldly spiritualist, she possessed an unapologetic, earthy humor and raucous love of fun. During any get-together at their apartment, the air would turn blue with cigarette smoke and uninhibited discussions of anything and everything, with some of the best stories those that Jane would gleefully tell on herself, as she does here in a tape-recorded conversation from April of 1977:

> I remember I had a couple stories in TOPPER and GALLERY and I went down to the [Elmira] newsstand to pick 'em up . . . and the man who ran the store didn't want to give me the magazine; he got a bag and he was gonna wrap the magazine in the bag—he was embarrassed that I would ASK for it! And there was a whole bunch of businessmen in there too, and this about 9:30 in the morning—I said to the guy, what are you doing? He said [*whispering*] putting it in the bag! And I said [*yelling*] what are you putting it in the bag for? And he said, Lady, it's not a very nice magazine! And I said [*yelling*], for gods sakes, I WROTE for that magazine, my NAME is on the COVER, I'm not ashamed to take the god-damned magazine home! And he was really embarrassed, like, oh lady, what are you doing . . .

Compassionate, intellectually adroit, gifted with a wonderful "what the hell" playfulness, she was at the same time the most serious, intensely focused person I ever knew, sometimes bluntly so. Yet she never demanded any official respect or formal decorum—merely a regard for one's own being and the possibilities within it. When she died at the age of fifty-five, she was the published author of poetry, nonfiction, novels, dozens of short stories, and more than twenty books dictated by, or examining the phenomenon of, the Seth personality. Two other volumes of the Seth material were published posthumously as well as four volumes of the body of work known as *The Early Sessions*; publication is in the works of what is known as the Deleted material.[18]

With a few exceptions, all of Jane's books are in print and all of her lifework, including her voluminous personal journals, poetry, dream notebooks, essays and observations, extensive correspondence, interviews, and the Seth material in its entirety, have been placed in its own archives in the Sterling Memorial Library at Yale University in New Haven, Connecticut. According to the Sterling Library staff, Jane's is the most frequently visited archives at Yale; at last update, the archival list of her work is forty-seven pages long, and growing.

"Jane was and is a hero," ESP class member Vickie Smith remembers, "in the classical sense of the word. She was a Writer, a Poet, and I fully mean those capitals! She showed me a world I longed for but didn't think could ever be. And not just the psychic stuff . . . She made it okay for me to dream of a life of the mind, that even though I still may not have achieved, at least my mind can envision it . . . daring to hope, or think, or dream of something different."

3

None of That Girl Stuff Allowed

From the start, Jane and I maneuvered, you might say, around a contrary order of business. She and I were not girlfriends, or even best friends, in the way those words usually suggest; the center of our common interests precluded that. To me she was a creative mentor-comrade-mother figure who encouraged my writing and "psychic" abilities and demanded that I take them seriously. No one, including myself, had ever asked this of me, though I'd been writing since early childhood, as Jane had, and some of our poetry had appeared in the same literary magazines (such as *Dust* and *Epos*), twenty years apart. Our similarities were as striking as our differences, which themselves seemed—similar. And evocative. But of what?

Perhaps sadly, we didn't gab about homey everyday girlfriend matters like recipes or clothes (though we did analyze one another's food and body image beliefs). We didn't go shopping together (though on a few occasions I did Jane's Christmas shopping for Rob) and she came over to my house exactly twice (once as part of a walking routine she was trying to set up for herself). We didn't confide the details of our sex lives (outside of admitting to a mutual case of the hots for Mister Spock of *Star Trek* days) or yak about hair and make-up (though my notes mention that I trimmed Jane's hair on at least one occasion and I often wished I could muster the nerve to tell her to switch from the coal-black hair dye she used to something subtler). Actually we were quite oh so careful not to lapse in front of one another into mere "girl" stuff, about which we cultivated a snooty, secretly frightened, disdain.

No, our mutual interests were almost exclusively focused on writing and "psychic" experiences, and in analyzing what those experiences might mean. We shared a certain energy, a way of tuning in on things, and an overall worldview which was, oddly, both the center of our friendship and the thing that precluded simple girlfriend-being. We loved to examine the underside of events, extract meaning from coincidence and dreams, take off into the "idea construction" of the universe and fly anywhere and everywhere with it as our wits and intuitions decreed—flying while seated firmly in her living room, that is, because aside from periodic excursions to visit in-laws in Rochester, New York, and Pennsylvania, and one or two brief winter vacations in the Florida Keys, Jane and Rob didn't travel much in the usual sense, in the years I knew them, for reasons largely stemming from her steadily increasing physical problems.

Moreover, and despite the fact of her own youthful cross-country trips by motorcycle and car, Jane had a fidgety impatience with globe-trotting tales (something noted by Debbie Harris in her journals), a quirk I now realize reflected her powerful fears about time-wasting distraction and thus fed into the reasons behind her physical travails. Of course if you are a writer you cannot also spend all your time romping through the wilderness, but plenty of writers manage to do both in some sort of reasonable proportion. By the late seventies it was a journal-worthy event for Jane to ride along in the car when Rob went out to buy groceries, let alone walk anywhere at all. Her enormous will and ability to focus her creative energies simultaneously trapped her and freed her, a dilemma she was never able to resolve.

Still, our interior safaris were plenty wild and woolly fare, when we'd "click" on something at the same time—for me this was a definite snapping sensation in the meat of my brain, accompanied by a feeling of swiftness, or acceleration (exactly the same sensation as in the moment, when I was four, when I suddenly knew how to read all of a piece, as my mother was droning her way through a *Little Lulu* comic for the tenth time, pointing at every word as she said it). Sometimes these were crystal-clear, brightly-colored images, like motion pictures in the air, that we'd see simultaneously; or concepts that would come to us in a rush; or sudden whole universes that would drop into our heads faster than we could describe them—or anyway, that was how it felt; unseen journeys filled with true magic. We tried experiments with consciousness projection, or clairvoyance, both awake and in dreams; in one of the first of these in the fall of 1968, so my notes state, Jane picked up some precise images of my parents' house (which at that point she hadn't physically visited) as it had been when my grandparents lived there in the late forties, down to the wallpaper patterns and the narrow wine-colored carpet on the stairs. And I had many lucid flying dreams to her apartment at 458 West Water, where I'd try to identify objects Jane would leave in an envelope hanging on the door or in other agreed-upon places (I did quite well at this, too). Even today, I have vivid dreams of traveling to that old apartment to see what's there—and on occasion, Jane will be sitting at her library table by the windows, smoking, as I fly in.

"Hey, Sue-Belle," she'll say, "what's up?"

There were many other times when we'd just talk ideas, or examine events from that unofficial perspective that we connected with so easily—the psychic play of political events, the mystical origins of mathematics, ribald remarks and asides, goofy and grand plots for stories and novels, coincidence and what it might mean in the unofficial order of events, whatever came into our heads. This sort of thing was always there, in the background, between the two of us, to one degree or another, in even our most inconsequential chats. And in those grand moments of spontaneous charged speculation, I often felt, and I think Jane felt, windows flying open in the air, doors blasting ajar, highways appearing across distant unexplored landscapes, waiting for us to shoulder our backpacks and come on—for me a glimpse of my true characteristics and purposes in the world; Jane too, I think, though she had her own strong vision along these lines.

Sometimes I would also imagine that I was the only one who truly connected with Jane's mode of consciousness, because I shared it, to some extent—its flavor, anyway, or at least a concurrence in how the mechanics of the universe might work. And so these moments also represented the best of what we had to offer one another as friends, and as women writers of a certain psychological eccentricity in a time when this combination was not particularly advantageous. And yet, we rarely engaged this natural empathy in an overtly encouraging way. Some of this was a simple function of time and circumstance. But much of it was a result of my thoughtless misuse of that self-same rapport.

For it's too embarrassingly plain to me now that I spoiled much of this common ground between us with frequent demands on Jane's abilities and our friendship to help me solve personal problems (a regret that others who remember her mention also). This isn't unusual for friends in the ordinary framework of the world, but the sad fact is I wasn't fishing for ordinary advice. Many times—many, many times, probably less often than I imagine, but often enough —I'd call her up with some miserable complaint, feeling ignoble and churlish but half hoping, I am ashamed to admit, that maybe Seth would come through (on the *phone*?) with a few well-delivered words of metaphysical megawisdom on, shall we say, the Boyfriend Question—or family illness, or the recurrent bouts of hopelessness and depression that seemed to come upon me like cobwebs in the night, whatever—and solve it all in one fell swoop.

This never happened.

What usually did happen was that Jane would zero in yet again on the writing abilities she saw lying there a-waste in the midst of all this moping, and how I ought to be concentrating on them instead. About getting down to it, as she so often said to me. What being a writer took, what Jane had sacrificed for it, what she thought I should sacrifice for it (I had no idea). About writing every day, no matter what.

This was the standard advice she always gave me, and I actually came to resent it, as any child will do when a parent does, in fact, know what's best, and says so more than exactly once. Beyond that, and despite her own accruing difficulties, she was sympathetic toward anyone's pain and almost always took the time and energy to see what she could "pick up" on the situation—for example, her positive (and medically accurate) feedback on an eye injury my son Sean suffered (and recovered from) when he was twelve, or the impressions she wrote up on my mother's health problems (some interesting connections with aristocratic past-life attitudes), or her advice that I should "go out into nature" to relieve the depression (an obvious strategy that momentarily helped and one she must have yearned for herself as time went on). And though she didn't give formal psychic readings or speak for Seth in public, she did offer occasional private (and, I must emphasize, free) Seth sessions to people in physical or emotional difficulty, which included me, twice—once when I was having some minor but annoying female-type problems (the session focused on my ongoing subliminal self-punishment for giving my first child up for adoption) and again when "Ned" Watkins[1] and I separated (and which focused primarily on our gender beliefs).[2]

Nonetheless, Jane clearly believed (and perhaps correctly) that many of my predicaments were devices of my own invention, diverting my focus from the abilities she so adamantly insisted I possessed. And in that, except for the year and a half I took to write *Conversations with Seth*, I never thought that I lived up to her expectations. How much of this conviction arose from the insatiable hollow pit of my own approval-seeking I can't say; I had no clear, driving will governing my abilities and therefore no approval to give to myself. I knew she was disappointed with my lack of focus where it counted—where Jane thought it counted—and I couldn't bring myself to argue the point. Not that I wasn't writing, exactly—from an early age I'd been churning out stories, poetry, unfinished fantasy novels, daily dream records and journals and copious correspondence with friends and pen-pals; and during ESP class years I was making a living as a newspaper reporter and writing a humor column for the weekly Dundee, New York, *Observer*, of which I was also co-editor. But still, in Jane's eyes (or so I felt), I squandered time and energy on things that got in the way of my One True Work, which was not, by any means in her opinion, appeased by newspaper reporting, however it might pay the bills.

Sometimes she would really let me have it about this, but sadly, what I took from her exasperation was not the motivation and confidence I know she meant to impart. Instead, I would sit there hangdog, feeling worthless and jejune, convinced that I was nothing but a big, fat failure. This conviction had such an effect on me that when, for example, I read the draft of her introduction to *Conversations with Seth* in 1979, I concluded that she'd carefully worded her (actually quite wonderful) compliments so as not to reveal her true opinion that the book was stupid.

But this was, of course, my own projection. And so we could never quite bridge the differences in how we lived our lives, especially after I had my son Sean in 1969 and became a single parent—to her the ultimate distraction from one's creative pursuits. Too bad we never cut through to the chase on this one—my belief, invisible until fairly recently, despite the fact that it manifested in my life like an electronic fifty-foot billboard, was that *husbands* caused the annoying distractions and demands on your time and energy; it was men who were in your face all the time, not children, a child. So I would look across this (rather parallel) chasm at Jane and feel even more humiliated by my Impossible Man habits because it seemed that she and Rob had the perfect writer-artist relationship that I should have been able to attain and never quite managed. What was wrong with me, anyway? What a dope!

Thus it was a considerable shock to discover in Jane's private papers that she had many of the (really quite ordinary) relationship hassles with Rob as I'd experienced in both my marriages and otherwise, not to mention her similar troubles with depression and hopelessness, a discovery that left me feeling both relieved and . . . resentful. (As in, goddamnit, Jane! Why didn't you tell me you felt that way too sometimes? Why was it such a goddamned almighty secret?) In fact, reading Jane's copious, brilliant journals was less a necessary provision for doing this memoir than it was an addictive astonishment: once I'd read a few pages, I was hooked, not the least on what I found in there about myself (less than I'd hoped, more than I entirely enjoyed) and what Jane didn't, apparently, record. No mention, for example, of standing up with Ned and me at the outrageous scene of our marriage; not a word about the reception later at my parent's house—how could she not? And only one comment ("Fun!") after reading my first completed novel (I have no memory of what she might have said to me about it), and some stinging remarks about the Boyfriend behavior, and—well, these are Jane's diaries; if I'm going to snoop, however supposedly esthetic my purposes (and however open they might be to archives perusers, thanks to Rob's courageous decision to place them there in his lifetime), I can hardly complain about what I find.

Coincidentally, in the same time frame in which I first look through Jane's journals, an old friend of mine from high school days commits suicide, leaving behind a slew of personal papers and a computer full of who knows what, which his family reads through, of course, as anyone would—as I am doing, after all. Somewhat predictably, the family's reaction is an explosion of fresh grief and outraged questions about his personal life, and I find myself torn between a lofty judgment on living with what you find in writings not meant for outside eyes (how dare they sully my friend's dignity, I sniff, turning to a passage in which Jane records the dates and volume of her periods), and a wretched longing to know what the family discovered; to go through his papers myself; to know everything there is to know about someone who shared a forty-year friendship and revealed to me nothing of the shadows in his heart—much as Jane did, in fact, in many ways. Thwarted in this, my stomach churns, tears fall; I search Jane's words for any mention of my name.

4

Some Autobiography

As to my own upbringing, Jane made it abundantly clear, in the years of our friendship, that she viewed my background as one of privilege if not outright indulgence, far from her own experience of hardship and lack, and this assessment was true enough—as far as it went. But underneath the surface appearance of difference, seemingly so substantial and obvious, Jane and I shared a psychological context that was oddly reciprocal.

I was born in Elmira in 1945, the only child to parents who were financially comfortable, and, for their time and place, somewhat temperamentally eccentric. They thought religion was moronic, didn't give a hoot about the social status they had ample access to, and though we lived in a house crammed attic to cellar with family antiques, books, and furniture, seemed not to care a whole lot about material possessions—the stuff was just there, mostly inherited; we'd moved in with it all after my grandmother died to take care of my grandfather and his country-gentleman farmhouse on ten acres in Webbs Mills, New York, a bucolic crossroads six miles south of Elmira. My father was CEO of a car parts factory cofounded in the twenties by his father, son of an Irish immigrant. My mother, who had an education in the classics and could recite chunks of same in the original Latin and Greek, read constantly, grew huge, gorgeous flower gardens, took me on countless nature walks, did the *New York Times* crossword puzzle in ink, no mistakes, cultivated an intense interest in birds and local colorful human characters and seemed, in my memory of her, to be always thinking about something else, a state of mind I later came to appreciate. Her childhood had been difficult and insecure, with a gifted and unhappy mother who vacillated between wild, abusive behavior and loving apology (much like Marie Roberts); yet my mother always spoke warmly of her parents, and of growing up in the hard times of the twenties and thirties in and around Elmira and the Finger Lakes. Her own unfinished memoirs are full of optimism and humor.

In the years before television overtook the world, we spent long pleasant evenings listening to the radio, playing cards, working on various home projects, reading and talking about the news or current ethical questions, telling and retelling family tales. For years my parents shared an ongoing debate about heredity versus environment, which my father inevitably won by calmly goading my somewhat overzealous mother into preposterous corners until she dissolved into pounding the table and shrieking, "You son of a bitch! You bastard! You are lower than whale shit!" He could do this to anybody. Grown adults would end up screaming or weeping over discussions about things like sheep anthrax, while he merely smiled innocently, unperturbed.

For the most part my childhood was idyllic and peaceful, much of it spent outdoors roaming the woods and hills of the impossibly sweet, safe, and undeveloped fifties and early sixties, skating down the shale creeks in winter, or curled up indoors, reading. Basically I was left to my own devices, in an E. B. White sort of benign solitude. It suited me perfectly, or perhaps I suited it—heredity as choice? I was an early reader and by age five or six was perusing books, encyclopedias, newspapers, comics, *Popular Science* magazines, and whatever science fiction and fantasy I could get my hands on, all without censure. I started writing stories when I was seven, in black marble-backed notebooks, with pencils. Even today, the smell of pencils brings back the thrilling rush of those first stories, of words from nowhere appearing like magic on the blank page. My grandfather Baker gave me my first typewriter, a bulky Remington manual with a broken "p," which I tapped away on, hour after hour, for years. I often read in public, taking books with me wherever I went. One of my parents' friends, who claimed to be a psychologist, observed eight- or nine-year-old me with a book in front of my face at a restaurant table one evening and sat down with us to ask, "What's she hiding from?" Everyone stared at me and I pretended I didn't notice any of it and kept on reading as if deaf, a habit I still enjoy today, and one that Jane cultivated herself. I remember the thrill of recognition I felt the first time she told me how she used to sit alone in bars or restaurants—"with my nose stuck in a book or writing poetry with *great* goddamned disdain, and if anyone approached me I'd just keep right on with it and not even so much as look up, as if they were utterly beneath my notice."

Unlike Jane, I always had vivid dreams, odd brushes with "ESP," startling little vision-like encounters—the sort of thing my parents talked about too, sometimes, particularly my father, who once told me that while a Marine he'd been saved by a sudden impulse to volunteer for extra shore duty on Guadalcanal; the group of men who left were all killed by a surprise air raid on the departing barges. "I never volunteered for anything before that, or afterwards," he said. "Something just told me to do it." This was one of only two incidents he ever mentioned about the war. The other was a funny story about accidentally stabbing a horse in the behind, and recently I discovered a version of the same tale in a collection of urban myths. Whether it was his story to begin with, or one he simply passed on to let us believe that this time in his life hadn't been one hundred percent horrific, I can't say.

It wasn't until after he died in 1983 that I could even begin to consciously acknowledge what the three of us had always hidden behind good-sport humorous denial: He was an alcoholic most of his adult life. He was not a fallen-down drunk or a lout; his was the habit of nightly scotch on the rocks until ever-earlier bedtime, cocktails for endless hours before holiday meals (with family members who drank "socially" right along with him), ice tinkling in a Steuben tumbler full of booze set in plain view on the car dashboard everywhere he drove. Still, his demons lurked, and made their appearances in his nasty Irish wit meted out to whomever had the misfortune to be in the way, usually my mother and me.

My mother died of lupus (as her mother had before her) in 1985, a little less than two years after my father. They were young, in their early sixties; yet I can't imagine them wanting to be any older.

My adult life began abruptly in the summer of 1967. I was a graduate of Syracuse University's journalism school, living at home and working the graveyard shift on Elmira's daily newspaper, when I accidentally became pregnant one night, smoking way too much pot out behind the backyard family cemetery with a fellow I'd known since childhood. I had no conscious memory of the act, and only figured it out in retrospect, so to speak, several months later. I was terrified beyond reason at the prospect of telling my parents (as much for the marijuana as the circumstances), and this was 1967, remember, long before there were legal or even kindly options. My friend Dan Stimmerman had spent several summers on Martha's Vineyard, Massachusetts, and had told me all about the place and how wonderful it was. Now I pictured: Island. Approachable only by boat, or plane. Secluded. Safe.

So I left on New Year's Day 1968 (after that party at Jane and Rob's) for the Vineyard, driving my college graduation-present Mustang through a blinding snowstorm without a map, directly from Webbs Mills to Wood's

Hole, right into the ferry's maw in the last few minutes of what I later found out was the last passage to the Island that night. I parked my car and walked upstairs to the outside deck, where I stood in the freezing saltwater wind, in the gathering dark, as the ferry crossed Vineyard Sound and into Vineyard Haven Harbor and I watched the cliffs pass by and the gulls circle across the waves and felt as if I'd come to the place where I was supposed to be for the rest of this life and as many others as I might ever have, before or afterward. Even now, sitting here at my desk in the rolling blue hills of the Finger Lakes, in countryside that is not only beautiful but unlike the Vineyard today, affordable, I feel the same about the Island as I did in those first moments, crossing the dark cold sea alone, not quite alone, knowing the near future would be unbearably painful and yet mine.

I got a room in the first motel I found and the next morning went to a pay phone and called the Vineyard *Gazette* and asked to speak to old Henry Beetle Hough himself, renowned editor, essayist, and environmental spokesman for the Vineyard. He came to the phone and very kindly conversed with me about my job qualifications and the fact that he had no open reporter positions. I said, that was okay, but would it be all right if I called him periodically to check? Something in his voice changed, then; I think some piece of knowledge had passed between us even though I was still clinging to the habit of subterfuge. "Come on over sometime and we'll figure something out," he said. I hung up the phone and drove over to Edgartown and found the *Gazette* office without asking a single direction.

I was six months pregnant by then but could easily have been mistaken for fat; at least my parents, who never knew consciously about this child, had chosen to think of me that way. When I walked into the *Gazette* office, I had to step over a sleeping collie and squeeze my bulk past an enormous roaring Mergenthaller press and an actual working Linotype flanked by actual working Yankee pressmen sucking on pipes and speaking in genuine Yankee fo'c'sle dialect. The smell of ink and machinery oil and tobacco smoke and newsprint filled the room. I had entered the gates of Heaven. At that moment I would have died to stay there and sweep the floor with my college diploma.

Hough's office consisted of a captain's chair and rolltop desk literally piled a couple feet high with papers framed around a writing space the size of a yellow composition tablet. Henry was in his early seventies, small and spare, with bright blue eyes that appraised me in a friendly, accepting manner. Only later, when I'd observed Jane's brush with fame in America, did I realize he might have had to fend off adoring college kids yearning for a job on the *Gazette* a few thousand times before me.

I introduced myself. "Ah," he said. "The eager reporter on the phone just now." He asked how long I'd lived on the Island. "Since last night," I told him, and we both laughed. "I like you," he said, and offered me a job as social reporter for Vineyard Haven, ten cents a column inch, the only thing he had in the dead of winter. Maybe my condition didn't escape those bright Yankee eyes after all. I accepted without a second thought, without knowing what a "social reporter" was, and then I excused myself to go find a place to live, and a phone, so I could start doing whatever it was a social reporter did, which as it turned out was to collect gossip and dinner party notes from Islanders who liked to see their names in the famous local paper.

Of course ten cents a column inch didn't even pay the phone bill, let alone rent and groceries, so I supplemented this job with a string of others as I could get them and hold onto them in the midst of growing more and more visibly pregnant. I cleaned houses for a couple of dentists who soon fired me because my condition "wasn't suitable for a family environment"; worked as a typist for one of the first land developers to start parceling off Island lots in those innocent pre-Boom years; worked in the billing department of the local hospital and was promptly fired for my complete inability to do anything right (billing people who hadn't been admitted in decades, for example); ran the Island's Western Union station whose duties included calling in singing telegrams to reclusive luminaries; began entering the fabric of the Vineyard community and a life that I'd loved from the moment I'd stepped out on the decks of that dark, cold ferry.

I had my baby on April 22, 1968, and gave him up for adoption. Three days after his birth, my parents showed up on the Island to take me to my cousin's wedding in Rhode Island. I saw them driving off the ferry ramp as I walked along the street about half an hour after leaving the hospital. As I raised my hand to flag them down I realized I was still wearing the wrist ID bracelet; I pulled so hard on it that it cut my skin before it broke, and I threw it in a trash can and waved my parents to the curbside in the same smooth gesture.

They took a room by the local golf course and we played a round of eighteen holes that afternoon. I could see in their eyes that I looked fat and tired (they had no idea!) but they said nothing. For the most part they were lost in a bitter antipathy that attached itself to inconsequential bickering over ferry schedules and golf scores. No fun debates about the nightly news any more. My father drank two quarts of scotch a day, starting at breakfast. My mother had blue circles under her eyes and held her face in a rictus smile. I think I could have whelped a litter of puppies on the motel rug and they wouldn't have noticed. Altogether, we were an unhappy family portrait of denial and distance.

I stayed on the Vineyard that summer, working several jobs (social reporter, telegram sender; cosmetics, and, ironically, contraceptive counter drugstore clerk), but by early September, the urge to get back home that had been nagging at me since early summer (not to mention my mother's almost daily heart-wrenching phone calls) could no longer be denied, and so I packed my belongings back into my Mustang and drove away, off the Vineyard. Dan Stimmerman rode back with me from summer employment on the Island. Neither of us would see the place again until long after it had become a media-intensive enclave of the rich and famous, gone beyond us forevermore.

5

Going Back

A week or so after our return from the Vineyard in early September, 1968, Dan asked me, again, to go over to Jane and Rob's with him for one of their Friday night get-togethers. Just a fun party, he told me, and maybe she would speak for the ghost. I resisted at first—I was very put off by Dan's description of Jane as "the woman who speaks for a ghost," which had all the trappings of stuff I'd grown up to abhor, but I remembered that New Year's Eve party fondly enough, and Dan insisted that I needed to tell Jane about a vivid "astral projection," as we called it, that I'd experienced just before leaving the Vineyard—*needed* was the verb he emphasized—so finally, and with more anticipation than I wanted to admit, I gave in.

Jane and Rob's longtime friends Maggie and Bill Granger were there, possibly Ned Watkins and his current girlfriend, some others. The room was large yet cozy, furnished with a casual make-do air and the warm glow of small incidental table lamps. The old sofa-bed couch was covered with a bright blue spread and the coffee table was a sanded and polished door set up on screwed-in wooden legs. Rob's paintings filled the walls; the dowel room divider creating an entry space between the living room and apartment door was packed with books, as were floor-to-ceiling shelves set up for Jane's manuscripts and the ever-burgeoning notebooks of the Seth material (about which I knew basically nothing). Jane's work desk occupied the bare floor in front of the big bay windows, with her manual typewriter, stacks of paper, and a cup full of pens and pencils at the ready. On the living room side of the bathroom door was a full-length mirror, which to me was the strangest thing in the place: whenever anybody went in to take a pee, which was fairly often, given the wine and beer we all consumed, the mirror would sweep the room and show you to yourself. Well, strangest unless you counted Willie the long-haired cat, who scratched and/or bit anyone who came near him, including, on occasion, Jane and Rob.

Neither Jane nor I made any notes about this highly non-portentous meeting, as far as I can tell, though my dream diary contains this entry on September 22, 1968: "A figure combining Zorba the Greek and the Bird-man of Alcatraz," which is not an altogether inaccurate portrait of Jane—or, for that matter, of myself. (She and Rob had only a vague memory of me from 1967.) I remember that we all made jokes about Maggie Granger's dislike of animals that night—not for the last time—and that I described some of the vivid dreams and clairvoyant experiences I'd had from early childhood, including the out-of-body, or flying dream, or what-ever it was, that I'd experienced while on the Vineyard.[1]

Somewhere during the evening I began to develop the bizarre idea that Jane, whose forthright demeanor virtually ignited candor from everybody around her, was about to swoop down into the cortex of my brain and come up with a detailed impression that would reveal my still tightly-held Martha's Vineyard secret to one and all, a possibility that (along with the wine) made me woozy with anxiety. I became so convinced of this, that Jane or this Seth person could somehow read my mind and inadvertently embarrass me by reciting its contents, that a day or two later I called her up and asked if I could have a talk with her in private.

She said, sure, come on over, and I don't know what she expected—certainly not the tortured confession about my lost child that I wrestled out of myself that September afternoon. I don't remember what her reaction was; probably neutral. From her perspective, she had secrets that were much more keep-worthy than mine: the fact that she and her invalid mother had lived on welfare, for example. Or that she was beginning to have trouble getting up and down the stairs. Or that her hands were not working so hot any more. Secrets she kept with the same charge of shame as I'd cultivated for my own.

It was during this conversation that she invited me to join her ESP class—the Thursday night one, she said, which was for "beginners"; the Tuesday night class was for "regulars." I remember swallowing my insulted reaction and saying, with more polite acceptance than certitude, that sure, Thursdays would be great, why not, it sounded like fun.

And of course, it was.

* * *

THAT LONG-AGO NEW YEAR'S EVE party had been fun, too, but more clamorous than anything I ever saw at Jane and Rob's place again, including the later ESP classes, which could be plenty loud and boisterous affairs. One fellow had passed out on his face in the apartment hallway that New Year's night, and Rob and another man had dragged the fallen soldier into the bedroom and dumped him across the coats piled on the bed. How hilarious this had seemed to everyone, including Jane and Rob. "We threw a couple'a people in there one time," Jane had yukked loudly about another such party, "and after a while I went in to go to the john and looked in the bedroom and noticed that the covers were moving around in a veeeery familiar position! What the hell, I didn't even know they knew each other!"

Later, after we'd become friends, Jane played a tape of her and Rob and the Grangers making up improvisational television commercials on their big old reel-to-reel recording machine (which did much duty throughout class years). On one of these tapes, Rob spoofs the ubiquitous aspirin ads of the day with a running, "First the headache starts up here and then it goes down here and then it goes around *there*, and then it goes into my *you* know and then it goes . . . " And Jane, in a perfect fake-sprightly sales voice, creates a brand-new product:

> . . . inflatable falsies. They are so easy and convenient! All you have to do is put your lips to the rubber nipples and *blow* . . .

"That's how we wasted our time before the Seth material came along," Jane said, in a disparaging tone.

Somewhere in here, in late September or early October, I took Jane a batch of my poetry and short stories—at her request? Must have been; I wouldn't have had the nerve to just foist it on her, since even my most hopeful appraisal of my own work foresaw a lengthy apprenticeship with the written word. Nonetheless, I was unprepared for her reaction.

She was absolutely fierce about it; almost predator-like in her passionate, and stern response. She handed the pages back to me and stared at me so hard my knees went weak—I thought she was going to tell me it was shit, how dare I insult her with this baby shit?

"You," she said, pacing out the words for emphasis, "Really. Have. It! *And* you'd *damn* well *better* start *using* it!" She continued to stare, waiting for me to—what? Disgorge the great American novel at her feet? I had no reply whatsoever. Although I had some natural idea that I had talent, Jane's enormous seriousness—an almost devouring seriousness—was shocking to me. I remember sitting there with her, at her work table, my papers in a messy pile between us, feeling exactly as if somebody had just handed me a package of such grave importance that I didn't really want to open it up and have to deal with the contents. At that moment, I just wanted to go home and put on my pajamas and eat ice cream.

"Get down to it, girl," Jane said, as she would many times thereafter. "You should be writing every day—every goddamned day. Set a schedule for yourself. Set it up around whatever the hell you have to do to keep body and soul together, but set it! Do it! You've *got it*! You do see that, don't you?"

I gulped. "Yeah." I didn't—yet I did. I felt like a little kid. Living at home again with my parents, I more or less wrote when the urge struck me, usually deep in the night when I was sure nobody would ask to see what I was doing. Later when I got a job as a professor's assistant at Cornell University, I set up my typewriter in my cheerless brick-walled Ithaca apartment and at least stared at the old machine every day. I longed for Martha's Vineyard and all that I'd left behind there, though mostly I put that aside and trudged on. Jane's ESP class was magic, no doubt about it, so maybe that would be enough. And I did feel that I was doing something there that I was supposed to be doing, even though whatever that something was didn't seem to be flying out of the typewriter, despite Jane's avid encouragement.[2]

6

The Strange Case Of The Chestnut Beads

Autumn, 1968. I'm over at Jane's, talking up a storm about something or other, probably Thursday night ESP class, which I've been attending for a month or so by then. While she's in the tiny kitchen fixing us some coffee, I go over and browse through the bookcase where she keeps her manuscripts and books of Seth sessions. Those don't interest me, but her collection of *Fantasy and Science Fiction* magazines do. There are at least half a dozen on the shelf, most of them from the fifties, I notice with sentimental amusement—the science-fiction era I'd cut my reading teeth on. I pull one of the magazines out and am leafing through it when Jane brings the steaming cups back to the table.

I say something to her like, oh wow, you subscribe to this great old 'zine? I used to read it all the time.

"Oh, yeah," Jane says, gesturing at the copy in my hands, "there's a story of mine in that one, called *The Chestnut Beads*."[1]

A gong seems to ring through the air. Spoons might have rattled on the plain china saucers. Maybe a bird flies off the nearby rooftop, startled at the sound. "Holy shit," I say, "you wrote that story?"

"Holy shit," she squawks, "you *read* it?"

"I sure did, in college," I tell her. "I never forgot it!" I flip through the pages, and there it is—*The Chestnut Beads*, by none other than Jane Roberts. "Holy shit!" I say, again.

"ROBBIEEEEEE!" Jane yells into the back studio and possibly Canada, "COME OUT HERE AND LISTEN TO THIS!!! SUE-BELLE'S READ *THE CHESTNUT BEADS* FOR CHRISSAKES!!!!!"

I don't remember what Rob had to say about this (though I'm sure it was succinct—he was always the cooler of the two, at least outwardly). I do know that Jane and I thought this was a really far-out coincidence. After all, I'd picked the issue with her story in it right out of the line-up, purely by chance—or something. But neither of us grasped just how far out it was, because half of the coincidence hadn't even happened yet.

The Chestnut Beads is a riveting tale about the end of the world by nuclear war, which by the time I read it in the fall of 1963 was something a lot of us growing up in that era had come to believe was inevitable. My classmates and I had practiced "duck and cover" under our desks in grammar school days, listened to the bomb shelter debates in junior high, sat anxiously in study hall that October day in 1962, our senior year, waiting to hear if the Russians would back down before the Cuban blockade—or not. My father had told me that morning, "If something starts, just get up and walk home. Don't pay attention to anyone, don't stop anywhere, just get yourself home." I still have vivid dreams about this scenario, in which I am walking through a dark and ruined landscape and the Webbs Mills house is far in the distance, in a circle of golden light, completely unscathed and always just beyond my reach.

I always imagined I'd survive well enough, somehow, albeit with some inconveniences; and privately I thought it would be a good thing to have the slate wiped "clean" of too many humans so we could start over and get it right next time. Such were my naive beliefs—not all that different from the story's intent. For *The Chestnut Beads* is also a fable of rebirth, in the hands of the women who survive and metamorphose into other, mightier versions of themselves secretly encoded into their psyches during sorority initiation rituals in college.

Interesting that around the time I was reading this story, the SU sororities sent representatives to the dorm to recruit new pledges. I had nothing but disdain for the sorority system and all that girly-girly stuff, as I thought of it—the whole business provoked everything I disliked (and feared) about my own gender, though I didn't understand my reaction back then. Effectively, this attitude isolated me from college social life, which was fine by me. I was alone, independent—apart, watching. This was my carefully-held self image. So naturally, I identified strongly with the transformation of the central *Beads* character Olive into the powerful Migma—a name like molten rock. Fierce. Immutable. Apart. A character the author had based pretty much on herself.

Also around this time, in December of 1963, back in Elmira, *The Chestnut Beads* author and her artist husband had started to get some decidedly odd messages on a Ouija board as part of their research for a book on ESP. My college dorm friends and I played with Ouija boards a lot that year—we even made a few "contacts," which gave us advice about whether or not to sleep with our boyfriends. Surprise! I don't recall the nature of the advice—for that matter I don't recall the nature of the boyfriends. The Ouija stuff was fun, mostly nonsense, but I do remember one response the board made to a question of mine: How old are you?

YOUNG AS A THOUGHT, OLD AS THE MIND, it replied. In an early Seth session—on the night of December 13, 1963, actually, when Jane and Rob were still using their Ouija board to communicate with Seth—Rob asks, "What is the mind as opposed to the brain?"

"BRAIN IS MECHANISM AND MIND IS SPIRIT," Seth-through-planchette replies. Rob's question is unrelated to the ongoing questions and comments both before and after this one. It is a perfectly straightforward query and a perfectly self-evident answer. I get a chill every time I read it.

In this same semester, I took the obligatory Philosophy 101 course, set in a huge lecture hall with a couple hundred students. Oddly, or so I thought at the time, the professor spent numerous classes digressing from the ennui of Emmanuel Kant and company to describe his serial dreams of himself as another person, a fighter pilot in World War I. These dreams, he said, would occur in clusters, sometimes for weeks, each one picking up where the previous one had left off, all of them in brilliant, sequential detail, including that character's name, military rank, memories of childhood and home, and even *his* dreams. The professor seemed fascinated, baffled, and alarmed—he presented this as if seeking an explanation from somewhere, anywhere. At one point, a student sitting behind me raised his hand and asked, in a sardonic tone, if reincarnation might explain it. This seemed to alarm the professor even more. So why did he bring it up?

Almost like a shadow of ESP class to come—concurrent with my reading *The Chestnut Beads* (though the connection was invisible to me then, of course).

Still and all, omnivorous reading habits naturally open up a never-ending labyrinth of interconnecting ideas and storylines, some of which imprint on the mind as vividly as any physical event. And to discover five years later that your newfound friend/mentor/creative-abilities mother-figure wrote this memorable tale is a pleasant serendipity, though nothing overly-spectacular by itself, really, since authors have to live somewhere (and Jane wasn't the first published writer I'd ever met whose work I'd previously read).

All of this is true—yet more than true. In 1978, long after I'd married and divorced Ned Watkins (whom I met in 1968, at Jane and Rob's place), when I was putting together the proposal for *Conversations with Seth*, it was Jane's editor at Prentice-Hall who pointed out that in *The Chestnut Beads*, the main character/Jane-figure's *child* is named Sue Watkins! Which of course hadn't meant a thing to me when I read it in 1963, or to Jane when she wrote it in 1957, or to either of us when we became friends in 1968. It *became* a coincidence only later, in response to events that had, as far as I was concerned, no association with that old story at all.

Then in 1994, in preparation for an article I was writing on *The Chestnut Beads* and these same coincidences, I read the story again for the first time in more than thirty years—and discovered some other rather intriguing connections in it between Jane and me that, if nothing else (and without belaboring the point beyond endurance), certainly demonstrate the amazing multidimensional nature of creative endeavors.

For example, much is made in the story's opening sequences of the Friday night get-togethers at the home of the mysterious woman named Lounze. It is during one of these gatherings that Olive is introduced to her husband-to-be, William Watkins. Remember, Jane wrote this story in 1957, when I was twelve. She and Rob didn't move to Elmira until 1960. By the time I met her in 1967, she and Rob had a long-established routine of hosting little Friday-night get-togethers with friends, and it was during one of these in late 1968 that I met Ned, whom Jane and Rob had known for about a year.

In the story, Lounze engineers this introduction for hidden reasons of her own. Jane didn't "engineer" any sort of set-up with Ned and me, but when I told my mother that Ned and I were going to marry, her first, infuriated reaction was to shout, "I suppose this is *Jane's* idea?" Taken utterly aback, I replied, of course, that Jane had nothing to do with it, why would she? But my mother was adamant in her conviction that this was all a scheme of Jane's, and she would not be dissuaded. She and I would have other confrontations along these lines, and I never learned from them; each time, it was a shock to discover the intensity of her anger toward Jane, whom she met only once, and that she viewed Jane, or more accurately, my friendship with Jane, as mysterious and vaguely threatening—as the *Beads* character Lounze is portrayed.

What I didn't mention to my mother that day was that—oops!—her grandchild (Sean) was already on the way. But in that, I suppose it's too ridiculous to point out that "Sean" is the Gaelic form of "John"—as in

Olive's first-born, Johnnie Watkins, brother of Sue, and a cute little twist I'd consciously forgotten until I reread the story; Sean and I always did have a more sibling-like than child-parent relationship, and hey, how far can you take this stuff, anyhow?

Well, I don't know. Here's some more: It is evocative indeed to contemplate the "larger-self" names that are given in *The Chestnut Beads* to the girls who join the sorority—it reminds me of the entity names given by Seth in Jane's ESP class (and other sessions) years later, and the explicit resonant significance that the *sound* of these names is supposed to have for those to whom they are spoken. This whole entity-name business initially made me uncomfortable, and still does, to some extent, though I intuitively understand it, and like my own, "Oranda," well enough (it does seem a tad girly-girly, however). In *The Chestnut Beads*, the characters display initial resistance to the "becoming" of these new names . . .

As Jane herself would later observe, the underlying nature of her own future endeavors appears throughout her early poetry and fiction; so it's not at all surprising to discover these kernels of prospective probable events embedded here—or in anyone's short stories or novels, or poetry.

Still, I wonder about intuitive communication, and the inner voices each of us responds to in moving toward our life's endeavors. Whenever I remember Jane talking about her early publishing days, when her fantasy stories were appearing in men's magazines like *Topper* and *Dude*, I am always taken back to a particular summer afternoon in the late fifties in Webbs Mills, where thirteen- or fourteen-year old me is waiting around in my friend Shirley's house while she finishes her housecleaning chores so we can go wading in the creek, or whatever. Every Saturday, Shirley has to clean the entire house, top to bottom, while her parents and two older brothers go away for the day. Somewhere in the back of my mind I think this is a rotten deal, though I don't say so. I offer to help her, but she says she's supposed to do the work by herself. So while Shirley is mopping the kitchen floor, I wander into the back room and find a pile of men's magazines moldering away in a corner behind some boots. Since nobody in my house would ever stop me from reading anything, I sit on the floor and start pawing through the magazines.

They're all issues of *Topper* and *Dude*, and aside from the photos of (by today's standards quite modest) naked women, what I specifically notice is that there's a science-fiction story in each edition. I've read half a dozen of these stories before Shirley comes in and sees what I'm doing, and makes me put the magazines back the way I found them so her brothers won't get mad at her, she says.

I don't remember any of the stories, though it might be fun to look them up, jog my memory—what might be the odds that one of them was written by a J. Roberts? As in, perhaps, a precursor to my reading *The Chestnut Beads* some five years later, in college? A response to a psychological connection already made?[2]

7

Really Great For Any Age at All

I said maybe three times to Jane, "You know, you're really great for thirty-nine," before she called me on it. This was in the fall of 1968, after I'd been in ESP class a while and coming over for those Friday night get-togethers on a more or less regular basis. I was twenty-three. Rob, at forty-nine, was a year older than my parents.

She and Rob were both there when she finally said something to me about my comment. Their body language suggested they'd discussed the subject at length and prepared, as a team, to respond. "I just don't know what you mean by that," she told me, her voice light and quick, not to be confused with jaunty by any means. "I mean, I just didn't figure you for it, Sue, you know? I think you'd better look at your own beliefs about age, and it isn't that I don't recognize what you're trying to say and all, but I guess what I'm trying to say is I'm really surprised."

I remember feeling pretty surprised myself, not to mention miffed, and thinking . . . whaaat? What's she talking about? I meant it as a compliment! But all I said was a meek, "Okay," and I never again told her how great she was for thirty-nine.

Except that she really was great for thirty-nine, or any other age, however it might have sounded to her, or what my age-related beliefs might have been at the time. Here she was, putting herself out on a psychological limb that nobody else seemed to know even existed, and doing it with impeccable integrity and balance, not to mention continuous self-assessment and creative genius, something in rare store anywhere. And letting a bunch of friends, fans, and strangers into her house once or twice a week for the sole purpose of *conversation* and philosophical exploration—not as strange back then as it is now, perhaps, with email and chat rooms and multi-channel TV appropriating the quiet hours, but still pretty wild, all of us there just to toss ideas and opinions and argument back and forth, for the sheer hell (and in the case of ESP class, $2.50 a head) of it.

And here the two of them were, Jane the writer, Rob the painter, unapologetic about structuring their lives around their art: Every day no matter what, Jane wrote, Rob painted, they explored consciousness and the meaning of reality, following their aspirations with the same dedication they'd felt from childhood. Their lives, in other words, did not come into focus with the emergence of the Seth material—rather, that body of work rose out of the focus their lives had already achieved.

I'd grown up around artistically gifted women who spent their energy kowtowing to the careers of husbands and mourning what they accepted as their gender's limitations. "A woman has to wear blinders," my mother told me often enough. "A woman can't look to the right or the left—she just has to look straight ahead and pretend nothing else is there." One of my mother's favorite authors was Dorothy Parker, whose story "Big Blonde" was in my mother's eyes the voice of Everywoman, of the humiliation and unfulfilled yearning that was a woman's lot. The first true despair I ever felt was upon reading that story, at my mother's insistence, when I was twelve or thirteen. The message was clear: You can't have what you want, men are dangerous, life is awful, you might as well drink. And yet, inexplicably, my mother looked upon fiction with great derision. "Fiction is a dodge," she said many times. "Only cowards write fiction." Though her invective was aimed mostly at novels, I hid my stories in desk drawers, and kept them to myself.

Later I grew to understand that in her assumption of inevitable disappointment, my mother was only trying to protect me from expecting too much. By contrast, Jane expected everything, creatively speaking, and her writing background sprang from poetry and fantasy, much like my own. So what if she couldn't run around the block? (A rueful question Jane grapples with herself, in her journals.) My mother could run around the block plenty, and break the men's swimming and diving records in college, and play a million rounds of golf, and still she ate herself up alive, repressing her own abilities with ferocious strength.

So as a couple, Jane and Rob seemed to me like something out of a science-fiction story themselves. They lived modestly, in steadfast make-do fashion (as with those cardboard studio walls Jane mentions in her letter to Blanche Price), keeping their wants and needs in check so as not to jeopardize the central vow they'd made to devote their lives to their art. In that way, they were quite radical to me—I knew other artists who lived spare lives, but this seemed a pretense or a grievous burden, rather than a methodical plan joyfully taken on to achieve life-goals. In effect, Jane and Rob were radical and conservative in equal measure. They didn't spend money on frills, or what I considered frills (or even essentials)—no bookstore bingeing, for example, or shopping extravaganzas of any kind, including food. In 1968 their car was an ancient Valiant with an unreliable battery; and here they were, roughly my parents' age, still renting an apartment furnished with home-made amenities and hand-me-downs definitely not of the antiques persuasion, still schlepping their dirty clothes to the laundromat or (something that used to give me a mild thrill of horror) washing it all in the bathroom sink and hanging it out on doorknobs or the backyard lines to dry.

"The checks I'd get from *Fantasy and Science Fiction* would cover our laundry for a couple months sometimes," Jane told me once. "We always managed to squeak by." She said she considered it a matter of pride, and love, that she'd never demand a "fancy house with all the trimmings" with the attendant mortgage payments, and thus "trap Rob," her words—trap both of them—with debts. Their tenaciousness bore its own fruit. When in 1975 they finally did buy their own house, they paid cash.

And they paid their work dues every day, no matter what. If they had a late-night party on a Friday or Saturday, or a New Year's Eve, and slept late the next day, they put in extra work hours to make up for it. And they kept track, no sluffing off, no matter what their other obligations. For years in her early journals, Jane logged in her writing time on charts, right down to the minute ("6–7:30, 1 1/2 hrs.; 8:20 PM–9:10, 1 hr."), along with the hours she put in selling kitchen knives or Avon products door to door, or whatever other part-time jobs she had, and compared these outside efforts with her writing schedule. ("Possibility of making out and to hell with depending on others in ordinary job," she writes for May 13, 1956, under notes for a full day put in. "My initiative only thing that will count . . . By God, we're not beaten yet by a long shot!") And then there was her insistence on not having children, in the face of tremendous pressure on women to do so, far more so then than now. All of this, all this carefully hoarded energy and mighty determination, poured into the creation of stories and paintings . . . What did my mother mean, "only cowards write fiction?" This all seemed fantastically brave to me. It was only when Jane demanded I do the same that I felt its potential as a prison. And so at times when I felt that Jane was ragging me about not having the proper dedication to my writing, I would think—yeah, well, Jane, at least I can run around the block if I want to. At least I can goddamned well get up and run around the goddamned block.

But of course I never said that. At the core of Jane and Rob's life was a secretiveness, more reticent than mere discretion, that held people at a distance, which I sometimes misinterpreted as a judgment. It was like a black hole, into which, depending on factors I could not decode, questions and comments would fall soundlessly, never to be heard from again. For example, I once asked them why they didn't publish the ESP class transcripts as is, in book form. "You don't understand the implications," Rob told me, and that was the end of it. No further explanation was offered.

At the time, I thought this meant that there was some awful discrepancy in the class transcript material that they didn't want to reveal. I couldn't figure what the hell else Rob could mean by "the implications." Now I think this had more to do with their sense of privacy, and of not wanting to turn the spotlight on the process, or performance, of Jane speaking for Seth in class, any more than it already was—they kept a careful accounting of balance there, too. Their focus was on the context of the material, which had to pass the muster of their artistic standards (Jane comments in her unfinished "Aspects" manuscript that the psychic field "has no understanding of what art standards are," for example); they also understood that too much public exposure might interfere with the essentially private process of producing it. Later, after I began to write with serious intent, I also came to understand that their secretiveness was a natural component of creative solitude, of keeping one's energy centered and the work whole.

* * *

BUT THE AGE THING—AH, YES, the age thing; there it was. I remember the night at Jane and Rob's with the Grangers on the eve of my twenty-sixth birthday. I was moaning and groaning with exceeding despair about how I hadn't done anything yet with my life ("haven't published a single novel!"), much to the disgust of everyone else, who were all at least fifteen years older than I was. Everyone but Jane, that is, who knew exactly what I was talking about, for she had yearned for the same, and still did, always would: making a name in the literary world.

"No, listen, it's the thing about being the rising young novelist," Jane chimed in. "One day you wake up and realize you're not a young anything anymore and where's the goddamned recognition, and what the hell happened, you know?"[1] But Bill especially would not be appeased. "Twenty-six years old and bitching!" he wailed. "Christ on a crutch! You've got so much time—shit, I wish I was twenty-six again! Just wait until you hit forty! You think you're miserable now! Just wait!"

Today, well past the age of thirty-nine, in fact having hit the age Jane was when she died, I can see Bill's point rather too clearly, as well as Jane's objections to my earlier conceit.

Yet I still say, Jane was pretty great for thirty-nine. She was pretty great stuff for any age. Any age you want to argue at all.

8

Friday Night Get-Togethers And Other Fun Times More or Less

It seems almost incredible now to remember that there was a time when Jane and Rob and I would walk from their apartment to nearby bars for a fun night out. Not only that I have a memory of Jane walking upright and free, but of the gracious old Elmira neighborhoods that surrounded us, and the lively downtown full of shops and specialty stores, five-and-dimes, movie theaters, restaurants and lunch counters, a hotel with a ballroom and elegant smorgasbord, a department store tea room, Mr. Peanut walking along the sidewalks doffing his top hat—not culturally a world-class icon, perhaps, but a cozy little city with a heart that is no more.

One of our favorite watering holes was the Steak Shop, a pleasant four-block walk up the street. It was small and dark and featured topless dancers, which in those days meant that the girls wore G-strings and pasties and kept their dancing feet planted on the floor. There was another place downtown where go-go girls, similarly attired, danced on raised platform stages while a jukebox blasted rock music; very with-it fare. Sometimes we'd go there; the walk was about the same. All mundane innocent small-town entertainment (though considered just a bit racy for early-seventies Elmira).

But it was Jane and Rob's friendships with the dancers that strike me as odd now, though it didn't occur to me to wonder about it at the time. Usually one or more of the girls would come over and sit with us during breaks and chat affably (in costume) over a drink or two. The conversations were inconsequential and homey, about kids and boyfriends, which seems hilarious to me now, the idea of sitting at a table in pasties and G-string talking about how your kid is doing in grammar school. I never saw any of these girls in ESP class or at Jane and Rob's place on Fridays, so where did they meet? Did Rob know them from his part-time job at the local greeting card company? I didn't ask.

Then there was the American Hotel, a colorful dive near the railroad tracks across town, with live music and a separate dance floor, pool table, pinball machines, sardine-can crowd conditions, and general agreeably seedy atmosphere. Jane loved the place, and in fact loved all bars and their spontaneous freewheeling racket and energy, as she said more than once. She and Rob would get up and dance to the fast music and sometimes to the slow. Jane's floor moves were a bit stiff and jerky, but she so obviously loved it—and they were good at it, too. They were almost always the oldest couple out there, and yet they not only fit right in, they were rather glorious to watch. Rob got into the music with a courtly sort of amused abandon—you could see he truly didn't care what anyone might think about this fiftyish fellow a-rockin' and a-rollin', and Jane, well, Jane just let go with the music, as much as it was possible for her to do by then.

We all drank cheap beer—me way more than anyone else. Except for a brief time when Ned and I were together, I was never with anyone, so once in a while Rob would ask me to dance with him. But I was, if anything, stiffer than Jane. I was awkward and self-conscious about fast dancing and didn't really like it (though I knew I was supposed to), and Rob didn't ask me on the slow, so I usually just sat out the music and watched the crowd.

But the energy and maybe the plain old exercise of dancing brought out something exuberant and free in Jane in a way that nothing else did. In that setting, she could yell and laugh and holler and make wisecracks all she wanted, and the hell with it—no worries about "annoying people," or about "going too far" hijinks-wise, as she wrote many times in her journals. She didn't mind the noise level at all—she'd just yell louder. And with it, she often let her other abilities fly free as well. She'd suddenly grab my arm and yell something like, "Hey, I'm gettin' something on the whole food thing, Sue, ya know . . . " and off she'd go with some pretty keen observations, and on occasion I'd start picking up my own images on whatever it was, and there we'd be, screaming "psychic" impressions at one another over mega-decible Three Dog Night while Rob looked on, imperturbable. He seemed to find it all sort of abstractly funny. "What are we going to do with her?" he'd say to me, with an affectionate nod in Jane's direction.

Certainly she had a trust of impulses in that setting (which in its way resembled ESP class) that I most assuredly did not. Though I didn't say so—I was only marginally aware of it myself—I wasn't especially comfortable in bars, for reasons of pique with music that drowned out conversation and a vague, unexpressed awareness that drinking scared and offended me, though I did plenty of it myself. And then there was the smog of cigarette smoke, which I disliked but never complained about—as who did, in those days? But for all the drinking I did back then—I would gulp down two beers in the time it took the others to have one, or less than one—I was actually afraid of what I might willingly do under the influence, and yet I would get as inebriated as I could as fast as I could and rely on—what? Some inborn radar I imagined I'd inherited to get me home safe and sound. Even though it had shorted out once, and was about to do so again.

In that vein I remember one especially crowded night at the American Hotel when Jane pointed out a cute fellow standing nearby, apparently by himself. "He's been looking over here for about ten minutes," she told me in a confiding tone, gesturing ostentatiously at the man in question. "Just for the hell of it, why don't you go over and ask him to dance?"

"Jee-zus, no!" I yelped, feeling myself going red as a beet. "Forget it!" Jane smiled and shrugged and said something like, well, okay girl, whatever . . . Did she feel sorry for me? Maybe. All I could think of was, oh crap, what if he comes over here and sits down and then I can't get rid of him? I pretty much spent the rest of the evening staring into near space and pretending to think unapproachable thoughts. "Ya know, Sue-Belle, it's just a dance, you don't have to marry the guy," Jane remarked at one point, and Rob leaned over and patted Jane's arm and said something like, Hon, leave her alone! And so she did.

It was in the American Hotel that Jane and I got into the past-life business with Brad, the unsuspecting bar fly who trailed over to our table with Rob.[1] The poor guy was depressed and inconsolable about his recent tour of duty in Vietnam, and when Jane started picking up on scenes from that time in his life, it was as if an electric current was suddenly plugged in between us. Not only did I start seeing the same scenes in my mind's eye as Jane talked, I started picking up on other images, of scenes from Brad's childhood and of another life he'd led, or so it seemed to me, in the Roanoke Colony in early Virginia. I jumped in to describe what I was seeing, Jane interrupted to add what she was seeing; and on and on, back and forth between us, some of the details of Brad's childhood vivid and (he gasped out) correct, and otherwise unknowable. We got so wound up in it that we forgot Brad was even sitting there—until he excused himself and basically ran like hell.

"You two scared that poor kid to death!" Rob admonished us. "What were you doing to him?" Jane and I looked at one another, blinking like frogs caught in a flashlight beam—where were we? The images we'd somehow picked up on, and—shared? Communicated? Opened up together?—began to fade, but the electricity of those moments hung on for quite a while. Where, indeed, did this stuff come from? How, and for that matter why, had we tuned in on this Brad character, a complete stranger? Probably one of the more dramatic examples of what you might call mutual instantaneous clairvoyant psychoanalysis, and neither Jane nor I ever quite knew what to make of it.

This was not the first time Jane had let go with both barrels in that setting, however, as I discovered recently, when I took my ailing computer to a local fix-it shop. By a series of happenstance questions I learned that Keith, the shop's owner, had run into Jane and Rob in the American Hotel many years before, 1969 or 1970, he said, and that the experience was, in his words, "creepy."

"She was persistent," he stated. "She pursued me!" According to Keith, he was standing at the bar with some friends when "this woman that somebody else identified to me as Jane Roberts," a total stranger to him, walked up and said she had a story to tell him that she thought he'd want to hear. Keith said he declined politely and Jane went back to her table, but that she approached him a few more times, until, Keith said, he agreed to hear what she had to say. The "story," as it turned out, was about a little boy, and as Jane went on, Keith realized that Jane was telling him something that had in fact happened to him when he was about four years old.

Briefly, Keith's story was that one day when he was four, he was playing indoors at the bottom of the stairs that led to the second floor of his house, and chanced to look up to the top of the stairs, where he saw a man standing there looking down on him. The man was entirely jet black—skin and clothes—and locked eyes with Keith until the four year-old turned slowly away and went into the kitchen where his mother and aunt were washing dishes. Keith said that he didn't tell anyone what he had seen, and went on playing quietly in the kitchen for the rest of the day. "The principal effect of it was that I became unusually quiet for a day or two afterwards," Keith said, and that over the years he told very few people about the experience. Basically, he just wanted to forget it.

So, Keith said, that night in the bar when he consented to hear what Jane had to say and she told him this story, he was a bit freaked out—*how* could this woman have come by this information? Apparently Jane gave her interpretation of the experience, though all Keith could remember of that was Jane's assertion that he had psychic abilities, and that he ought to come to ESP class, which he never did. "I don't have anything to do with that nonsense," Keith said.

Well, I thought, so you say, but then here you are telling me this tale (which wasn't the only instance of "that nonsense" in his life, as he would later admit). Plus, something about it sounded just a bit out of character for Jane; I'm not sure why—for one thing I have doubts that she would "pursue" anybody in this manner; but then, I wasn't there. If true, though, tuning into this total stranger's forty-plus year-old experience in such a powerful way must have intrigued her to the core. Why Keith? Why just then? What connections were operating between them that opened the door to these kinds of vivid (and completely accurate) impressions? I can imagine her questions.

* * *

One of the last times we all went out together, on a warm moonlit night not long before the flood of '72, a gray tiger kitten charged out of some bushes as we were walking home from the Steak Shop and followed us all the way back to Jane and Rob's apartment door. They took it in for a few days, named it "Parmesan" after the cheese for some oddball reason, and then gave it to a friend (they already had two cats). But the reason this incident sticks in my mind is the memory of Jane bending over to pet the kitten, straightening up, walking along, turning her head to call it, reaching down to pick it up, moving apparently without another thought except of the tiny creature trotting along behind us in the street-light shadows of a time and place that would vanish sooner than any of us could imagine.

Sometimes, remembering this childlike and ordinary fun, it seems that an entire world slipped out of our grasp back then, when we weren't looking—or at least it did out of mine. Or maybe not. Maybe none of us is really as dumb to our lives as we sometimes mourn; as I certainly did later, when Jane could only walk in my dreams and time had moved us all in its relentless current toward rendezvous somewhere north of the Polar Star and I came to realize, as Jane and Rob came to realize, that her physical problems had eaten up her life, taken away everything except, in the end, her ability to speak. And even then, what was there to speak about, except her physical condition? Everything else was gone.

* * *

SO EVENTUALLY JANE AND ROB were going out less and less, which was fine by me—I liked their place; it was comfortable and intimate, always fun, always open to any old idea anybody wanted to bring up and hash. Usually Maggie and Bill Granger would be there, maybe some local artists, occasional friends and fans, sometimes a few people from ESP class, all of us sitting around tossing ideas, dream recall, remarks, funny stories, and opinions back and forth—no television blaring, no loud music, and except for a few rare occasions, no Seth. Even more remarkably, at least to me now, looking back, and unlike much social discourse today, there was an almost complete lack of conversational Darwinism among us who gathered there—no political or philosophical grandstanding (though we had our share of arguments) despite the divisive nature of the times; and moreover, no Seth-agenda underlying any of it, including, or especially not, from Jane. Lots of reality-behind-the-reality dissection, though, and a few experiments with class-type fun stuff like table-tipping and—as Jane recounts in detail in *Adventures in Consciousness*—one rather unusual evening (even for us) during which Jane, Rob, Maggie, Bill, and I all spontaneously began to tune in on selves from another lifetime (so much so for Rob and me that we let the personalities "come through" to some extent) while my friend Tim, a clinical psychologist, just sat there, watching. But the thing was, that so-called past life scene—in which I felt, and partly let loose, a headstrong child's defiance of a severe, details-oriented person Rob had supposedly been—captured something in exaggerated terms that existed between Rob and me in the Now, though far in the background, like the undercoating of a painting: invisible to the conscious eye, essential to the form.

He and I would run into those aspects of ourselves again, in less amenable guise.

Then there was the night Jane "arranged" a birthday party for Rob—this might have been his fiftieth, in June of 1969, though I have no notes about it—not by the usual means of phone or invitation, but by "sending out vibes," as she put it. "I didn't plan anything," she said later, "I just sent out mental messages for people to show up." Not only did they show up . . . and show up . . . and *show* up . . . but among those who packed into that living room were friends Rob hadn't seen in years, an amateur magician who gave an impromptu performance, a tap dancer who climbed out the window and danced on the adjacent roof for our amusement, and even a neighbor who decided "for some reason" to bring a cake—fifty-some people over the course of the evening, or so we figured later. "I think I might have overdone it a little," Jane laughed, obviously pleased with herself.

But for the most part, our Friday night social life was everyday, homey fare. Bill Granger could always be counted on to tell stories about any war machine ever invented, especially fighter planes and submarines. Maggie and Bill traveled a lot, too, and brought back great tales, such as the time their plane was hijacked to Cuba. (No one was hurt, though Maggie's camera was confiscated, and Bill's chronic ulcers were given an extra squeeze watching the potholes and tree saplings whisk by as their jet rolled down the too-short Havana runway toward, he most sincerely hoped, takeoff speed.)

We'd take turns bringing wine and beer; Jane and Rob would provide cheese and cold cuts and crackers arranged on plates in the closet-sized kitchen (where I used to amuse myself by adding loony items such as "anteater butter" or "grackle livers" to the Spartan grocery list hanging on the wall). There were never any dinner parties or anything so formal there, just snacks, and maybe ice cream or pie, if someone brought it—goodies such as ice cream or pie were not exactly staples in Jane and Rob's pantry. Jane, and others, smoked constantly. Today I wouldn't sit in a room with a smoker for thirty seconds, let alone hours and hours in a small space gone blue with the stuff; but then it seemed, well, a bit much sometimes but essentially a normal part of life.

Fondly remembering those evenings, my long-time writer friend Barbara Coultry ("Bernice Zale" of *Conversations)*, commented in a 1999 email to me, "Picture: We're at Jane and Rob's, a social visit with fine tendrils of nerves threading the air. Sometimes I felt there was a strange rivalry between you and Jane. It reminded me of a mother/daughter relationship in which each of you would slip back and forth between the roles. As a psychic, Jane was, for a while, the mother, but person-to-person, she was more the daughter. Jane seemed very intense socially, as if she were trying way too hard to be normal. You, on the other hand were (and still are) a natural socially, and I think she may have leaned on you a bit that way."

On occasion Jane would read her poetry to us. I've never liked readings (or for that matter live performance of any kind) and this always made me uncomfortable—what can you say afterwards except wow, that was great?

And the truth is, I didn't like a lot of her poetry, but there was no way in hell I could ever tell her that. She considered it the core of her being, and who was I to criticize? Besides which, if anyone dared so much as rattle a beer glass, let alone, god forbid, chomp a cracker while she was reading, she'd give you a look that could melt cement until you knocked it off. So we'd sit in careful silent attention, and she'd read, sometimes for half an hour or more, in her quick, precise voice.

And whatever you might think of the poems, you could tell, listening to that voice—Jane's own, as were all her voices—that poetry was indeed the wellspring of her mystical nature, the place from which everything else—the Seth material, the *Oversoul* novels, all of it—had begun.

* * *

IT WASN'T LONG BEFORE I WAS USING Jane and Rob as a means to escape family holiday gatherings whenever they offered, or I managed to wangle, an invitation. Christmas Eve and New Year's Eve were sure bets, along with occasional Thanksgiving nights. They provided a kind of alternate clan experience, maybe some version of an ideal in that regard. And yet I find as I look back that I miss both groups with a keen and inescapable weight.

I have a photo taken at my aunt and uncle's house on Christmas Eve, around 1975. In it, I am sitting on a sofa between my mother and my father's sister, who are baring their teeth at one another in the characteristic expression of that charming pre-dinner cocktail hour in which horrible things are said to one another in pleasant, even jocular tones. As usual I'm about twenty-five pounds too fat and, perhaps to celebrate the holiday ambience, I'm wearing a wool crewneck sweater and lined wool pants with woolen ragg-knit socks in a house that was typically heated to a minimum of seventy-four degrees. In the background, my father is safely asleep in a recliner with a big, dopey grin on his face—perhaps this is the year he has given the impromptu shaving demonstration with the bone-handled electric knife my aunt and uncle had thought was such an elegant gift idea. Or perhaps it's the year my uncle launches into the tirade about how disgusting animals are, citing many graphically detailed examples to prove his argument, in particular a zoo gorilla he once observed eating its own feces. Desperate to keep myself indifferent and the conversation sprightly, I try changing the subject by saying hey, funny you should say that because I had a dream last night about gorillas; to which my uncle replies that as regards this supposed coincidence and everything else I have to say along these lines, I am the one who is full of shit.

"I don't believe anything you say is true," he tells me kindly, and my mother laughs, and so do I, and as soon as I can manage it, I leave—graciously, I'm sure—and flee to Jane and Rob's place, where, so my notes have it, we spend the evening comparing dream-threads (part of my gorilla dream included Jane in it, running along a street with me), histories of vile holiday remarks delivered by relatives, and numerous forms of possible retribution involving shit, and the throwing, burning, splattering, or disguising as hors d'oeuvres with olives on top thereof.

Did Sean go to Jane and Rob's with me that night? I don't remember specifically (I would usually stay until midnight or so, way past his bedtime), though he did go there with me on occasion, as well as to ESP class now and then. The first time two or three-year old Sean saw Jane speak for Seth, he burst into maniac giggles, stood up, and threw his treasured binky—a full-sized thermal bed blanket—right over Jane's head in a whooshing tent-like effect, which didn't disturb her trance state in the slightest—Seth just kept right on expounding, even when I pulled the blanket off and Jane's hair floofed all over her face in snapping static chaos.

But if you take that family scene around the Christmas tree, and factor in that all the people there were educated, well-read, interested in the mysterious and by no means wrapped up in any sort of philosophical allegiance, and moreover accustomed to a home setting that featured discourse, however skewed by the cocktail hour—do that, and you can almost catch the strange parallel threads weaving in and out between those scenes, between different kinds of families—those of blood and those of some other kinship; threads of purpose and intent pressing against the confines of roles and beliefs we could not quite figure out how to avoid. And by this last I mean both groups, each in its own peculiar way.

For example, there was the night Willie the cat jumped into Maggie Granger's lap. Maggie's intense dislike of animals, especially cats, was a standing joke with Jane and me (and it's interesting to me now to note the parallels here with my uncle's judgments), which I suppose served to cover up how annoyed we really were with her about it—something Maggie would pick up on some level, of course. Naturally, Willie loved to rub against Maggie's ankles in that special attraction cats have for those who detest them. So Rob would shut Willie in the coat closet (and later, their second apartment across the hall) for the evening when Maggie and Bill came over, but he must have forgotten this time, or else Willie managed to push the door open.

Maggie was sitting in Jane's rocker, talking and gesturing animatedly with a cracker in one hand and wine glass in the other, when suddenly,

WHOMP!—there was Willie, right in Maggie's face, right on her, and Maggie reacted as if a hornet's nest had fallen from the sky. She let out a shriek, threw her cracker and glass against the wall, and jerked away from the cat so hard the chair almost tipped over.

Of course, Willie also went berserk and ran like hell while the rest of us—not Maggie—laughed ourselves sick. You could tell by her expression that she was horrified and nauseated, but did we sympathize? No! (In the back of my secret, nasty mind, I thought she got what she deserved . . . Don't like animals, huh? Take that!)

On the other hand, Jane and Rob always had awful cats—only one of them, the short-lived Billy, would let you pet him without running away or trying to bite or disembowel your hand. Willie was okay in that regard, but barely—one of those cats that allows you two pats, tops, before nailing you. Maggie had probably observed this in the past, and figured Willie for an eye-gouger. Maybe she wasn't so far wrong, at that.

When Jane and Rob took in Rooney the stray, I talked them into having the cat neutered—took him to the vet myself to have it done. He was spraying all over the walls and bookcases, yet they acted as if they'd never heard of neutering as an option. When Rooney died, apparently of urinary tract disease, I remember that Jane expressed resentment that they'd had it done at all. For a long time I thought she blamed me, or the operation, for the cat's death, and then I read her poem, "A Lyric to Rooney" in *Dialogues of the Soul and Mortal Self in Time* and was simultaneously enlightened and mystified. "We had him fixed,/He grew fat and seemed content/but opulent,/sagging somehow," Jane writes; "So, did we betray him/with our sympathy?

> . . . he was always sick.
> We kept him from his death too long . . .
> He might have lived
> without our food,
> scrounging around the neighborhood,
> and dying in one last
> March battle,
> seasons later,
> while the spring moon's
> yellow eyes, brighter than his
> at last enclosed him.

Well, as moving as this poem is, and as much as I resonate with it, it's still to me an equation of proportion: unfixed tomcat = problem; fixed tomcat = solution. Ironically, I now realize, and despite our jokes about

Maggie's attitude toward animals, Jane was just as baffled by my sentiments as by Maggie's, if not more so. To her, I must have seemed a bit heartless, or managerial in my way—this even though she and I shared profound empathy for the natural world. She'd seen me cry openly in ESP class because I'd hit a rabbit while driving to Elmira; this much to the disgust of class member Warren Atkinson, who called me a hypocrite because, at the time, I ate meat. Jane and I had many discussions about our love for animals. Yet in class one night she remarked that I possessed "the type of consciousness that would dissect a flower to see what made it tick." Well, a flower, sure—and maybe a *dead* animal; but this remark left me hurt and confused, as if she were accusing me of being some kind of vivisectionist! Was she expressing sorrow and anger for Rooney's death? I don't know.

Not long after the Willie incident, on a cold and snowy Friday night, Jane and Rob and I drove up to Maggie and Bill's house in the hills overlooking Elmira. Bill gave a tour of their interesting clutter of travel mementos and told stories about his unsuccessful attempts to foil garbage-can raiding raccoons with ropes tied around the cans in elaborate supposedly lid-securing sailor's knots. The raccoons got in the cans anyway, but not by chewing through the ropes—they untied the knots. We had a riot with that one, Jane and I especially, carrying on about Maggie's aversion to animals and here they'd attracted genius knot-thwarting raccoons to their yard, and what kind of beliefs did that reflect, and so on. Though Maggie and Bill never really clicked with the you-create-your-own-reality idea, or really any of the Seth stuff, they enjoyed bantering it around as much as any of us did; and Maggie (who was a reporter for the Elmira newspaper) interviewed Jane many times over the years about her latest books, future projects, and ideas.

Agreement wasn't what mattered to Jane—it was the interaction with engaging people that she enjoyed.

"I think of class as . . . my equivalent of a salon which fits into old ideas about writers gathering great people around them, encouraging them; being paid court," Jane remarks in her journals, reflecting the tenor of these little social gatherings, too, even when it wasn't always so amiable among us.

Because sometimes it was anything but. Such as when Bill went off on a tirade of his own, mostly of despair, in which his extraordinary storytelling abilities would turn in on themselves and offer up a hellish sucking vortex of war or environmental ruin to come ("That boy of yours will never know what a forest or a cow pasture looks like!"), and all of us would feel dashed to pieces for days afterwards. Sometimes he'd reduce me to tears, particularly if I objected to his certitude (an interesting parallel with my father's conversational techniques), and pound my protests into the speculative ground, almost mercilessly, or so it felt, because of course I shared his fears to some extent. We all did, who doesn't? And Jane would try to respond in defense of everything.

One night I gave Maggie what I thought was a hot news tip: A contractor friend of my father's had told him about being part of a work crew hired to do masonry work for the military in what was apparently a secret nuclear warhead storage facility in Romulus, New York, a village some fifty miles north of Elmira on the east side of Seneca Lake. I told this (and other details) to Maggie in a spirit of wow, here's a thing to investigate, maybe uncover a hot story, but her reaction wasn't even as benign as disinterest. Indeed, to my surprise, she was quite hostile about it.

"Oh, if there were such a thing up there, everybody would know about it," she said dismissively. There was a small silence.

"Gee, Maggie," Jane said, in a voice unusually tentative for her, "isn't this the way stories like that get found out, through tips like Sue's?" To which Maggie replied, "Oh, we hear all sorts of stuff all the time, we only follow up on reliable leads." And that was that.

We all sat there.

Swiftly, Bill jumped in with another of his airplane stories and nobody ever mentioned the hot news tip again, least of all me. Years later, after the Nuclear Freeze movement had come and gone and the Army finally acknowledged they'd been storing decommissioned (they said) nuclear warheads underground at the Romulus depot, I thought about calling Maggie up and saying I told you so, but I never did. So maybe those Friday night get-togethers weren't as unlike traditional family gatherings as I wanted to believe.

* * *

NED WATKINS HAD BEEN INTRODUCED to Jane and Rob by a childhood friend of Dan Stimmerman's (the Dan connection) and was also in the regular Tuesday night ESP class, which I started attending somewhere in the late fall of 1968 (about the time Jane dropped the Thursday night class altogether). He and I liked one another well enough, though we didn't have all that much in common, really, other than our friendship with Jane and Rob, with whom we went to a New Year's Eve party that

December of 1968. I remember nothing of that party, not where it was or who else was there; all I remember is drinking way, way too much, waking up the next morning under the covers of Jane and Rob's living room sofa-bed, looking at the pile of my clothes on the floor next to me, and realizing that someone else—I had no idea who—was lying underneath the covers with me. When I lifted the blankets and saw Ned's face, my immediate thought was, *Well, I guess it's back to Martha's Vineyard I go*, and for just an instant, just the briefest of instants, really, my heart, as they say, leapt for joy.

9

The Meat Market Marriage

So Jane and Rob stood up with Ned and me when we were married in February of 1969. We decided to use the justice of the peace in Odessa, the tiny village overlooking the south end of Seneca Lake where Ned had grown up. Neither one of us was overly enthusiastic. I was pregnant again and felt, as Ned must have felt, caught in some relentless seawave of Dumb. We couldn't figure how to get out of it—all we could do was swim as best we could. Neither of us had mentioned the underlying incentive to our parents, who declined to attend. So Ned and I collected Jane and Rob from their apartment and drove the twenty-five miles or so from Elmira to the grocery store the justice owned on the main street of Odessa. I don't think we even called him first. We just drove on up, assuming he'd be there, and he was.

I have a vague memory of the four of us riding along the wintry country roads, chatting brightly, the sun glinting off the gunmetal snow and skies the color of a chlorinated pool. For my wedding day I'd worn a brown wool dress with black piping around the neck and hem. Size sixteen. With matching brown loafers. I don't recall what the groom's attire was. Jane and Rob, dressed rather better than the happy couple at the helm, were crammed into the narrow back seat of my '67 Mustang, which was about as comfortable as hardwood bleachers and required a complicated feat of gymnastics to access. I don't know how Jane managed to crawl in and out; I'm ashamed to admit that I didn't notice. She sat rigidly, her knees bent in a position that I'm sure must have been torture, though she said nothing about it. They regaled us with the story of their own marriage ceremony, which had taken place on December 27, 1954, in the living room of Rob's brother's house, in Tunkhannock, Pennsylvania, with his parents attending. That setting had been informal too, as well as the in-home reception following it, but as for informality—well, as the saying goes, they hadn't seen nothin' yet.

The JP was hacksawing a side of beef behind the back counter when we came in the store. He was wearing a blood-spattered white bib apron over a plaid flannel shirt and jeans with rubber work boots, also splashed with blood. Ned imparted the purpose of our visit and the JP sighed and said sure, no problem. Graciously, he put down the saw, removed the apron, and wiped off his hands before leading us outside and up a long flight of narrow covered stairs into his JP chambers, a dismal second-floor room with a messy rolltop desk and pale green milk paint covering the wainscoted walls.

Jane had a terrible time getting up those stairs—it was clearly an ordeal for her, worse than (or possibly exacerbated by) the struggle she must have had with the car seat. As Ned and the JP and I climbed the stairs ahead of them, Rob said something to Jane in an oddly emphatic tone, and I glanced back and saw that he was half-carrying her, pulling her up step by step because Jane's knees wouldn't bend far enough for her to manage them on her own. A shocked chill penetrated the state of slam-dunked numbness I'd entered some days before. Until that moment, I hadn't realized how physically impaired Jane was by the arthritis-like stiffness she occasionally referred to as "the symptoms." My response was to look away and keep going. What else was there to do? Stop the whole procedure?

After the ten-minute ceremony, Ned asked the JP how much we owed him. "Whatever you think it's worth," the Justice said.

"You got change for a five?" Ned asked. Jane laughed loudly. As it turned out, Ned had it exactly right.[1]

The deed done and paid for, we trekked back down the rickety stairs, the JP went back to chopping dead meat, and the four of us drove to my parents' house for a reception of sorts. We must have stopped to see my new inlaws, but if so, I don't remember it—I was way too far gone in pretending that all of this was just a terrifically *fine* thing for us to be doing. In fact I was so detached that I experienced the peripheral vision blackout usually associated with fainting. I could only see directly in front of me, and even then everything was a blurred pearly gray, as if my eyes had been coated with Vaseline.

My mother had laid out the dining room table exactly as she did for elaborate holiday meals—the linen tablecloth and napkins, the antique Havilland china, the sterling silver, the lead crystal water glasses, the antler-handled carving knives, the fancy hors d'oeuvres tray, the candlesticks, the drinks, the smiles. I don't remember what the food was. Jane sat straight as a ramrod across from me at the table, acting chipper as a finch trapped in a cage. Rob was relaxed and jolly, conversing easily with my parents; but he was their age, and held no grudges about the comfortable circumstances in which they lived. Of course by that hour of that special day, my father had consumed a quart of scotch, maybe two. At one point in the meal he turned to Ned and roared, "Remember this, boy—if you ever hurt her, I'll nail your balls to a cliff and kick your ass over the edge!" It was the only thing he said to Ned the entire afternoon.

My mother and I laughed hysterically—nay, we screeched. I didn't even dare look at Jane.

Finally we could all escape and the four of us went back to Jane and Rob's apartment and took some Polaroid photos to commemorate the event. Of those half-dozen pictures, I remember only one of them clearly: in it Jane, looking no more substantial than an elf, is standing between Ned and me, our arms carefully draped across her shoulders and her smile seemingly cut from ice. By then, after all that climbing and crouching and social deportment, she must have been in agony. But she hid it well, at least from me. And all those photos are lost now, for when I tried to find them again in 1999, I discovered that they had vanished from my collection and Rob's too, which is strange indeed, as he and I are both meticulous packrats when it comes to holding on to such things, "for the record," as Rob would say.

All this happened on a Tuesday, so Ned and I stayed for ESP class, during which Seth delivered a lengthy (and actually quite poignant) monologue to us about "the ceremony of the skies and trees and even of the grass," and on "looking into the face of vulnerability to find joy." Well, at least Seth was hopeful. Then Ned and I went back to my desolate little apartment on the edge of the Cornell campus and tried to make a go of it.

Jane later told me her impression of my parents, as people stuck by virtue of their clothes and furnishings in an outmoded time frame, especially my mother. While not exactly untrue (the house was floor to ceiling antiques with red velvet-flowered wallpaper in the dining room, for one thing), these remarks struck me as hilariously funny: Did Jane ever get a load of her own clothes in that regard? For that matter, who among us was not stuck in some sort of time frame, some element of our past to which we wished we could return? Or maybe I misinterpreted Jane's words; maybe she meant something else and was trying to be polite, I don't know. I never told Jane the impressions my mother had of *her*, however. In fact I never mentioned it at all, to anyone, until writing about it now, in this memoir.

That this should have been the only discussion Jane and I ever had about this entire event struck me as sad much later, looking back on it across more than three decades and seeing for the first time the void that existed between us. In those moments, Jane and I were acting like teacher and student, engaged intellectually in psychic analysis but without the intimate warmth of true friendship, and this was by and large the mode in which we operated, though I didn't recognize it then, or in my life as a whole. So much else about my relationship with her was so glorious that this lack hardly mattered, and the truth was, we were both comfortable within its limits. But it was precisely this emotional distance that made it almost impossible for us to get around our expectations—basically Jane's expectations—and be stupid in front of one another, a gift that intimacy bestows. Instead, I felt her disapproval—of my actions, my parents' lifestyle, my acquiescence as opposed to determination—and I think she must have been wary of mine, or anyone's, though I had none toward her that I was aware of (none that I would have dared express, anyway). No wonder, then, perhaps, that those wedding day photos, the only ones taken of Jane and me standing side by side, have disappeared into another world.

Seven months later, eleven days after Sean was born on October 7, we visited Jane and Rob and they used two packs of film taking pictures (which survived intact) of the three of us. Maggie and Bill Granger were there, and I remember Bill picking up Sean and cuddling him and calling him "Little Peanut," and Rob speaking in wonderment, again and again, about this tiny new person in our midst, and Jane acting sprightly but saying little; and that I nursed Sean in full view of everybody, as I often did in ESP class, which must have appalled Jane on levels I can't even begin to imagine.

* * *

BUT NED AND I HAD AN AWFUL TIME—it just didn't work. Had I been able to understand that what I wanted was a child, not a husband, maybe we could have avoided the mismatched marriage trauma altogether; though given the times and their lack of good will toward single parents, I doubt it. Obviously, though, I'd acted on this urge before—and both times, my conscious mind had been effectively blotto during the mechanics.

Jane and Rob did their best to help us, including an invitation for a private Seth session, during which Ned and I were each gently skewered, you might say, with some keen analysis and recommendations for repairing the marriage.[2] We divorced anyway in 1970, though the insights applied beyond that framework—not only to me, but in a universal manner (typical of Seth's remarks), and in its way, to Jane, or more accurately, to the differences between Jane and me that always seemed so . . . alike.

"You have felt for a long time that you were between the devil and the deep blue sea," Seth told me that night. "That you had a mind and a womb, and that somehow the two did not go together. Regardless of past life influences, which did exist, and granting some other interior reasons, you had children to prove that you were a woman, both to your mother and yourself. Then, you thought, you could be quite free to use your mind and your other abilities, and no one could say a thing because you could always say, 'Obviously I've proven my womanhood and I'm free to use my mind.'

"Many subsidiary issues fall into place here—the attempt[s] at times to . . . hide the womanly nature of which you are basically ashamed."

I paid little attention to these insights. For one thing I couldn't really see what relevance they had to the problem at hand. Much later, long after Jane was dead, I would read these passages over and think that my head must have been made out of wood all those years, not to have caught on from the moment these comments were made. Almost as if Jane and I had purposefully set up opacity, rather than empathic clarity between us, as a method of exploration.

For it was the issue, so to speak, of our womanhood, and what to do about it—prove it, disprove it, attack and punish it, hide it or revel in it—that formed the space between us that was simultaneously so invisible, and yet so unmistakably our central argument.

10

The Seat of the (Somewhat) Unconscious

One of the more astonishing things that ever happened to Jane and me took place on one of those Fridays, and up until now I've been too self-conscious about the details to include it in print (I cut it at the last minute from *Conversations with Seth*). It's not just the personal aspects that bother me—it's the sheer wildness of the event itself, which, had I heard it from somebody else, I probably would not have believed.

Late 1969 or early 1970: Ned and I and the Grangers were at Jane and Rob's, talking about the energy-focusing experiments ESP class had been doing while in the relaxed-alert state officially recognized in brain-wave hertz measurements as "alpha." Specifically, class had tried some playful healing imagery, which produced some immediate results, as Jane told the Grangers that night. Or at least the energy recipients thought so, which temporarily, at least, amounted to the same thing. Bill and Maggie listened to this with great interest. "Why not test it out right now?" Bill suggested affably, in a spirit of fun. "Hey, why not?" Jane said. None of us, least of all me, expected any big deal to come of it. It was just alpha stuff, light and inconsequential.

Besides, my enthusiasm was somewhat dulled. I had been suffering mightily from the so-called "female" problem of trichomonas, an amoebic infection that is now quickly cleared up with oral doses of Flagyl. In those days treatment basically amounted to hot baths and applications of gentian violet, which took a while to be effective; and open, violently itching sores could and usually did appear in the interim, which was the case with me that evening. I was in sheer misery—for one thing it hurt to sit down—but didn't let on; it was, after all, humiliating. I'd talked with Jane about it earlier in the day, seeking from her, as I so often did, an answer behind the problem. She'd offered her sympathies but said nothing further, which was even more embarrassing, as I thought her reaction must mean I'd offended her, somehow, by mentioning it to her at all.[1]

So there we were, me just hoping to distract myself, playing with this alpha healing business—whoop-dee-do, I thought; borrr-ing. Nonetheless, at Jane's direction, we all closed our eyes and imagined going inside Bill's stomach. He'd had serious ulcers for years, often having to subsist on food like plain mashed potatoes and weak tea. We sat in silence. I floated off on a sequence of disconnected images until abruptly, vividly, I found myself standing in the middle of a bombed-out battlefield, complete with carnage, shredded and torn earth and trees, and the distant thunder of guns—an image of Bill's stomach, I knew. A minute later, we all came out of it, and I told Bill what I'd seen. Jane had perceived similar images, and she pointed out the obvious connections with Bill's physical symptoms. It made sense to him, though he couldn't quite articulate why. "Jeeze, wouldn't you know, I'm carrying around the original Battle of the Bulge," he joked. "Hey, anything you can do in there, be my guest! Take out the whole damn thing, for all I care!"

Jane laughed, and let it go at that. Then she suggested, without further explanation, that everybody try the alpha thing on me.

"The room fell quiet," according to my notes. "I tried slipping into a receptive state, suggesting that the reasons for [my] condition would become clear, and that my body would heal itself. We all sat there for maybe a minute, traffic noise droning on outside the windows . . ."

"Then, suddenly," my notes continue, "I felt a sharp tingling sensation, something like a mild electric shock. I opened my eyes in surprise. Jane was looking at me in what I recognized as a deeper state than alpha—something like the Seth trance, but different, parallel to it—resembling it in some fashion, but with a feeling of concentrated purpose.

"I couldn't help grinning at her steady stare. 'Ye-e-e-s?' I mugged.

"Jane said, 'It's the woman thing again, Sue.' The others looked up from their alpha daydreams. 'It has to do,' Jane went on, 'with blaming your womanhood for issues that aren't really related. It's—you're making divisions all over the place where none really exist.' As she said this, I thought of all the times I'd felt that I could be a woman, or I could be a writer, but not both; and that each side, each choice, resented the other. It connected."

My notes go on to say that Jane described some other impressions she had of the reasons for my symptoms, but I forgot the particulars almost immediately—because as she talked, I began to realize—and this is where it gets tricky, even now, after all this time and contemplating—I began to realize that I was no longer uncomfortable, sitting there. "Was I that numb from two glasses of beer?" my notes ask, but I already knew otherwise. I got up from my chair and went into the bathroom and checked.

The trichomonas sores—open, fiery-hot burning-itchy sonsabitches, as anyone who's had this nasty scourge can tell you—were gone. *GONE*.

And I mean—gone. Presto-chango. Poof! Not there. Not a trace.

Momentarily, I thought I'd gone crazy. Seriously nuts. That an entire time period, maybe a couple of weeks, had passed by and here I was in Jane and Rob's bathroom again, thinking that only a couple of minutes had passed since—since before, when the sores were right *there*. Where they now were not there at all. But no, it was the same Friday night; everybody out in the living room would agree with that, I was sure. But what was this, anyway? What had *happened* here? I was shocked and really quite upset. Scandalized, in fact. I returned to the living room and waited until the general conversation started up again, and underneath the cover of voices, I told Jane what had happened—what I thought had happened.

She reacted enthusiastically, but guarded, too. "Hey, people, did you hear that!" she said. "Sue had this female problem, and now it's gone!" She grinned at me, but she was uneasy about it herself. Bill made some sort of joke—he was embarrassed, and really, so was I. Ned said nothing at all. He just stared at the floor, nonplussed.

Jane and I looked at each other, and went on to other subjects. And we never talked about it again.

To this day, I've never scrutinized the meaning of this healing—or whatever it was—experience. But for my notes, which I wrote up as soon as I got home that night, the whole thing seems impossible to me now, as if I must be misremembering it, or that I dreamed it, or made it up and confused it with something real. Except that it *was* real—one might say super-real, but was it that? Does this sort of natural healing go on all the time, beneath our conscious knowledge? Had the frivolous little alpha thing somehow clicked, nudged my natural healing abilities just so, turned them into high gear? Or more discomforting, had we suddenly harnessed our mutual energies in a mighty illustration of what is possible? And if so, what did this mean, exactly, in the ordinary, daily world, to each of us? If we could, in effect, get better any time we wanted to—then how come, in effect, we didn't?

* * *

BUT JANE DID EXPERIENCE SOME remarkable instances of "natural healing," the most intense of which occurred in August of 1973, when her blouse sleeve caught on fire in the kitchen at 458.[2] According to her notes, Jane screamed and Rob rushed out of his studio and ripped off her blouse, "but my hand was a mess of third degree burns," she later wrote. "The sight of it really frightened me as badly as the pain and I knew I had to do something quickly. I calmed myself down, sat in a chair, and began a self-hypnosis procedure to dull the pain, first of all. When this took effect, I talked to my body, telling it to repair the tissue easily and quickly. An hour later, to our relief and amazement the hand looked completely normal . . . Magic again, I thought, because self-healing does seem magical to us and when it happens, for a moment we know that we've suddenly done things right, with brilliant true competence . . . so why don't we do that more often?"

And in the arena of so-called female problems, Jane had accomplished similar feats. At age twenty-five, after she miscarried, at home, at three and a half months ("a rabbit test had said I wasn't pregnant," she notes), she didn't seek medical attention for four days and only then to find out what had gone wrong with her diaphragm. In her unfinished "Magical Approach" manuscript,[3] Jane says, "I was relatively innocent of the dangers that could be involved—which is why I came out of the entire situation so well . . . I was examined and given a clean bill of health. I didn't need a D and C or any other medical procedure."

The second instance happened in 1958, when she was twenty-nine. She'd had a continuous period for forty-five days—exactly as long as she'd been waiting for a check to arrive from a story sale. Finally, she writes, though she was not in pain or overt physical distress, she consulted Rob's family doctor (the same one who'd given her the ill-fitting diaphragm), who told her, as she recalled, to just go home "and buy some scotch and have several drinks," instead of worrying about it, or about paying him for the visit. When her check arrived in the mail a few days later, Jane notes, the errant period stopped. "So . . . the body can respond to our nervousness, and our upsets," Jane observed. "Both incidents reinforced my belief in the body's ability to heal itself."[4]

Likewise, in 1979, in the midst of writing *Conversations with Seth*, I also experienced a runaway period, which lasted for six weeks without letup. Of course I called Jane to ask for help (I didn't feel ill, but it was, to say the least, inconvenient). Somewhat mysteriously, Jane said only that she'd think about it and get back to me—and when she did, a few days later, all she would say about it was that "the womb is the seat of the unconscious," which she repeated, emphatically, three times. Her tone was oddly reticent, as if she couldn't bring herself to tell me some gawdawful truth behind the symptom, or as if I must be an idiot not to see what was right in front of me.

In fact, it was indeed right in front of me, as it had been time and time again and would continue to be for years to come, hammering away, unfazed by guilt or woe, until I *got* it. From the moment I'd signed the contract for *Conversations*, I'd been involved in an endless round-and-round argument with the man I was seeing, my soon-to-be second-ex. He disapproved of the subject matter and spared no effort to belittle my writing aspirations as a whole. Yet in the same breath he would implore me to marry him. Incredibly enough, my notes about it say this: "Other than [the nasty remarks], he's very loving." (*Other* than?) I wanted to break off the relationship but couldn't quite let go. And why not? I didn't know why, or so I'd convinced myself . Meanwhile, my period flowed on and on.

And yet I must admit that I thought Jane's remark about it was just plain dumb. I had the temerity to be short with her on the phone, not even offering her so much as a thank you for her time. A correct observation, I had no doubt, but *so what?* was my ungrateful reaction. Peevishly, I decided to get my own answer this way: I'd sit down and write a spontaneous poem, and whatever appeared on the page would be it—like automatic writing, from me to me. Somewhat to my surprise, the lines I scribbled were halfway decent, and directed, with vehemence, toward my man friend. In part the poem read:

> You battered me with fists of words,
> you bruised me with your tongue,
> you slashed me with your lips until
> my bones welled up in blood.

It went on for five stanzas, no holds barred—violent and raw with indignation. So I called Jane back and read it to her. "Right," she said when I finished. "Exactly right—you got it. It's the *woman* thing again, Sue, don't you see? That *division*." (I didn't dare mention the insults leveled at my writing—and why not? Because I put up with them?) Jane said nothing about the poem itself.

In the midst of all this—talk about the unconscious boiling over—Jane called me one day to announce her somewhat abashed decision to title her next book *The God of Jane*. "Do you think it's too audacious?" she asked me. I told her I thought it was an absolutely wonderful title, and audacious as hell besides, the perfect combination. "I figured you'd say so," she laughed, and the minute I hung up the phone I sat down and wrote a poem in response, which I called "The God of Sue." Some of my lines make this observation:

> She loves desire,
> She loves to love,
> but as for being loved, ah well—
> sometimes She simply isn't
> sure She wants
> the person who comes with it.

"Not bad," I told myself, and without thinking any more about it mailed a copy off to Jane. She ended up including it in her book. "I was delighted," Jane writes in *The God of Jane*, "that someone else was so enthused, and that the concepts could be used in such a highly individualized way." But then she adds, "Sue's poem also surprised me in that it visualized the God of Sue as She—reasonable enough, and almost a feminine manifesto—but when I thought of the God of Jane, for example, I just didn't think of sexual elements at all."

Reading this passage in the published book, I remember thinking . . . feminine manifesto? C'mon Jane—for chrissakes what in the *hell* are you *talking* about?! Whaddya mean, you didn't "think of sexual elements?" Bull-shit!

Not for the first time, our respective creativity saw what neither of us could quite get through our conscious heads. Eventually, I had a D and C, which took care of the wayward period, but not the rest of it, the underlying cause. It would take many other tricks of magic and realization, and a few other related physical symptoms, before I began to fathom what I'd been telling myself all along. But by then, Jane was gone.

II

The Honest Appraisal (Yowch!) And Similar Tales Close to the Bone

Not that we hadn't tried to breach these gaps before. One day in 1972, in her second apartment, the extra one Jane and Rob rented across the hall, the one with the huge oak tree just outside the windows where Jane set up her workroom—one day she said to me, "Let's be really honest with one another."

"Uh, huh," I said, smiling, as I usually did when I felt apprehensive. "Sure. Why not?"

Jane lit a cigarette and brayed a loud and equally uneasy laugh. She was at her desk and I sat facing her in a green aluminum lawn chair; I think I'd dropped by with some ESP class transcripts I'd typed up for her. It was a late spring day, a few weeks before the June 23 flood would roar down through the Chemung River Valley and devastate Elmira and every other community in its wake, and change everything.

Since April of that year, eighteen-month old Sean and I had been living in our own apartment on the river side of West Water Street, just a block from Jane and Rob. I had a full-time job as a typesetter in an Elmira print shop. I no longer had a car, but work, Sean's babysitter, the grocery store, Jane and Rob's, were all an easy walk, and I often enjoyed just ambling along the pleasant leafy sidewalks or the riverbank, towing Sean (and his ever-present binky) in the red Radio Flyer my grandfather had given me for Christmas when I was three or four.

It was a long way from Martha's Vineyard and the life I'd left behind there, but it was simple and sweet, and what the heck, I told myself, someday when I hit that best-seller list . . . someday, I'll go back and find that life, and pick up where I left off. Unlike Jane, whose goals were clear-cut, I had no real plan worked out as to how to achieve this, or what it was, exactly, that I wanted to go back to. It was a distant, amorphous dream of a place that had something to do with literary achievement and something to do with avoiding the more difficult details of the present. I was spending my evenings writing elaborately detailed erotic mini-novels starring myself and the characters from *Star Trek*; I had nothing else to write about, or so I believed. Except for Jane's ESP class and its splashovers beyond Tuesday nights, I lived in a small, protected world inhabited by Sean and my parents, Jane and Rob and Friday night or ESP-related friends, books and newspapers, and the unremarkable daily grind of a dull job.

So now, here we were, Jane and me, sitting together in her sunlit workroom, having always, up to now, pretty much avoided the nitty of our gritties, and we're going to be "really honest" with one another? My stomach began churning up an acid storm. Actually I was more afraid of what she might want from me than anything she could say in return. I came from a family that was simultaneously without guile and accomplished at keeping things unspoken, a status I maintained in the world at large. Anyway, Jane and I had already done the secret-telling bit in ESP class,[1] so what was this all about?

I remember clearing my (rapidly shrinking) throat and saying something like, well, okay, you go first, I dare ya, ha ha, and, confirming my suspicions, Jane immediately said, "So tell me, Sue-Belle, what do you think about my looks?"

Today, looking back on this, I realize that what she was fishing for was some encouraging feedback about the appearance (or, as I'm sure she secretly hoped, nonappearance) of her physical problems. By this time she was more or less stiff all over (some days not so much so as others), and very thin, though bright and quick, not at all "disabled" looking, whatever that means. Her teeth were somewhat crooked (and were, unknown to me, loosening in their sockets, the effect of a receding gum line), but her luminous eyes and good-natured grin tended to negate these frailties. She wasn't beautiful in the standard sense, but she was by no means unattractive, especially when she was filled with ideas, laughing and animated and radiant. In fact, Jane had been (as Walt Zeh observed) a striking beauty, a self-evident distinction that is mentioned in such diverse places as her high school yearbook and in the (to modern eyes mind-bendingly sexist) bio for her first short story, "The Red Wagon," in the December, 1956, *Fantasy and Science Fiction* magazine, in which editor Anthony Boucher breathlessly refers to her as "a stunning little brunette who ranks high among what [writer Cyril] Kornbluth calls Boucher's Belletristic Beauties," then manages to pull himself together well enough to acknowledge that "she can write—freshly, imaginatively, and sounding (God bless her!) like no one else in or out of our field." It's hard to know whether to scream or applaud.[2]

But that day in her apartment, she wasn't radiant or stunning—in fact I thought she looked defeated, though at the time I had little if any comprehension of what could possibly defeat Jane Roberts. No way was I going to give her any negative suggestions, in any case. If I'd known just how needy she was for reassurance, I would have—but I don't know what I would have done. I was twenty-seven; Jane was forty-three. About reassurance, I knew squat.

What I finally said to her was that I thought she was "handsome." I couldn't say "beautiful," and I knew she wouldn't believe it anyway. Intuitively, I realized she would appreciate the reference to male good looks—it fit her ideas about the intellect, for one thing. Besides which, it was true.

"Handsome," she repeated. She considered that a moment, looking out the window, smoking, and then said, "I guess I like that. I guess I'll take that." She let out a sigh. "Sometimes I think I look like a monster."

I said something in reply like, well, shit Jane, I feel the same about myself half the time, which seemed to soothe her a bit. "I suppose," she said, looking away; but in fact I had no concept of the depth of Jane's fears, or how damaging the source. I'd heard my parents expressing hatred for themselves, especially about aging, so Jane's remark seemed ordinary to me, something to skip over lightly and ignore.

Then I lost my head and tried to explain something that had come to me a while before—that I thought her physical stiffness was reflected by Rob in his painting style, especially in his human figures. That either he was expressing a belief they shared, or that rigidity was a creative framework they each used, or something like that. I didn't phrase the thought very well, and I could see that she didn't like it much—after all, I was criticizing Rob's work, something neither of them would put up with on behalf of the other. Finally she said, "Yeah, I see what you mean," in a defensive tone and so I shut up and we didn't discuss it further. It was her turn.

Ho-kay.

First she told me that I was a "good-looking gal" and so ought to lose ten pounds or so. Well, that analysis was no special surprise—I heard it more or less constantly from my parents—but I still felt a small surge of melancholy to hear it from Jane. It was only a lead-in to what she really wanted to say to me, which was, again, that I "really had it" as far as writing went and I should "get at it," and get at it now; that I should be "at the typewriter" for a minimum of six hours a day without fail.

"I guess I thought you'd be more dedicated to it by now than you are," Jane said to me. "But if you're gonna do it, gal, then you've got to screw yourself into a chair every day no matter what, and just . . . do it." Her eyes were dark, intensely serious. "You're either a writer with a capital 'W' or you're not—which is it? And if you're the writer, then you'd jolly well better get to it, right?"

I said nothing.

"Well, I guess maybe that's what you have to figure out," she said, at last. "Either you do it or you don't."

What could I say? She'd reminded me of this often enough that it had begun to feel like nagging—this was "honesty"? Sitting there in the hot seat, it occurred to me, if dimly, that I'd used this forum to give her some positive feedback and she hadn't done the same in return. Maybe I had a naive idea of what honest appraisals were all about. What did looks have to do with it?

Then she went through the thing again about how surprised she was that I'd "had a kid." Well, I was surprised too, actually, though it wasn't as if I complained about it; I thought having a child was perfectly, unassailably fine, in fact—but this was the Nth time we'd been down *this* road by then, and so I thought, okay, Jane, let's get off my ass about it, all right? But I didn't say anything. Instinctively I knew that having a child or two, or writing in the hours when the kids were in school or sleeping, wasn't the point. The point was something else, something darker, something more emotional and threatening than either Jane or I could get to, even though we shared it—whatever it was—to a large extent. Maybe all women do; maybe everyone does, regardless of gender. After all, in those years, it was still men who were typically expected to trudge out the door every morning and support a whole family by themselves.

Actually, all this was quite disheartening, though I didn't let myself admit it. I realized that she was expressing tremendous respect for whatever abilities I might have possessed, but all I could focus on was what I read as disappointment. The thing that had drawn me to Jane in the first place was the fact that here was a woman whose intense concerns, whose *career*, in fact, revolved around essentially playful questions about the nature of consciousness, and who was delving into same and writing books about it unlike anyone else in her time and place. Thus on one hand I sought her approval and on the other wanted to be free of its judgment, a too familiar paradox.

But the thing was, Jane and I never had any meaningful discussions about writing technique, or the vicissitudes of publishing, or anything else specific about our shared craft. She never *asked* me how many hours I devoted to writing or what I might be interested in writing *about*; she assumed, and more or less correctly, that I had no particular objective either way, and I wasn't about to admit to all those *Star Trek* potboilers as a defense. No, it was all about getting down to it, planting the self in front of the typewriter or frittering it all away—no middle ground. Maybe she thought she had nothing else to share, or maybe I just didn't know enough to recognize these gems when they were offered. More likely, though, what I was hearing was the voice of Jane's fears for herself projected on me: that if she let go and did anything she wanted—as I obviously could, by compare—then look what would happen! She might become fat, unambitious—*pregnant*! And the irony is, I was in a position to snap back with a reciprocal "honest" appraisal, if I'd only had the insight at the time to say something like, Jane, you've proven you're a writer with a capital "W"—now why don't you jolly well attend to your *physical* condition?

But it wasn't that simple. There was a question of dignity and self-image tied up in this that rose out of, and fed into, her physical hassles in a vicious cycle.

For example, one day not long before *Seth Speaks* came out, Jane asked me, "What name do you think should go on the Seth books as author?"

I stared at her, caught off-guard. Was this a trick question or something? Did she mean the author's name should be Seth? Should it be Seth/Jane? What should I say? I couldn't figure out *what* to say—it all suddenly felt like a trap. She and Rob sat quietly, waiting to hear my answer. I must have hesitated too long, because she laughed and said, "Jane Roberts."

"Oh, well, sure, of course," I said, seeing at last what she'd been getting at. But once again I felt that I'd failed a test. Only years later, when I read through her papers, did I understand the mine field this question presented, universally applicable.

"Felt I've been in an inferior position," she writes in the unfinished "Aspects" manuscript, "pushed to the wall to prove my worth—fraud or saint—no firm ground between. Ridiculed or looked up to. Impossible strain . . . If I didn't prove ESP, etc., then I'd be object of ridicule—rejected by intelligent society . . . a stupid second-rate psychic instead of respected writer.

"Seth got all the respect and I had to deal with the nuts."

Reading this, all I could think was—oh *why* when I had the chance, when she asked me that question, didn't I just come right back with "Jane Roberts"? What in hell was I thinking?

* * *

BECAUSE IT WAS "THE WRITING THING" that connected us. Whatever our mutual or secret fears about it, it formed, even more than so-called psychic stuff, the cusp of our experience. I remember the day—though I don't recall clearly when it was, probably early 1970—when Jane received word of her advance from Prentice-Hall for *The Seth Material*, $2,500, for them at the time an absolutely stupendous amount of money. She called me up and I went over and helped her and Rob consume a celebratory gallon or two of red wine, which always gave me blistering headaches, though I didn't care that afternoon. Jane was already pretty well looped when I arrived, whirling around and whooping it up (and thus still fairly mobile). I'd never witnessed such throes of joy about a writing success—she was the first person I knew who'd *had* any. I remember that she flopped down on the sofa with her feet dangling over the arm and yelled "Twenty-five hundred dollars! Twenty-five hundred goddamned dollars!"[3] at the top of her lungs, and the three of us laughed and hollered and carried on like maniacs well into the wee hours, or so I assume, because one moment I was sitting in Jane and Rob's living room and the next moment I woke up in my bed at my parents' house with no memory of anything after about nine o'clock the previous evening. My car was out in the driveway, so I knew I must have driven home, across the Walnut Street bridge over the Chemung River, through the winding streets of southside Elmira, and out the country highway, six miles, to the Webbs Mills house—but in what condition, I had no idea.

Weirdly, this incident was an uncanny recreation of one of the preeminent scenes from my childhood—the night, in 1951 or thereabouts, when my parents and I went out to celebrate my mother's radio quiz show win of $250, which for them at the time was also a stupendous amount of money. To land the prize, my mother had correctly recited a poem by Edna St. Vincent Millay. Elated, she got absolutely smashed and rode home with her feet sticking out the car window, yelling "Two hundred and fifty dollars! Two hundred and fifty dollars!" and my father had to drive down the middle of the Walnut Street bridge to avoid whacking her feet against the girders. *That* incident had scared the bejeezus out of six- or seven-year-old me, though when Jane did it, it was funny . . . funny, too, the like amounts of money and the physical proximity of both events, involving alcohol—and literature—years apart.

* * *

I DID JOIN JANE'S WRITING CLASS for a while, mainly in an effort to show her that I could live up to her idea of seriousness. Aside from journalism school, I'd never taken a creative writing course and was in fact deeply suspicious of the whole idea. But this was Jane, and I imagined plunging into some kind of directed project; a novel, maybe, or interconnected short stories; something I thought I couldn't manage on my own. This group met on Wednesday afternoons and besides me included Hope, who was writing an historical piece about a thirteenth-century monk who harbored a few secret sins; Fran, an older woman who lived up the street from Jane and was working on a mystery novel; and several others who came and went over a period of time.

I choked in that class. Jane would ask us to write a couple paragraphs on this or that, or present a viewpoint through which to explore nuances of character or whatever, and I could not squeeze out one word. Not one. I'd go in the other apartment, go downstairs and sit on the porch, sit in the bathroom, whatever. Nothing. A blank; as if nothing had ever existed in my head at all, every time. Performance anxiety, obviously—what if I wrote something and Jane pronounced it crap in front of Hope and Fran? Or worse, handed it back to me without comment, lips pursed in disgust? Though Jane found this funny, and told me not to worry about it, I was humiliated, and soon dropped out.

Related incident, vividly etched in my memory, 1979: I give the first draft of *Conversations* to Jane to read over, at her request, so she can put together an introduction. It's a huge manuscript, two big boxes full, typed up on the cheap foolscap I used to buy for $1.50 a ream. Jane reads the whole thing in less than a week, calls me up and says—okay, I'm done, c'mon down and we'll talk. I drive to her house in a sweat, thinking, oh, boy, she's gonna tell me it stinks.

Jane's sitting at her work table in the corner by the fireplace. She has the manuscript in front of her, all tidy and neat. I sit on the edge of my chair, nervous as a jackrabbit in front of the hounds. Jane lights a cigarette, takes a deep drag, looks at me very seriously, an affectionate—I'm thinking pitying—smile on her face. I can't utter a word. In fact I think my throat has broken. In another minute I am going to soil myself.

"Well, ya know, it's like this," Jane says. "You did a really excellent job, ya know? A really excellent job; I mean that."

"Wow, really?" I croak. "You really mean it?"

"Yee-ah," Jane says. "Really great. But the only thing is—" she suddenly lunges forward in her chair, eyes wide—"*Jesus Christ, Sue, you made me sound like a god-damned fuckin' sailor!* Do I really *swear* that much?"

"Uh," I say, "uh, well—"

"You'll have to tone down the swearing!" Jane says. "For the sake of the reader, you know." So I take the manuscript home and edit out some of the swearing—reluctantly, I might add. I didn't think I'd exaggerated her speech habits at all—in fact, I thought I *had* toned it down.

* * *

JANE ALSO LET ME READ SOME of her unpublished fiction, including *Cast of the Witch*, a fantasy novel about women with psychic abilities, and a couple of autobiographical "straights." I thought some of the writing was stilted, some of it wild and free—much like Jane, much like any work in draft form. Now, reading her journals and a small selection of her other work for this memoir, I realize that the novels were a tiny percent of her tremendous output—the product of someone who did, in fact, plant herself in front of the typewriter for hours and hours, every single day.

Thus I think of Jane's relentless determination not to fritter away her time. I think about the definition of "time" and how it is that some of us seem to experience it as a fuller, perhaps fatter, dimension than others seem to do. I wonder if sheer will, pressing against the idea of time, changes the way a person utilizes its alleged parameters. I conclude that there is no other possible explanation for what Jane accomplished in her writing lifetime.

I look over her voluminous notes, dream records, journals, notes attached to the journals, daily records, charts of story submissions with earnings, expenses and editor comments; these plus the virtually continuous outpouring of novels, short stories, poems, and ideas and outlines and revisions for same throughout her life, all woven in between part-time jobs, occasional socializing with friends, frequent and thorough housecleaning (along with the furniture rearranging that Jane so loved to do), visits to in-laws, and numerous other details of daily life, not the least of which included the needs and joys of married life and several moves between Florida, Sayre, and Elmira. And then there are the volumes of published and unpublished Seth material, the 252 Seth sessions delivered in the years of Jane's ESP class, her published nonfiction books, the *Oversoul Seven* novels, her unfinished autobiography, her "Sinful Self," "Bali," "Aspects," "Magical Approach," and "Heroics" manuscripts, and the works she dictated to Rob from her hospital bed in the last two years of her life, to mention some, by no means all, of her output.

Her journals from the fifties are staggeringly detailed, with notes categorized in such topics as "Mood, Discussion, Activities, Specials"; "Correspondence"; "Avon [hours worked]"; "Worries"; "Symptoms" (which include comments about "thyroid drops" and other indications of her slowing-it-down symptoms even then); "Significant Events–Main Topics of Thought"; "Psychic Aspects of Day"; "Mood"; "Period" (about which Jane worried every day that she wasn't having one); and, of course, "Writing," in which she records her writing time to the minute and evaluates her efforts against a daily expected minimum.

Reading these records—of which I've indicated a mere portion—one becomes overwhelmed with the sense of the sheer weight of life; of anyone's life, and certainly this one, which was measured to a large degree throughout its span by the weight of paper; pages and pages, stacks, piles, reams of paper, all filled with millions upon millions of words, only a fraction of them thus far published. And along with every page filled top to bottom with words, there are ghost words, probable words, ideas springing off the page and spinning into the air, ideas and words sprung free. And yet even these are part of the weight of a life and never vanish, but are recorded somewhere, if only in dreams and notions of dreams.

So I think of Jane, who weighed no more than a child most of her life, and the weight of time and how she used it, and something mystical comes to me, some meaning, that I can't explain. It is deeply mysterious and yet perfectly plain. And it comforts me, situates me more clearly, in my memory of her and the friendship we established between us, which was no more significant than I remembered, and certainly no less. In the end, I had it figured about right.

Only one real pique in all those journal notes—an entry in August of 1959, in which Jane describes a talk she and Rob have about how aware they are of their childless state in the midst of friends and neighbors having children; this during a particularly worrisome month in which Jane became convinced she must be pregnant (she wasn't) . . .

Thursday, August 13, 1959

. . . after being so miserable about it for the past few days that I couldn't even write, I find myself *accepting* the possibility calmly.

Rob and I had a long discussion last night. Certainly we didn't "want" children and at the thought I grow panicky but panic as I've found, disappears before common sense and intellectual scrutiny. If I *am* pregnant I'll make a novel about it . . . a woman who is a writer fighting against the woman-role . . . undergoing pregnancy and delivery—And [so] it's Florida in any case—for a child, the sun and sand!

Saturday, August 15, 1959

My period is starting! Late I imagine because of the bug I had earlier in the month. Oddly enough, though, we *have* decided to try for a child this year or next!

I read this last entry and I think, oohhhhhhh really? Say, Janey-O, was there some little thing you forgot to MENTION in all those discussions you initiated with me about the god-damned having-a-kid question? Eh?[4]

But Writer with a capital "W"—what is that? Am I it? Or not? How will I ever know for sure? In my low moments, and in some exuberant ones, this remark has always haunted me.

12

The Flood And What Washed Up There

In mid-June of 1972, Hurricane Agnes rose up out of the Gulf of Mexico, crossed the Florida panhandle, and traveled up the east coast into Pennsylvania, where it parked itself over the Susquehannah River basin and proceeded to dump nineteen inches of rain in five days on the headwaters of the Chemung River Valley. On June 23, the Tioga, Canisteo, and Cohocton Rivers crested simultaneously in Corning, New York, where the Chemung River forms, creating a wall of water that smashed through a dike and surged downstream, overtopping levees, dikes, and flood walls and inundating communities for hundreds of miles along the way.

Corning residents had no warning of what was about to happen; in Elmira, evacuation orders were given by bullhorn from fire trucks only an hour or so before waters overflowed the twenty-three foot dike that runs along downtown's riverbank. Thousands of homes filled to the second-story roofline; dozens more were swept off their foundations and demolished. Overall, more than 100,000 people were displaced, twenty-one died, and some $750 million in damages were left in a stinking wasteland of muddy destruction and despair. And though Corning would eventually revive as a thriving tourist town, Elmira's business district of diverse family-owned stores, already under pressure from the new shopping mall west of the city, was essentially destroyed, and many of its quaint old neighborhoods—including the one in which Jane and Rob's apartment was located—fell into decline.

The flood served as a turning point in the lives of everyone who experienced it. I know it certainly did in mine. In Jane and Rob's case, the effect was less overt—their apartment stayed high and dry—though it did precipitate a chain of events that included buying their first home and, as a matter of simple logistics, a change in the climate of their friendship with me. A few months after the flood, I moved to the village of Dundee, some forty miles north of Elmira, and I live in that area today. I might have stayed in Elmira and probably would have returned to my parents' house had it not been for this move, which was a psychological one as much as anything, and for which I have always felt regret and relief with equal, and apparently unresolvable, intensity.

* * *

I'D RENTED MY WEST WATER STREET apartment by the river with no more thought of flood danger than imagining rocks falling on me from the moon. It was on the ground floor in a spooky old brick building with arched doorways, a flagstone foyer, and a huge back yard next to the steep, grassy river dike. At one time, the apartment next to mine (occupied in 1972 by a couple who were also members of Jane's ESP class) had been the office of my childhood pediatrician—moreover, my place had been the office of my mother's gynecologist when she was pregnant with me some twenty-eight years before. Sometimes I contemplated the murky symbolism behind all this. It was to get murkier.

I loved that apartment—really, it was much larger than I needed for Sean and me, but the rent was modest and the neighborhood was simultaneously lively and cozy. Maybe a little too cozy where my parents were concerned, as they persisted in dropping in on me at odd hours unannounced—but of course they were only concerned about us, weren't they? And then Jane dropped in on me unannounced one spring afternoon, to my complete surprise, which made up for everything. I opened the door and there she was, in jacket and a brimmed hat, a huge grin on her face.

"Hey, Sue-Belle," she said, "I was just out walkin' and thought I'd stop by and see ya." I gestured her inside and she plopped down in an overstuffed chair that looked firmer than it was—she sank down in it, and a look of sudden panic passed across her face. I said something like, that chair eats people all the time, I should put a sign on it. But she didn't seem amused—she couldn't move around well enough to get comfortable in the thing, and I was too embarrassed for her to ask if she needed help.

After a minute she relaxed a bit, awkwardly, and we chit-chatted for a while, and she got to her feet—with effort, but on her own—and said well, she should go on and get back to work, and she left. From out the side window, I watched her walk back up the street, slowly and carefully, but essentially peppy and fine. She kept her hands tucked in her jacket pockets.

I was overjoyed—Jane had come over to see me! She and Rob had been there one other time, with Maggie and Bill, but this struck me as more girlfriend-like, more egalitarian, if you will. I remember images racing through my mind of Jane and me rushing back and forth on the tree-lined street, manuscripts in hand, conferring with one another about plot and character, point of view, dialogue and denouement, publisher advances and royalty rates! Everything I hadn't been able to extract from her Wednesday writing class and wanted so much from her, above and beyond the sense of magic her ESP class gave me, and the perspective she and I shared in that context (though oddly, it was somewhere in the spring of '72 that I quit going to class for a couple of months because I was too uncomfortable with what I read as slavish worship-attention on the part of other people there, or maybe it was simple jealousy on my part for her attention).

So my reaction to her visit was self-centered glee, utterly missing the iceberg beneath her deceptively simple statement that she was "just out walkin'." I wish I had understood the state of her fears for her physical condition by then, or just how badly she was faring (with periodic, though temporary, improvements), or how much she yearned for positive reinforcement in the physical triumphs she did achieve. The fact is, I had only a glimmer of any of this, partly because Jane was so secretive about it herself, an attitude she questioned even as she held onto it.

"I'm too farting serious about everything," she remarks in her journals in April of 1972. "All I've got is some stupid stiffness—it's not as bad as we project—and I can get flexible—way to farting hell with it!"

Around this time, Jane told me that she was looking for a good sturdy bicycle to take a ride on once in a while, so I lent her my old Schwinn, which had foot brakes and one gear—forward. The thing must have weighed almost as much as she did, and had a seat big enough to accommodate a circus fat lady, but Jane took one look at it and told me she loved it.[1] I think she might have ridden it in her back yard a few times, with Rob helping out. I had a spiffy new ten-speed that I rode back and forth to work sometimes, so I didn't think about my Schwinn again until way too late.

* * *

WHAT I REMEMBER MOST ABOUT THE weeks before the flood was the endless rain. Days and days and days of rain. Going to work in the rain, coming home in the rain, grocery shopping in the rain, listening to the rain all day and all night. The river began to rise, of course, but that was normal enough. The Chemung had flooded Elmira in the past, but now there were all those sturdy dikes to protect us, right? I called Jane that Thursday night, June 22. They told me I could bring Sean and stay with them, if I felt uneasy about the river—an incredibly generous invitation, I only realized much later. They rented two separate apartments on the second floor (one essentially for Jane's workroom), but still, as far as I knew they'd never opened their place up to anyone else, and somebody with a two-year old in tow besides.

I thanked them, and said no, it was okay, Sean and I would be fine. (My parents had called that same morning and suggested they come get us, and I'd told them no, too.) And so I went to bed that night more distressed about having to get up and go to work in the rain the next morning than anything else.

Somewhere around dawn, I woke to an eerie wail of sirens punctuated by megaphones bellowing orders for everyone to evacuate immediately. I got up and looked out the window. It was actually nice outside—the rain had let up, and the sun was trying to break through the clouds. The sirens and voices moved on down the block and I very nearly went back to bed. Sean was still asleep and I didn't have to be at work for a couple of hours. Leaving as ordered didn't occur to me—I dismissed it as somebody else's panic, not related to me at all.

What finally jolted me out of this oblivion were the screeching and banging sounds coming from the adjacent apartment. I opened the door and there were my neighbors, running back and forth across the foyer carting armloads of record albums, of all things, into their waiting car. "Get everything up on shelves!" they yelled at me, without stopping. I couldn't see what all the fuss was about, but I decided to go look at the river anyway; Sean would be safe in his crib for a few minutes. I sauntered down to the riverside dike and up its steep slope to see what was what.

I got a good look, all right. The river was right up to the top, exactly level with my toes, lapping almost gently in the grass. And from there the river just went on and on into the morning grayness, stretching out flat like an endless silver plain across Elmira's southside. And then a three-story house swept past and crashed into the Walnut Street bridge. I recognized the house; it was one I'd often admired as I drove past it—miles upriver, on the way to the mall. Now I watched as the force of the current sucked it under the bridge and shattered it into kindling.

At the same moment, I realized I was hearing a sound—I didn't know what it was; it seemed to fill the sky. In fact, I looked up, trying to see what it was. It was like a great wind roaring through a forest. And still, I didn't get what was going on. All I could do was stand there, transfixed by the wonder of where all that water was coming from.

Finally, I walked back through the yard and went inside to wake up my son. The phone rang. When I answered, my mother's voice screamed, "What are you doing there? Get out, get out, get out!" I started to say something, but my father grabbed the phone from her and shouted, "You get that boy and get the hell out of there right now!" And yet even as I assured him that I was just about to leave, I felt no particular hurry. I thought, oh, all right, I'll go up to my aunt and uncle's in West Elmira for a while. I figured the water would make a few puddles in the back yard and that would be that.

I took with me exactly four things: diapers and a pack of manuscripts stuffed in a pillowcase, my typewriter, and my pocketbook. Five, if you count Sean, and six if you count his binky, which was technically his carry. I didn't take extra clothes for either of us; I did not even take my cat. It wasn't until I drove up to the corner of Walnut and Water (in a car lent to me earlier in the week by my new man friend) that I understood the source of that enormous roaring sound. It was the river, pouring over the cement dike in an explosive roar, filling West Water Street like the overflowing bathtub of the gods.

Startled into sensibility at last, I floored the gas pedal, zoomed around the corner, and raced up Walnut Street with the flood literally surging at my wheels. My uncle was on the phone to my mother as we pulled into his driveway, far above the flood's reach. It was the last call anyone could get through to Webbs Mills for weeks, but at least my parents knew we were safe. That afternoon, I took Sean to stay with his grandparents in Odessa. I didn't see him again for nearly two months.

When I remember what I lost to the river that day, what I think about is this: My childhood stories and poems, buried in a mud-filled desk drawer, and the sterling silver baby ring that Rachael Clayton of ESP class days gave to Sean when he was born. But all my dream notebooks, which were packed together in my nightstand drawer, came through dry and unscathed, even though they, like everything else, were submerged.

* * *

THE WATER RECEDED BY SATURDAY afternoon. I drove through the muck to my apartment and pushed the door open. I was horrified, of course. All the furniture was flung about and overturned and everything was covered with mud. My Siamese cat had survived by floating around on the same overstuffed chair that Jane had sunk into; it was the only dry surface in the place, and the water hadn't quite made it to the ceiling. Even the walls were coated with slime. The cat never did recover his voice—from then on he could only croak like a broken door hinge, and who can blame him?

Outside, people were standing in the reeking knee-deep gunk, immobilized, speechless. Again, sound filled the air: the adjacent river booming along just below crest mixed with a huge, hissing roar, and everywhere an overpowering stench of petroleum and natural gas. It occurred to me that the gas lines must have ruptured, and what were we all doing here, waiting to be blown to smithereens? I don't know why we were allowed to come back so soon, or maybe there was nobody available to stop us. The only thing I could think to do about it was to go over to Jane and Rob's and see if their place had come through intact.

I waded up the street through the mud and noise to 458. The front porch steps were piled with debris, so I went around back, thinking to take the stairway that led up to the second floor hallway door. It was then that I saw Jane and Rob's old car in the carriage house garage. It was half-buried in muck and one of the tires was flat.

My heart slammed against my ribs. In that second I was utterly convinced that they'd tried to get away and had been caught in the garage by rising flood waters. I was overcome with the certitude that Jane and Rob were dead in their car.

I slogged my way to the garage as fast as I could and threw open the passenger-side door. You must understand that I thoroughly expected to see Jane's corpse fall out; I saw this plainly and vividly in my mind's eye as I ran up to the car. In those moments, in the midst of that stink and destruction, the roaring gas lines and the pounding river water—in those moments, the only explanation in my head for the car's presence was that Jane and Rob had drowned in it, and were still sitting inside it, upright, together, Jane's hands clutching a pocketbook—later, privately, I would laugh at myself about this, but at the time, running up to that car, into the filthy dimness of the garage, it was so unmistakably clear that this was what had happened that I was shaking violently all over and screeching in a high-pitched ululating wail as I grabbed the door handle and yanked it wide open.

Only muddy water gushed out, soaking me to the crotch. Whimpering and moaning and gagging, I leaned against the fender until I could stop gasping for air. They hadn't driven away and I knew they hadn't walked away. Then I saw my old Schwinn over in a corner, buried in sludge, ruined. I'd gotten it for Christmas in 1953, when I was eight years old. I thought of my Radio Flyer, left behind in the basement storage room of my apartment house. How many people were just now thinking these same thoughts, up to their knees in mud and ruin?

I don't remember if Rob called to me from his studio windows, which overlooked the back yard, or if I just went up the back stairs to their apartments. The waterline (later measured at ten feet) hadn't reached the second floor, but the building stank, as the rest of Elmira stunk, as it would stink for years to come every time it rained.

Rob met me in the hallway. "Looks like your car's done for," I told him, but I never explained how it was that I knew it. Rob handed me a towel and I wiped my jeans off as best I could, left my shoes on the stairs, and followed him into the second apartment. Jane was sitting at her table in front of the tree-shaded windows, smoking. All three of us were subdued; probably we were more than a little shell-shocked. I sat in the lawn chair and put the towel under my feet.

We exchanged stories. Jane and Rob had decided to remain behind when the evacuation orders sounded, figuring the house was sturdy enough and their second-floor apartments would be safe. Nonetheless, Rob had moved his paintings, their journals and files, and all the notebooks of Seth material up into the empty attic. At the last minute, with water pouring in the basement windows, he'd gone down cellar and leaned across a doorway to shut off the water heater and furnace valve.

"At first," Jane said, "it felt like an adventure," but as the river surged higher and higher up the sides of nearby houses, they began to wonder if they'd made the right decision. "I realized that with my physical hassles I'd never be able to swim out of there or even get into a boat, probably," Jane said, somewhat apologetically.

I said something like, "Jane, nobody can swim through a flood," but I understood the point: for them, escape had become effectively impossible. As Rob later recounts in his notes for *The Nature of Personal Reality*, they "sipped wine and used light self-hypnosis to take the edge off" their fears, but as the hours crept by and the river kept rising, Rob suggested that Jane try to get something psychically on their situation. Her subsequent predictions that the water would stop halfway up the first floor windows, that they would be safe if they stayed where they were, and that the Walnut Street bridge would be washed out, all proved to be correct.[2]

"I guess we made our stand with our life's work," she said, and I made a half-joking reference to *The Chestnut Beads* and its bomb-shelter parallels. There was no hot water but they had plenty of food, and curiously, even hilariously, the electricity had stayed on throughout. And why was that? Nobody else in the surrounding neighborhoods had electricity for weeks.

Then Jane invited me to stay in their apartment—their original one across the hall, where ESP class was held—while I cleaned up my place and got some semblance of order back into my life. It was an extraordinarily gracious offer; and I accepted it and spoiled it in the blink of an eye. I asked if my new man friend could stay with me, as he'd also been flooded out. Jane's reaction to this request has been mercifully erased from my mind, though she obviously agreed. I already knew she didn't like the guy, and he had plenty of other options. The imposition on Jane and Rob's good will was somewhere out beyond boorish.

My friend and I ended up staying there for about a month, and the daily scenario went something like this: I would go over to my dank, wrecked apartment and spend hours shoveling, scraping, scrubbing, tossing, crying, and accomplishing little more than pushing mud and ruined objects out to the curb (all my books, all of Sean's baby clothes and toys, all our furniture, all . . .); then I'd drag myself back to 458 to wash myself and the single set of clothes I had to my name in stinging ice-cold water delivered by the head-to-toe nine-nozzle shower Jane and Rob were so goddamned fond of, put on the old bathrobe I'd found unscathed in the top shelf of my closet, hang my wet clothes out on the line to dry for the next day, eat a couple of sandwiches, and collapse on the sofa in a state of sheer exhausted delirium more or less resembling sleep. At first my friend pitched in to help, but after a few days he decided that his time would be better spent sitting at the table in front of the bay windows composing an epic poem for the ages about the awful devastation wrought to all by the flood. This, he assured me, was his true destiny.

So he'd sit and write all day while I cleaned. Did I say a word about this? No! After all, it wasn't his place buried under two feet of river silt and petroleum effluvium, right? Did I bring him cigarettes and beer from the blocks-away corner grocery upon request? Of course! I was going out anyway that morning, wasn't I? Indeed I was. Evenings he'd read aloud to me from the newest installment of his grand opus, which went on for more pages than even the so devastated might be inclined to say about it. Eventually, he self-published it in booklet form and ceremoniously presented Jane and Rob with autographed copies. I remember that Jane smiled politely and said thank you. I remember that I imagined Rob walking through that living room every day, past the epic-in-progress, to get to his studio in back. I remember thinking that maybe I could drink a big glass of flood mud and drop dead on the spot, and be done with it.

Somewhere in here—was it the Tuesday after the flood?—the Boys from New York showed up for class, unaware of what had happened to the city. "We knew there'd been a hurricane," Rich Kendall remembers, "but we drove to class anyway, because we didn't realize the damage that had occurred. When we got out of our cars in front of Jane's house, Army National Guardsmen with bullhorns told us to get off the streets because it was past curfew. When they asked us why we were there, we decided to say we were visiting friends.

"Due to the flood, class had been canceled, which we weren't aware of, and Jane was very surprised to see us. She let us hang out in her apartment across the hall where she usually did her writing. Only about six people were there. Seth didn't come through, but that was okay. This was the first time Sue Watkins and I connected, though we had been sitting in the same class for months."

What I remember about this little un-class is the sensation of rediscovering my own psychological ground—the only way I can describe it—in the rambunctious banter that always accompanied the New York Boys, however many or few of them there were (they had much the same effect on Jane). Whenever I reconnect with that ground, there is a ripple effect that never fails me. Not long afterward, my landlord told me he'd decided to gut my apartment and start over; the wood floors and plaster walls were ruined beyond repair. I'd been scrubbing them for what seemed like years, and so he made a deal with me for six months' free rent in an unflooded third-floor apartment in return for all the work I'd done. Given the lack of hot water, no furniture or clothes, and an abundance of fleas in the upstairs place, this wasn't such a great gift, but it was more than a lot of people had. The Red Cross gave me a new mattress and sixty-six dollars in food stamps, my aunt gave me a sleeping bag and pillow, I managed to salvage the top part of my rolltop desk and a few items of clothing, and my man friend announced that he was moving in with a woman he knew who lived across town. Things were definitely looking up.

So I collected my stuff from 458, most of it manuscripts and photographs rescued from desk drawers and laid out across the floor on paper towels to dry. As I was stacking the few boxes out in the hallway, Jane called out to me from the second apartment. "Can you come on over for a minute?" she said. "I'd like to have a conversation with you about some things."

Some things, eh? Great. I could tell by the tone of her voice that this was not going to be about "things" in the news. I walked over and schlumped down in the green lawn chair. Jane sat in front of her work desk, smoking. The principal's office was in order.

Jane got right down to it, I'll say that. In a light, careful voice, she asked me if I were "in love" with this guy. No, I told her, I wasn't "in love" with him. "I don't even like him very much," I said, voicing an opinion I realized had been there all along, but hiding, like a trickster brain tumor with a particularly uncouth sense of humor.

Jane just looked at me, momentarily speechless. "Well," she said finally, "I could understand it if you were carried away by passion."

"Passion?" I was very embarrassed by my conduct with this man, but I had no idea how to think about it—none. My own motives and feelings were a complete blank to me. I had acted almost automatically, without any conscious appraisal of what I was doing, or choosing to do. Worse, this state of mind about men felt completely normal. "Well," I said to Jane that day, "there might have been a little lust at first, but no, I don't love him or anything like that."

She screwed up her face and lit another cigarette. I prepared myself to be dressed down, though that didn't happen, exactly. She'd already seen me through a lot of previous moping over a former ESP class member, who was married and with whom I'd had one brief, very intense, and essentially platonic encounter filled more with romantic scenarios of a fantasy future together than anything else. One Tuesday he didn't come to class and Jane took me aside and told me that he'd sailed off to the Bahamas with the wife of a local college professor. This was the exact adventure he had concocted for us, no inkling of any other applicants for the first mate job, and not even a goodbye or a hint of goodbye. Standing with Jane in her little kitchen as she told me this, class noise receding into the distance, Jane's eyes sharp and alert, I remember thinking, how come Jane knew about this and I didn't? But I had kept my face placid and serene as the rising moon.

Jane, who wasn't fooled, had said, "You're better off."

"I know," I said evenly, without emotion, and I did know it, though I was utterly stricken, as much by my own stupidity as anything else. You'd think I'd learn the first time, though togetherness fantasies were not the allure with Flood Man. No fantasies there at all. I have no clue as to what it was. Maybe it was revenge, who knows.

So anyway, here we were once again, Jane and I, in her leaf-shrouded work room, and she's trying to figure out what the hell's going on with me, and *I* certainly have no explanation.

She went on to talk about how impressed she and Rob had been a week or so before this, when the gas utility was finally turned back on and Flood Man—who considered himself a gourmet cook, largely because of his prodigious use of butter and cheap wine in everything—had stuffed and roasted four Rock Cornish hens in the dollhouse-sized oven of that minuscule apartment kitchen and taken two of them over to Jane and Rob as a surprise thank-you dinner gift. Jane talked about this incident for several minutes, trying to acknowledge something redeemable in the man, I'm sure, carrying on about how sumptuous those two "squabs" had seemed to her and Rob. Since I was the one who'd bought the fucking hens, I wasn't especially impressed—I was, in fact, mystified by Jane's rapture over it all. But I didn't say so. I didn't say much of anything. I could hardly bear to look her in the eye.

Too bad, too—here again, as so often happened between us, we were standing at an intersection, a crossroads as it were, in one another's belief mysteries, with some degree of insight available between us, if we'd been just a little more . . . what? Brave? Unashamed? Less indignant? I don't know. Something.

Jane left the squab question and went on to her next point, which was to remind me, as if it had no relation to her previous remarks, that she and Rob "often have bachelors over who are into this stuff," meaning the Seth material, and that she would have me over too, on those evenings, if I wanted to meet some of these eligible fellows. She was looking at me with her most penetrating stare, and so I replied, sure, that would be all right, why not? Ask me over any time.

So with the bachelor suggestion out in the open, and my positive if rather limp response to it under her belt, Jane let go and lit full-bore into Flood Man and his rather flamboyant blend of odious characteristics, starting with a stunt he'd pulled right after the flood had receded, in which he decided to "test" the National Guardsmen's anti-looter policy by going out after the mandated curfew and purposefully walking past their armed perimeter and then back through it, even as they'd yelled at him to stop. Nothing, perhaps unfortunately, had come of it, but Jane said to me, "That sort of thing just shows that he's childish, and a freeloader, so what you're doing with him, I just can't see."

Of course, she was absolutely right—I couldn't much see it either, but what was I supposed to say? All I could feel in those moments was abject humiliation, profound and deep (as I feel now, remembering all this and seeing once again before me the beginnings of behavior patterns that I would repeat for more time and energy wasted than a moth around the flame would believe possible). All Jane's words meant to me was this: I was a stupid baby. Period.

"You know, Sue-Belle," she said, "it's just a matter of cutting the wrong guys dead." She gestured a guillotine chop as she said this. "You don't give 'em a second's chance, you just cut 'em dead." She shrugged—her expression said, what's so hard about that? *Chop*. I grinned weakly. I had the "cutting dead" part down pretty pat—it was the "wrong guys" thing that I couldn't quite figure out, but one can always hope.

Right in the midst of this conversation, I suddenly realized I was about five seconds away from a cataclysmic attack of diarrhea. I barely made it to the little bathroom, which was down a short hallway adjacent to the room where we were sitting. It was violent and noisy, and I was of course even more horribly embarrassed; it seemed that no matter what I did, every part of my body conspired to degrade me at every turn.

When I came back out into the living room, Jane, no stranger to bodily humiliations, smiled in a comradely way and said, "Well, I don't know, Sue, but it seems to me you literally just want to run like hell from all of this." And what could I say? As far as this entire subject was concerned, she was exactly right.

It was then, at the end of this conversation, that Jane first presented her idea that she and I try some sort of "dream-intensive writer-study of psy-time and stuff, just to see what we get," and keep records, and maybe later write it up "in some form, maybe a book." And also that she and I could have our own mini-class, "really delve into the ideas, just the two of us, see what happens, what the hell," she said.

When I look back on this, I am just stunned by the obvious regard she had for me despite everything. She clearly figured that our mutual interests and abilities outweighed any asinine thing I might be caught up in at any given moment. Yet we never followed through on this idea (though we talked about it often enough). Other things interceded, including her new publishing possibilities, my move to Dundee in November of that year, and Jane's increasing physical difficulties—after the flood she did not venture outside the house until July 13, when according to her notes she walked half a block two days in a row, and then didn't go outside again until August 30.

And of all of it, of all the things that were ripe for comment about this entire sorry experience, what appalled Jane the most, apparently—for it was the one thing she never mentioned to me directly—was disguised as a housekeeping issue, which I discovered much later while reading a copy of the Deleted material. At some point therein, Jane makes the remark that "Sue Watkins lives in a pig sty," which absolutely dumbfounded me. I couldn't figure out where this came from, since she only visited me two times, and while no doubt the place had its share of baby toys and clutter lying around, a pig sty? Hardly! And so I grumped about this to myself, picking at it like a scab for years. A *pig sty*? C'mon, Jane! What a thing to leave for the record! How could you?

Then while reading her journals and other manuscripts, I came across a reference to the "slum" she thought Flood Man and I had made of the apartment back there in 1972. "Sloppy . . . no discipline," the passage reads, "not using abilities." Well, I doubt it was a "slum," but now I had an answer to a heretofore mysterious moment in ESP class later that year, when out of the blue Jane had turned to me and delivered a quasi-evangelical monologue on how "a writer's home is the temple of our work" and should be "respected and cared for, and so we should keep it clean," all in a meaningful tone, while looking straight at me and gesturing expressively. I was baffled by her direct manner—it wasn't as though I disagreed with her, so what was this about?

I think what it was about was the simple mistake everybody makes at one time or another: being generous and then regretting it, and not knowing how to get out of the consequences. The other side of which is realizing that one was part of the unwanted "consequences" involved. That, and Jane's (quite literally) unbendable ideas about work, and her fears along those lines as she projected them on me in a day-to-day living situation. In that regard, she might well have perceived me and Flood Man as a kind of bizarro version of her and Rob, and there I was *scrubbing floors* all day while the male (sitting at Jane's old work table, yet), indulged and protected, spent his time grinding out (in Jane's opinion and mine) second-rate fare. (The implications of that image must have seared her to the bone.) Of course Jane's affection and best hopes for me were behind her reactions, too. But for the most part, I think her housekeeping displeasures—a traditional female-role chore, amusingly—were symbolic of the larger issues that our relationship embodied and played out for us both.

* * *

"HELLO MOMMY, I MISSED YOU," Sean said when I saw him next, after all this was over, sometime that August. It was the first complete sentence I heard him speak. He was not quite two years old.

I cried.

13

After the Flood And Into the Soup

Sometimes I drive past the house in Dundee where Sean and I lived, eons ago it seems, for most of the 1970s, after the flood. It's one of those big old places with a wide front porch and trees around it that graces vintage neighborhoods everywhere. The Agway building next door burned down a while ago, though the woodlot across the street has endured and the trees, like Sean, have grown impossibly mature. I wrote *Conversations with Seth* there, sitting in front of the window that looks out over the sidewalk toward school, three fat drafts on a typewriter in a little less than a year. Rent was fifty dollars a week for the whole second floor, two bedrooms and all utilities included. Thus was the simplicity of rural upstate New York.

Throughout these years, I drove to Elmira every Tuesday to attend ESP class, and on weekends when Sean and I visited my parents I'd go over to Jane and Rob's on Friday night. In between visits I wrote letters to Jane and Rob about intriguing dreams I'd had, or other interesting "psychic" type experiences, or just descriptions of what I was working on or what I was up to. Nothing had changed, and yet everything had changed.

I was making a living as a stringer for the Elmira daily (twenty-three cents a column inch) and as co-editor of the two-person weekly Dundee *Observer* (fifty bucks an issue). My colleague Susan Benedict and I (known locally as the Snoop Sisters) spent many hours attending municipal meetings and local events, driving to fires and accidents (often in the middle of the night, with our kids bundled in pajamas and blankets in the back seat), copying countless police reports, retyping mountains of news bits and stuffy press releases, and pulling the inevitable all-nighter to get the paper on the stands every Wednesday no matter what.

In and around this substitute for actual employment and other mundane details of life, I began to write every day—maybe an hour or two, sometimes more, clacking away on my old manual typewriter (later upgraded to a Selectric) after Sean went to bed. Sometimes I'd spend all weekend at my desk, lost in the magic of storytelling. ("My Mommy can't come to the phone right now," I heard Sean inform a caller one Saturday afternoon, "*she* is an *authoress*.") I kept elaborate dream journals and wrote poetry and short stories (some of which were published in small quarterlies), won fiction prizes, and garnered the usual quota of rejection slips. I wrote three novels, one of which sparked an enthusiastic response from an editor at Avon, who later sent it back without explanation. I wrote a weekly humor column for the *Observer* that won first place in the New York Press Association's newspaper competition, and almost sold to a national features syndicate (I chickened out on the commitment and declined the offer). Eventually, all the hours I'd spent interviewing local folks, asking questions and recording the answers, sitting in coffee shops listening to gossip, dallying with my future ex on his dairy and horse farm, and generally living the small-town life, all segued with my friendship with Jane and Rob and became part of *Conversations* and later *Dreaming Myself, Dreaming a Town*,[1] books that sprang as much from ordinary life as they ever did from extraordinary experience.

In other words, I had a life that encompassed other lives, outside the context of ESP class or the familiar surroundings from my childhood. Unlike my job schedule in pre-flood Elmira, I could be home when Sean was home; even better, I quit the party drinking—became quite self-righteous about it, in fact. A complex of interests rose up before me to explore: the horse world, the antiques and collectibles trade, running a small business, gardening, the mysteries of a village with its generations of secrets and joys (all of which I wrote about in one form or another). Sean and I grew up together in Dundee, and it was there that I began to appreciate everyday life as it was lived by people whose psyches seemed so different from mine and turned out not to be so dissimilar after all.

And yet my desk drawers were filled with unfinished stories and novels, scraps of ideas that went nowhere, outlines of writing projects, all great material that I set aside for an hour or two of schmoozing in the local restaurants and later could not recreate. "You're either a writer with a capital 'W' or you're not," Jane's voice whispered, more or less constantly. So despite my successes, I felt suspended between two worlds, or portions of my own being—never quite committing to either for fear of leaving the other behind. The same fears, I realize now, that fueled Jane's tremendous creative energies and simultaneous will to shut off all other choices.

I remember the afternoon, a week or so before Christmas in 1974, when Jane asked me if I'd do some shopping for her for Rob ("Find him a couple nice shirts, something with-it," she said) and so Susan and I went to the mall near Elmira to see what we could find (for some reason I settled on shirts with a natty dude-ranch flair) and then took the packages over to 458. Susan had never met Jane, though she'd heard me talk about ESP class often enough. I felt quite daring about this little escapade, though I'm not sure why, except that I know I wanted some sort of affirmation from Susan, my down-to-earth newspapering pal, who had a phenomenal understanding of what real news was, and the things people found interesting about the world and each other. I suppose I was looking for something pithy from her about a mentor relationship I often didn't understand myself.

Susan and I sat on the floor in front of the sofa, our elbows on the coffee table. Other guests were there—Maggie and Bill most likely—and did most of the talking. We chatted about this and that, nothing special. I don't remember Jane's reaction to my shirt choices. When we left I gave Jane a copy of that week's *Observer*. Susan's only comment, according to my notes, as we drove home that night was, "How come I keep meeting people who deal with ideas like they were real?" (More recently, she recalled her only impression of Jane as ". . . a business woman who enjoyed what she was doing, and didn't have much else she considered interesting.")

The next time I saw Jane, she said, "Well, Sue-Belle, I can see what you two gals are up to," and gave me a look that implied—significance. But of what? Gals? *Gals*? What did she mean, "up to"? Something more than the perks of managing an eight-page 2,000-circulation, no-profit weekly with antiquated typesetting equipment? A feminist thing? What? Jane didn't explain, and, as so often happened, I was too intimidated by her expression to ask. I think I was afraid she'd tell me that I was making an ass out of myself—it certainly wouldn't be the first time we'd had *that* conversation.

And it is true that Susan and I used the newspaper as a context for spoofing news methods—mixed in with serious, occasionally crusading, subject matter. Were we indulging in self-aggrandizement, albeit unconsciously? Is this what Jane meant? I don't know.

Jane later said to me, "Your friend Susan is to you as Maggie is to me," which was true enough—Susan had a similar lack of affinity for animals, and both she and Maggie basically thought the Seth stuff was okay to a point, but really kind of a bunch of highfalutin' gobbledygook. And they were both in the newspaper business, and earthy, motherly friends to each of us in a way Jane and I couldn't be to one another.

Not long after this, my newspapering inclinations led Jane and Rob and me down a small side road that came close to derailing—not to mention distracting—all of us, and our friendship. Susan and I were always thinking up ideas for other kinds of periodicals, though we never followed through on any of them—not enough time, for one thing, and we enjoyed imagining such publications more than actually doing what it took to get them in print. One day as we were sitting in the coffee shop tossing these ideas back and forth (what about a monthly news magazine, or a weekly four-pager specializing in local business news, or a weekly specializing in people-features), one or the other of us—it could have been either—said something like, what if Jane's class published a newspaper? (There were no such publications at the time.) And with that, the concept stuck in my head and took root.

In my dream journals early in 1975 is a page in my handwriting with lists of necessary equipment and supplies, article ideas, interview possibilities, columns, cartoons, a section on dreams and coincidences, even an extensive mailing list and royalty share breakdown for a newsletter called, "The Sumari Journal, featuring Seth Class Transcripts."[2] I presented this idea to Jane, who immediately took to it, somewhat to my surprise—I was only half-serious about it myself.

She and I talked about this on and off for several months. We came up with some great content possibilities for it—playfully, no prototype issues or anything that concrete, but our attraction to the whole thing was undeniable. Like my stint on the Vineyard *Gazette*, Jane had once worked as Society Editor for the *Saratogian*, and so to some extent shared my affection for newspapers in general. On the other hand, as with the newsletters Susan and I thought up in our restless hours between *Observer* issues, neither Jane nor I was really too keen on the realities of such a venture. And then we started to get silly, making up outrageous jokes (in the spirit of those long-ago, ad-lib promo parodies) about what we could include in the thing. I suggested a "stupid belief of the month award"—we could hold a competition for it, readers sending in their dumbest root assumptions! Give out prizes! Trophies! Hold annual banquets! We bantered back and forth in this vein almost every time the subject came up—I suppose for one thing it was our way of avoiding any serious commitment to an official newsletter and the organized status implied, something that made us both squeamish.

And so one afternoon we were really going at it about this hypothetical paper, egging one another on and roaring with laughter, when Rob burst into the living room from his studio like a wrathful avenger and chewed us out but good. He spoke to Jane, though it was meant for us both. "What do you think you're doing, making fun of people like that?" he scolded. "It isn't funny, it's cruel, and you're being childish!" He stood glaring, hands on hips, as furious as I ever saw Rob get about anything.

"Hey, we were just kidding around," Jane offered feebly, but she sobered up as though she'd been slapped. Rob said nothing. He just glowered at us for another moment, and marched back into his studio and shut the door.

I was mortified, stunned and furious myself—what the hell, we weren't making concrete editorial plans, I knew how to run a newspaper, for chrissakes. We were, yes indeed, *kidding around*. But I said nothing. Jane lit a cigarette, her hands shaking slightly. She was trying to get control of herself, I could see. Her face was bright red and she had tears in her eyes. "Well," she said, finally, lightly, not looking at me, "he's probably right." I couldn't think of anything to say, and I made an excuse and left soon thereafter.

Later I wondered if we'd just annoyed Rob with all the racket we were making that day—after all, he was certainly no prude expecting obsequious devotion. We'd offended him, though, no doubt—or I had. And recently I found this note in my dream journals for Friday, February 28, 1975 (the same day my *Observer* humor column won its category in the New York Press Association contest): "Seth did say that [The Sumari Journal] paper, in our terms, 'was meant to be,' and would succeed, but to 'temper our humor with wise compassion'"—though where this remark was made (in class? In the Deleted material?) or when, is a mystery; I could not locate it anywhere. So maybe Jane and I weren't as funny as we thought. Maybe we were expressing some pent-up animosity about a host of things. Maybe we had a few stupid beliefs to work on ourselves. Maybe, on the other hand, Rob needed to lighten up a little.

The next time we talked about the subject—one Saturday night in June—"it was decided," according to my notes, "not to do the Sumari Journal. Rob seemed to have the strongest objections, mostly aimed at what he called 'a concept of sadistic humor,' meaning mine. Also, neither want to end up with an 'official publication,' and I can't blame them for that . . . But all the same, Rob's remarks cut. I felt put down and pissed off."

I was hurt, but it's interesting that in this same time period, I was offered a job on a weekly paper published by a former member of Jane's ESP class—the self-same object of my earlier unrequited love-mope, in fact, returned from his oceanic trek (without the professor's wife). Responding to the tug of old fantasies among other things, I drove to his office for an interview. Weirdly, he used most of our conversation time to make crude jokes and sarcastic comments about Jane, and some of it was pretty damned cruel indeed. I ended up declining his offer and disabused of any leftover attraction for the man.

The parallels didn't escape me, and apparently I wrote Jane a letter about this encounter, as she brings it up as part of a dream interpretation in her unfinished "Aspects" manuscript: ". . . reminds me of something [this fellow said] to Sue about my classes; to the effect that I counted on them to let me be the star of the show . . . and not to laugh when I read poetry. It still now shocks me; why should they laugh? But [there's the] idea that women have any kind of limelight only when or if men allow it . . . and ridicule is always beneath the surface if the woman usurps the male's abilities . . ." (Hmmm, I mused, reading this—perchance this applies *too* well?)

In any case, several newsletters and at least one quarterly magazine (not to mention dozens of web sites) focusing on the Seth material have sprung up over the years, so the best of our original intentions at least lived on, perhaps despite ourselves.

* * *

"SO," ROB SAID TO ME, "WHY DON'T you write a book on class?" It was 1978, all apparently forgiven and forgotten. The idea hit me like a brick. I looked at Jane, who suddenly perked up, eyes wide and bright. "Hey, why not?" she said, as if it had just hit her, too. "You could use your newspaper abilities, report what went on, the ESP experiments and stuff—"

"Yeah, interview everybody who was there, get their dream records, show how those correlated—"

"—use excerpts from the sessions," Jane added. "Prentice would love it, I could write an intro—"

"Hey, why not?" I said to Rob. He was smiling innocently—too innocently.

"It would be a massive undertaking," he said, but I sluffed that remark off—Rob was always talking about projects as "massive undertakings." In my mind, I was already gathering up the information, organizing it, typing it up, correcting the galleys, autographing the printed page, cashing the royalty checks. Not for the first time would I delude myself into thinking that a creative project would be a cinch, or that I could let other voices do all the talking and leave myself out of it, like a good reporter should. So I took up Rob's challenge, went home and wrote a proposal just as if I knew what I was doing, and sent it off to Jane's editor at Prentice-Hall.

The headstrong girl got her comeuppance. Which is, I suppose, what the severe old teacher had in mind.

14

"The Work" And Other Puzzles

Dream, November 11, 1970: I am looking for an apartment in Jane's neighborhood, but the rents are all outrageously high. I look up through the windows of 458 to see not one but three Janes standing there. One is flighty, one is heavyset and mannish; the third is Jane "herself," at her writing table, which is piled high with work. All three lecture me about developing my writing abilities, then express their fears to one another about their contrasting characteristics, particularly the "flighty" and the "real" Jane . . .

"You see," Seth told me later, in class, "Ruburt's way is too expensive—it is too expensive to follow another's way, and that is the message of the dream."[1]

* * *

JANE WOULD SAY TO ME, "I'D LIKE you to carry on my work."

I never understood what she meant by this, exactly. She never really explained. It went without saying that speaking for Seth wasn't what she meant. It was nothing that literal, not to mention ridiculous—Seth was a part of who Jane was in the same way the forty-year old Jane was part of the twenty-year old Jane, or as her novels and poetry were part of her, as her thoughts were part of her; not handoffable, in other words, to anyone. I don't even think Jane knew what she meant by it, or even if she reflected on it much (I could find nothing about it in her journals).

No, whenever she made this statement to me, it felt less like an offer than a challenge—one I never quite met, mostly because I didn't really want to meet it—or was afraid to try. And so I always had the underlying sense that somehow I wasn't keeping my part of the bargain with Jane, whatever that bargain was.

Occupying the other side of this oddly-minted coin was the fact that my friendship with Jane and interest in "her work" clearly disconcerted my immediate family, especially my mother,[2] who was utterly convinced that Jane was exerting some sort of devious influence on me to do—what? An obscure *something* I could never fathom—marry people at random? Produce a master race? Go door to door handing out Seth leaflets? ("Was it Jane's idea for you to get pregnant?" my mother demanded, when I told her of Sean's pending arrival.) She refused to elaborate and I was too indignant about her accusations to try bridging this gap between us. (Interesting that Jane's mother had nothing but scorn for the novelist Caroline Slade, whom Jane considered *her* mentor).[3]

So there I was, largely alone, threading my way among people who frequently seemed disappointed in who I was, or so it felt at the time. All of which is a common, perhaps universal experience, and one that Jane herself endured without surcease (as she says in *God of Jane*, "little in my life, from its start to now, has ever seemed to fit any norm"), though she had Rob; and to me, then, having a life partner like Rob was enough to make up for everything else. But the outward structure of our backgrounds was so different that Jane tended to see my hassles as fleeting things of no great consequence (which in fact they were, by and large) while I considered her past, as she described it, exactly what a real writer ought to have—the destitute upbringing; the stories about her poetry scandalizing the orphanage nuns; the cross-country motorcycle trips with her first husband; the science-fiction writers' conventions in the fifties, where she was one of the few, if not the only female writer; the disapproval heaped on her for not wanting children (even a chiropractor once told her she should go home and have a couple kids)[4]—all of it seemed to me deliciously colorful and novel-worthy, and in many ways, as Jane herself acknowledges, it was.

But from the moment she started delivering the Seth material, Jane found herself caught up in a different kind of argument: an intense, deeply personal struggle with how to present herself as its author and maintain her somewhat oxymoronic stance as both creator and questioner, while simultaneously not destroying the spontaneity of its expression. On May 5, 1972, she writes in her journal:

> The psychic stuff literally came out of the poetry . . . As long as it was just ideas it was okay. Science fiction too: the same ideas in a story are accepted as provocative, daring, far-out and what a great imagination you have, but start

> saying but this is true and look out—Do they give you a prize for writing a book . . . no, they want to know: is the book true? Are the ideas real? Are you a fraud? All before they'll even listen to the lovely ideas; they don't want you to make them bring the ideas out into real life either. The same idea[s] in poetry they'd accept as original and compelling and great.
>
> Before they were lovely dreamy ideas, now suddenly they have to compete with what people call facts . . . you have to work at them and live your life around them . . . and live up to them; and everybody is watching for you to make one wrong step so you have to watch it you don't dare go too fast for fear of making a mistake and they'll all say, aha, the ideas are wrong they aren't facts at all and you're a fraud; . . . and like with reincarnation they want to know precisely how everything works when that isn't the point at all; and they have to have it all in black and white with dates and details very matter of fact; you've got to prove it where in a story or poem they'd just say, hey what a great idea.
>
> Being Seth is fun and wildly creative beyond my understanding and anyone else's too—but it's got to be explained down to the smallest details—prove what he is or I'm a fraud; but prove it in stupid terms . . .

Sadly, until I read her journals for this book, Jane's anguish in this regard was largely invisible to me—sadly because I share many of the same dilemmas. We could have been much more help to one another, not as problem-solvers in the usual terms, but more as comrades who shared similar literary standards and ambitions.

Sharing ambitions wasn't what Jane meant by "carrying on" her work, though. There was something on the inside of this statement that was about more than writing novels or speculating on ideas in the Seth material. Some of it had to do with an unspoken acknowledgment of our mentor-protégé alliance; some of it, particularly before the Jane Roberts Archives arrangement had been made with Yale University, was about simple mortality. But at least a portion of it was about something neither of us could quite get a handle on, though I sensed it lurking, as I'm sure Jane must have, in the corridors of her remarks about my having "had kids."

We had two or three strange encounters in ESP class about this, in the form of reincarnational dramas, which we resisted playing out—for one thing we both understood that these little scenes represented a crafty way for us to work out underlying issues that we were too inhibited to bring up directly, at least in front of people. Or maybe it was indeed a close encounter of the other-life kind; interactions of *aspects*, as Jane describes them in chapter 1 of *Adventures in Consciousness*:

> I was . . . questioning the students when something else caught my attention. First dimly, then more vividly, I began to sense the presence of an invisi-

ble personality beside me. That is, I didn't see him, but felt his emotional reality quite as strongly as physical vision could ever show it.

I'd "met" this same person in several previous classes when he told me mentally that he represented a past life of mine. Then, supposedly, I'd been some kind of jealous leader, demanding utmost loyalty. My friend Sue had been one of my followers. Now he wanted to confront her, feeling that she was going her own way this time and not following in his footsteps, as he thought she should have.

What to do? I try to be spontaneous in class, at least within reason, so I said, "Sue, that other one is here." I laughed—only to me it wasn't my laugh but his: richly sardonic, indulgent, and amused all at once. I felt a strange facial expression from the inside and realized that my features were adapting it.

Sue just stared at me. "Yeah, I know he's there, and I wish he'd go away," she said.

At the same time I began to feel much bigger and stronger than I am, physically, as this other personality really began to rouse himself. An anger against Sue—*that* certainly wasn't mine —rushed through me. He wanted to confront her, directly, speaking through me. That wasn't fair, I thought. If he had a score to settle, he should contact the person *Sue* had been. Sue and I as ourselves would have nothing to do with it. So, firmly, I tried to hold myself aloof, and to end the matter I called out, "Time for a class break everybody!"

But I didn't quite make it. As people began to mill about, I heard that laugh that wasn't mine directed at Sue again. "I've looked at you with this expression on my face many times," "I" said. "You should know it well."

Sue cried out, of all things, "I've got a two-year-old defender this time," meaning her child, and "I" answered scornfully, "That's one of the most foolish remarks you could have made to me."

But now I decided that the affair had gone too far. I didn't approve of this other-self's grand manner or the tricky way he'd tried to come through, when my attitude toward him was plain. So this time I closed off completely—it's just a matter of saying "no" and meaning it—and I realized that earlier, I'd only half wanted to end the confrontation. I'd wanted to close the personality out enough to prevent his speaking, but not enough to prevent me from probing into *his* reality. Now he just disappeared entirely.

"We're going to have to work that through sometime," Sue said.

"Yeah, but let's wait," I answered, and we grinned at each other, content to let the episode rest.

We never did get back to this, which was just fine with me. Picking up impressions of other-life information and playing with them was fun, up to a point, but I didn't like overt playacting and I especially didn't like whatever this was between Jane and me. It made me feel put-upon and lectured at, not to mention embarrassed. Yet I secretly enjoyed the opportunity to at least suggest defiance, and really, I'm sure that I meant the "two-year-old defender" remark as a joke—well, maybe not (obviously it found its mark). Maybe what I really needed to do was stand up for *myself* a little in the face of Jane's wasting-time pronouncements. Why, after all, did this shame me so much? Was I judging myself, already believing in a lack of worth?

Nonetheless, and for whatever reason, the "carrying on her work" issue came to a head in late 1979, not long after an informal ESP class get-together that would turn out to be its last. Jane had decided to end regular class meetings soon after she and Rob moved to their new home in 1975, a decision that I thought was not an especially good idea for her, though I couldn't help but agree with her not wanting to deal with the weekly thirty or forty person jam-fest in their new living room (which was smaller than the one at 458, and not as segregated from the rest of the house). And then there was the prospect of all those people using the one small, rather privately located bathroom, the after-class housekeeping chores, and the lack of room on the narrow, hilly street for parked cars; all in all, the house did not lend itself to a weekly crowd.

Still, and aside from my personal regrets about class ending, I wondered about her giving up that unique social interaction,[5] though even that wasn't without its maddening aggravations. As Jane gripes in her 1972 journal, "V. asked me in class, 'In *Oversoul Seven* you wouldn't write anything that isn't true, would you, that you don't believe?' Christ now they want me to prove my fiction. Fiction can be truer than facts but they keep after me they're so incredibly stupid . . . Nobody asks if a painting is true."

Jane and I had talked now and then about the possibility of another kind of class—a "core group," as she put it, of about ten people meeting every two weeks or once a month to focus on one or two areas, such as coincidences, or dreams and their interconnections with waking life, or impulses and precognition, that sort of thing. We discussed this several times, sitting at her round wooden table in the corner by the fireplace, in that new house that was so cozy and yet so—enclosed. Her hesitation about it, she said, was that it might get out of hand numbers-wise; that she was too sought after at that point to keep it small and focused; that eventually it would get out that she was holding such a class (after all, how could either of us have kept from writing about it?), and that would be that. And she didn't like the idea of keeping it secret, either—she hated the notion of exclusion, but how else could it be set up? In her 1977 journal, she also talks about an idea for some kind of seminar, "at least something for summer." As she puts it on November 4 of that year:

". . . something definite with a whole plan of action behind it . . . see psychologists, in a weekend seminar sort of thing; then maybe those in other fields; but the idea is to further acquaint them with Seth's and my ideas so that they apply them in their own fields; so that they can help people directly . . ."

But she wasn't in very good shape by then, and this embarrassed her so painfully, besides causing her physical pain, that she really didn't want to open herself to anyone's comments (or, as she perceived it, criticism) about it—she wasn't "perfect," so how dare she set herself up as any kind of group leader, was her lament. And little that I or anyone could say helped her much with that, though there were times when her difficulties didn't seem to matter so much to her, or when she stopped worrying about them, at least momentarily; or times when she would seem to be on the mend—shoulders not so stiff, walking better, her hands flexible again—if only for a little while.

Anyway, sometime in late 1979, the house next to Jane and Rob's place came up for sale. I drove up to see them one day and noticed the realtor's sign, and how cute the house was, just the right size, and private, with woodsy back and side yards and a front-facing attached garage. Jane and I talked for a couple of hours about how neat it would be if I bought it. "Then you could really get involved in my work" Jane said, genuine excitement in her voice. "We could really get into some great stuff, hold our own goddamned class."

I was gathering up a head of steam about this myself. There were many attractions to the idea. I was at odds anyway—I was restless with my life in Dundee; *Conversations with Seth* was about to be published and so I had some income to bank on, and Prentice-Hall seemed interested in other book ideas I'd come up with (including another one suggested by Rob).[6] The house itself was fairly inexpensive, somewhere in the $30,000 range, and up on the hillside away from flood range, so *that* scenario would never repeat itself. Also, it was a twenty-minute drive to my parents' house—a mixed prospect for me, though not without its comforts, and certainly a good thing for them and Sean, who could go to Elmira schools, much preferable to Dundee's, where he was having a miserable time. Finally, though I'd miss my friend Susan and our *Observer* projects, I was ready to move on. Sean and I could both start over, away from the circle of rumor and innuendo that comprises the downside of any small-town life. And then there was the prospect of "our own goddamned class," as Jane put it—an opportunity that thrummed with portent, not the least of which was (I have to admit) my own personal access to Seth.

But I didn't have a down payment, and so I decided to ask my parents for it.

Well, to put it mildly, and which shouldn't have surprised me, they went absolutely ballistic. For starters they flew into a rage about how I was not, and never would be, capable of owning *any* house, from which my mother jumped on a train of conviction that this house buying notion must be *Jane's* idea, and therefore proved that she wanted something from me, which I was too naive to see. In response to my (rather heated) demand to know exactly what this something was, my mother replied (I hesitate to say "smugly," but there it was), "If you can't see what it is yourself, I'm not going to tell you." We went around and around like this for most of an afternoon. My mother was intensely, increasingly, one might say exhaustively, incensed about the next-door proximity to Jane, quizzing me nonstop about it, long after the down payment question had been beaten dead, punctuating her remarks with accusations that were so offensive, so contorted and bizarre, that I actually stopped being angry and became somewhat afraid for her sanity.

All this even though such a move on my part would have been to their benefit—more so as the years went by.

I never resolved this with my parents and trying to assess it now, in the context of the present, is as disturbing to me as it was when it happened. Did it all rise up from some hidden well of jealousy? Fears for Sean? Something horrible from my mother's past? Unconscious knowledge, never expressed, of the real reason I'd gone to Martha's Vineyard—like projected waking dream elements they couldn't otherwise interpret? Or—a much more difficult question—were they in fact expressing, in wildly exaggerated, protective terms that I could not dismiss, my own unadmitted hesitations?

For what would "getting involved in" or "carrying on" Jane's work really have meant to me? Would I have become more serious, sooner, about writing; more successful in the publishing world? Or would this probable move have stifled my other interests to my ultimate detriment—would I, indeed, have acceded to the role of adjunct?

Or would Jane have relaxed a bit, spent time outside with me, tending a garden we'd create together, maybe even—gasp—hit some yard sales with me on Saturday mornings, joking and laughing about the amazing junk we'd find as we drove along, fifty cents for a lamp shaped like a chicken or an art glass vase she could use in a painting, and who knows what characters and coincidences and dream connections we'd have run across along the way and written up for amusement, analysis, and posterity?

I'll never know in this life, though things do have a way of working out for the best. Nonetheless, whatever the source of Jane's offer, I was flattered but resistant, even a touch resentful—had I no work of my own to give? Did she mean the drudge work of sorting and editing? Was Rob included in the package? At times I had the impression that Jane wanted him to be, if something happened to her—and in a Deleted material session not long before she died, Jane says to Rob, "Maybe you can marry Sue and carry on my work." (Reading that, I had to laugh; so like her not to want Rob to be left alone, but jeeze, Janey-O, how about checking in with me first, ya know?)

So even in the face of Jane's obvious regard for me, I automatically reacted defensively, as if "her work" and "my work" were at some sort of odds, or as if the one could overrun the other, and submerge it—exactly the way those so-called reincarnational selves of ours (and my mother as well) had tried to express it. And I still feel this defensiveness, even though ironically, and contrary to what I think I want to do, I seem to be fulfilling at least some small version of Jane's request.

When I told her (without mentioning the details) that no down payment was forthcoming and the house idea was kaput, she expressed disappointment, and that was that. We never discussed "the work" issue again.

In the end, perhaps my parents were exactly right to refuse to help me move into that house, even at the "expense" of my not living closer to them. Maybe on some other level of communication, they understood my "too expensive" dream better than I did. Maybe my "two-year-old defender" remark wasn't delivered as humorously as I'd like to remember it.

15

Cross-Corroborating Beliefs And Odd Stuff of Which Counterparts Might Be Made

Reading through Jane's journals has offered up endless discoveries about her private life, some of them delightful and some of them disturbing, and some of them so ironic and timely and parallel to my own life that I have to laugh out loud even as I cringe with self-recognition. In the course of our friendship, Jane and I only half realized that our backgrounds and beliefs paralleled one another's, and we never really explored it—mostly for lack of time, but also because our accompanying attitudes got in the way, sometimes absurdly so.

Cases in point . . .

The Writing Thing

From the start, I was as attracted to the idea of this memoir as I was oppressed by it. I wanted to capture something of the person Jane had been, and I resented my feelings of responsibility toward that task. I enjoy writing about Jane's ideas and yet I feel like something of an interloper for doing it (ye gods, "the work"!). I've occasionally entertained fantasies of throwing everything even remotely related to the subject, dream notebooks and all, right into the burn-barrel and be done with it. Usually accompanying this mood is a too-clear memory of the day I gave an autographed copy of *Dreaming Myself, Dreaming a Town* to someone from whom I craved approval. He opened it up, flipped through the pages, scanned the passage with him in it, tossed the book down on his messy desk, and said, "I just wish you'd do something of your own for a change." He never mentioned the book again.

I carried his remark like a stone in my heart for a long time. I suppose it will always rattle around in there to some extent. Because, of course, it fits my secret fears to a T. And in all the years that I knew Jane, I had not an inkling that the same remorseless clamor went on in her own head from the moment the Seth material began to be published—including the same burn-barrel fantasies, which Jane actually carried out at one point. "After I decided not to do any [more] science fiction, I had this great big bonfire out in the back yard," she said in a 1977 radio interview. "Tears were rolling down my cheeks and I burned all my science fiction, whether I'd sent it out or not, except for one manuscript called *Cast of the Witch*—I just missed [it] somehow, and found [it] some time later." Jane also used to say that she sometimes imagined her and Rob burning all the Seth material before they died, "two scrawny old people dancing naked around the fire, and to hell with it and everybody else."

But until I started reading Jane's journals, I thought that my quandaries about all this were mine alone. I was wrong. For example, this journal passage from March 26, 1972: Jane's editor at Prentice-Hall has just told her that he'll offer her a contract for *The Education of Oversoul Seven* before he sets one up for *Adventures in Consciousness*; this would be Jane's first hardcover novel.

> Today, Sunday, suddenly at desk thought comes with relief; well that gets me my respectability back . . . a novel.
>
> As a writer I feel free to do anything I please, investigating anything, saying anything; where I can say well I write books in other fields too you know or something; gets me away from the psychic image which I experience as confining with a whole bunch of ideas around it I don't approve of or like; and more dos and don'ts than I can manage, and taboos and expectations.
>
> As a writer I feel free to be as psychic as a bird, do what I please, and use my abilities psychically quite freely. When I think of me as a psychic I get hung up because I seem to be in the company of so many nuts. Writers may be as nuts as anyone else but it's a nuttiness that doesn't bug me—there's no dogma attached . . . which makes me think now twice [about] speaking for Spiritual Frontiers.[1]
>
> Yet my writing has been excellent describing my psychic experience but that's because when I'm writing I think of myself as a writer. Writing a good novel might just free me from this fuck I've been in . . . and publishing it; and free me . . .
>
> I can expand and write novels and so-called psychic books too . . .

In our conversations about writing, which were almost exclusively confined to Jane's admonitions about getting down to it x-number of pages a day, she never, in my recollection anyway, confided any of this to me—either that or it went over my head (we did talk about our mutual aversion to the "psychic" and "new age" images and associations she disliked so much). Had I understood, maybe I would have said something to her like, come on, Jane, if you want to write novels, take a couple years off and write novels, what's the big deal? But I suppose she never quite dared take the chance, except for the *Oversoul* trilogy, which she refers to in her notes as "lessons in fiction form." But what about just writing stories having nothing to do with any of this? No "lessons," no "psychic" overlay, just characters dealing with life?

"I don't think I could ever write a straight novel again," she told me one day, after I'd read two of her early autobiographicals. "I've just gone somewhere else with it now, and I guess I couldn't pretend otherwise and stay inside that old framework." And yet of course, stepping outside that framework has its own risks; I didn't understand how great these were for her, at the time, even though they are not unlike my own, or any artist's. For one thing she was horrifically afraid of ridicule, something she'd experienced on an almost unimaginable scale throughout her childhood, and thus felt in exquisite razor-sharp terms that line, real or imagined, between forging ahead and going too far—another reason for her physical expression of "holding back."

"Jane was a lady of great ability and determination," Rob writes in a September 20, 1984 letter to Walter Zeh, shortly after Jane's death. "She suffered greatly because her work met with much ridicule. Not many know this, because on the surface it seemed she did so well. But her talents were highly controversial, and she was largely ignored by establishment disciplines."[2]

The Money Thing

Jane had a certain automatic response to the idea of "rich" people, and, with some justification, considering the contrast in our childhood years, she saw me as coming from wealth (a dramatically exaggerated assessment of circumstances), which she felt obliged to "overlook" (her word for it). Maybe my friendship with her and my innate abilities despite this unfortunate handicap encouraged her to look this belief over—I don't know. We couldn't even begin to get across this one to compare notes.

I recall a moment in ESP class when I was bemoaning the spread of housing developments in the rural countryside around Elmira, something I'd cried about from the time I was old enough to notice it. In particular, I said that I had always been afraid that the people who owned the farmland bordering my parents' property would sell it off for house lots and ruin everything. What was now a peaceful rolling field would be destroyed forever. I was working myself up into quite a state over this when Jane broke in to ask, "How much space is there between your parents' house and this field?"

I looked up at her, surprised. "Oh—about three acres," I said, "but that isn't the—"

"Oh, well, shit, Sue, for chrissakes!" Jane said, in a curt, dismissive tone. "Three whole acres, what the hell?" She turned away and started talking about something else. Stung, I sat there trying to compose a blistering wildlife defense statement to add as soon as I could butt in, when Jane turned back to me and said, "You should watch your attitude about people who live around that neighborhood."

I said, "What attitude? What do you mean?"

"Your attitude." Jane was staring at me intently. "You need to watch it." And that was all. It didn't get through to me until much later that she'd interpreted my suburban-sprawl mope as snobbery. And was it? Possibly, I suppose—I thought it was reasonable alarm for the state of green space and the natural world, but maybe Jane was perceiving something else.

Around that time, in the only private Seth session I ever had, which was devoted to connections between my "secret" son and me, Seth made pointed comments about the unconscious blame I was projecting upon myself for letting the baby go. "You blamed yourself for financial reasons, though consciously this would be the last thing to come to your mind," Seth told me. "Subconsciously you wondered what social environment your child would *really* encounter, and whether or not you deprived him of the social and economic benefits that you have convinced yourself, consciously, you do not need."

At the time of this session, I remember thinking something like, yeah well, thanks a lot, Seth, I wasn't worried about that until you mentioned it! I'd assumed that economic standards were part of the adoption screening procedure; meaning, of course, that on some level I had indeed worried about "social and economic benefits," and who wouldn't, in my position? Or maybe I did have a money "attitude," as Jane put it. The funny thing was, she had the same attitude in reverse, not that you had to dig too far to find it.

I can't remember if the following transpired in class or during a Friday night yak fest, but it was in the apartment at 458. We were trading stories about funny encounters with strangers when Jane launched into a description of some "potbellied old rich men," as she put it, that she and Rob had run into in a local bar, and how gorgeous she thought Rob was by comparison. Well, Rob had always been dapper and slim, sure, but as Jane went on with this story (something about one of the unfortunate blokes asking how many kids she had at home, and her colorful reply), she kept repeating the words "potbellied" and "rich." Over and over, like a mantra—the potbellied rich man said this, the potbellied rich man said that, potbellied rich men all over the place.

After a while it began to sink into my head that I was very put off by this. Not that I didn't see where it was coming from, but I remember thinking, jeeze, Jane, what is your *problem* here? So what if somebody has a little money, or some pudge? It certainly wouldn't hurt if you had a little more of them yourself, I mused nastily. But I was well aware of some of my own uncompromising equations—religion is for cretins, for example (still a pretty fair assessment, in my opinion). So at first I said nothing. Besides, I wasn't all that convinced that rich country club types, potbellied or not, would be caught dead in the bars Jane and Rob and I liked to frequent. My guess was they'd been bullshitting about the rich part—but oh well.

Finally, I had to interject. "Come on, you make them sound like a bunch of drooling fools," I said. "What does a pot belly have to do with anything?"

"Oh, yeah, well, I guess you would see it differently," Jane replied, in all seriousness. I don't remember what my answer to that was, if anything—now it's funny: Did she mean that somebody with my so-called background would naturally go for the potbellied rich type, or that I'd excuse those unlovely traits as a matter of heft loyalty, or what?[3]

The Woman Thing and the Sex Thing

Less amusing than the potbellied rich man question—I was always happy to partake of a little man-bashing whatever the socioeconomic scale—was the lambasting Jane occasionally handed out to all the hypothetical women who in her opinion did "nothing" but (as I recall it) waste time living off their husbands' incomes rather than use their own abilities in the world. I'm not sure what set Jane off in this direction whenever she took it (and it is exactly the social assumption from which women were freeing themselves in those years); defensiveness, possibly, for her own refusal to toe some kind of role line. And for the most part, I went along with it—not that either Jane or I scorned women who didn't have formal jobs; this was, again, about "getting down to it," and the whole woman-writer arena scared me to begin with, conflicting as it did with every other choice in life, or so it seemed.

No, what began to snag my attention about this particular rebuke was how often Jane included the descriptive term "big boobs" as part of it, as in "women with big boobs who sit around all day watching soap operas," a sort of feminized version of the potbellied rich guys hanging around neighborhood dives. It wasn't until I'd heard her say this half a dozen times over the space of a year or so that I even realized it had been irritating me from the start.

It took me a while to work up my nerve to respond to this (there was a calling-attention factor that embarrassed me), or even figure out what it was that irked me about it. When I finally did speak up—I think I said something like, "You know, Jane, I resent the 'big boobs' thing and your equation of it with 'stupid'"—she immediately acknowledged my point, and apologized profusely, though my impression was that I really hadn't gotten through to her about what I was talking about—that her apology was sincere, though puzzled.

This is not to fault Jane for some dreary lack of political correctness, or meant as an indictment of sexual wit, something most people relish, and rightly so. Jane possessed a psychological luxuriousness that did not judge itself, not to mention a shamelessly earthy sense of humor. Beyond that, all of us have assumptive ways of speaking, and facing others' reactions is a natural learning method, in itself innocent of harm. Later Jane would call me on my equally careless and frequent use of "skinny and run-down" as a pejorative, and I was as oblivious to the personal affront as she apparently had been.

The fact is, these respective remarks beautifully illustrated the self-limiting beliefs we each held, and the results thereof. For Jane: big = stupid; for me: skinny = sickly. Yet neither of us ever quite saw this correspondence. It was always just at the edge of our conscious appreciation, there but not there, ready to open up a huge well of connections that we never quite made.

So obvious—so tricky. But then, the entire "woman thing" as we called it, seemed to each of us (privately and for the most part unconsciously) like the shoals of the Lorelei, just waiting to wreck the *real* plans we'd made for ourselves. Though she didn't consider herself a "feminist" by any means—"I never thought of myself as anything in those terms. I thought of myself as a writer," she once said—Jane seethed over any hint that her work was being patronized because she was female, which was one of the reasons she kept herself so thin (read: male-like). For her, "curvy and sexy" (a.k.a. "big boobs") meant "frivolous," as she puts it in her journals. She would have none of it. (She even wonders, in her journals and notes, if the expression of Seth as a male voice rose out of her beliefs along these lines.)

Keep in mind here that we are talking about the sixties and seventies, when it was still difficult for a woman to get her own car insurance, let alone recognition for her own success, or keep her own name. For instance, as late as 1974, the Elmira newspaper wanted to refer to me as "Mrs. Ned Watkins" in an article on a journalism award I'd won, four years after Ned and I had divorced. This was standard fare in most newspapers: women didn't make news with their own first names (the same paper referred to Jane as "Mrs. Butts" whenever it ran an article on her latest book). I flew into a rage about this to Maggie Granger, who was, to my surprise, not especially sympathetic. Policy was policy, Maggie said, and though Jane chimed in on my behalf (Maggie and I ended up having quite an argument about it), the funny thing is that I can't even remember if the article ran in the Elmira paper at all.

For both Jane and me, our identities were fiercely, perhaps fearfully, tied into the writer-image, so no wonder the name question sent me into such a tizzy. Like Jane, I didn't consider myself a feminist (though I got my back up just as easily as she did about many of the same issues); I was a writer first, which to me encompassed everything else. And also like Jane, I had the idea that being female was what got me into trouble (this despite some of the real trouble that my writing, specifically news reporting, occasionally got me into). Somewhere in the midst of all this, Jane called me up one afternoon to tell me that in the previous night's session, Seth had said to Rob: "Tell Sue that she would be better off if she thought of herself as an individual who happens to be a woman rather than as a woman who happens to be an individual." It made perfect sense, and I was disappointed as hell. *That* was the answer to my ruffled feathers? But of course, it was (and it applies universally).

In her journals for May 30, 1974, Jane records a dream in which I appear in a "pink long prom type organdy dress with a real flower maybe a rose pinned to it":

> [Sue] looks great but then I see she has a lot of makeup on and some red makeup on her nose.
>
> She tells of an incident . . . driving with some man he makes a pass at her. She gets in deep water or the car actually goes into water, anyhow it's over and she's laughing . . . She's on couch. I sit on floor [*the reverse of how we usually sat*] by coffee table, do a yoga exercise and generally loll and cavort not completely normally free but damn close and happy about it.
>
> Sue to my way of thinking representing female aspects carried too far? Overdone? So a guy makes a pass, she gets in deep water only here we're laughing because it's all over. Her nose is made up red . . . Recall old kid ideas, masturbation or sex showed on your face; the mark on Sue though also reminds me of a clowns makeup—women or maybe sex made you look like a fool too . . . Here though we're laughing at the whole thing and I'm doing yoga and cavorting on the floor hopefully meaning I'm in the process of freeing myself.

Though I was somewhat offended when I first came across this dream in Jane's journals, I had much the same feeling, by itself shameful to me, that being a woman "or maybe sex" did make you look like a fool. In fact, not long before this, on May 12, 1974, I'd also dreamed of being in "deep water"—of another, or an alternate, flood; here, as the waters began to rise, I went to Jane and Rob's place with Sean and all my books; this time the water came up into the second floor (second chance?), but their apartment was on the third floor, and we were safe. With them, no man friend around, I'd escaped the "deep water," and looking like a fool (ah, but to rewrite the past).

So it was our womanhood that threatened what we each saw as the "real" person, the writer. And thus each of us donned a protection system. She stayed rail-thin (no curves) and physically immobile; I kept myself just heavy enough (not obese, not out of shape; in fact I've always been fairly athletic), just safe enough, without drawing too much attention to the act of hiding. Certainly "being a woman" was what had gotten me pregnant, right? The writer just wanted to sit at a desk and type, didn't she?

Or so I'd ask Jane, kidding around—she should know. According to her (and this is a persistent theme in her early journals), she and Rob worried constantly about a possible pregnancy—*constantly*. "So we tried not to do it too much," she told me once (a statement rather eye-poppingly disaffirmed by her own journal notes). "Every month we'd worry about whether I was going to get my period, and if it was a few days late, I'd really get in a state. A couple of times when I was late I'd go to the local doctor and ask him, 'Is it the menopause? Is it?' and he'd say, oh, girl, you're way too young for that, and I'd say, like hell I am! I'd rather have that than the alternative!"

Not until much later, remembering these conversations, did I think to wonder, well, jeeze, Jane, what about the Pill . . . that came along in 1962 or thereabouts, didn't it, and anyway, what about a diaphragm or an IUD, or . . . but who was I to talk? (I wasn't privy to her birth control methods until I read her journals.)

While they lived at 458, Jane and Rob always had stacks of magazines around, including lots of *Playboy* and *Penthouse*, sometimes *Gallery*, unblushingly out in plain sight. I made jokes about this a few times ("Say, Rob, you get these for the still life models?"), and in reply, Rob would say, with complete professorial detachment, "Yeah, you know, that's all valuable information that wasn't available in the years when I was growing up," and smile as guilelessly as a cat. The downstairs tenant supposedly lent them his copies, though the sheer numbers seemed to me like an awful lot of nudie magazine subscriptions for one person . . . maybe they were pulling my leg. I was always just a tad uncomfortable with this. I can't say why, exactly—I didn't mind looking through the 'zines myself, either in front of them or privately. Maybe it was something of the same reaction to the thought of one's *parents* having sex. Egads! Not that Jane was especially reticent about that, either, if the subject came up.

"If it wasn't for goddamned oral sex, my goddamned sex life would have been dead years ago!" Jane roared one Friday evening in 1973, in the midst of an envious discussion of the tubal ligation I'd decided to have, considered quite a radical thing back then, though not quite as radical as yelling out intimate details to the amusement of half a dozen people, perhaps; but then the times, they were a-changin'. "Valuable information," indeed.

Parallel Dreams

It's not possible here to include all of the interconnecting dreams that Jane and I recorded over the years (I didn't realize how many there were, actually, until I read her dream accounts in 1999). It would certainly make for a unique form of memoir-making, but the obvious problems with this idea involve the delicate issues of convoluted background explanations, personal details, and the bugaboo Boredom Factor that quickly renders all dream-records except one's own into dull mud.

Still, we had some beauts. Not that it's unusual for friends to have similar dreams—anyone who keeps such records will discover this soon enough—but the thing was, when our dreams did correlate, it was more than just like images making appearances; the underside of events, or issues, were addressed in strikingly similar fashion. And we didn't have any sort of consistent dream-share schedule, so we weren't predisposing the subject matter or any particular set of dream-symbols to any great degree. For the most part these connections were spontaneous.

For example:

> From Jane's journals, September 20, 1971:
>
> Am in car with bunch of people on way to St. Jo's Hospital [in Elmira] where we are to help a man there. Then turn around remembering he is at Arnot [Elmira's other hospital] instead.

> From my dream notebooks, September 20, 1971:
>
> [A friend of my mother's died September 19 at Arnot Hospital.] I drive to class. Jane and some others and I decide to go back to Arnot to help [this person] realize he's dead. I stop at a gas station to get directions and the attendant points out [the person's] name in a book. "He's dead," the attendant tells us.

Here, Jane's notes state that she didn't know about the death of my mother's friend until the afternoon of September 20, when we compared these dreams. We'd had numerous discussions around this time about how dead people might come to *realize* they're dead, so it's interesting that the details of our dreams centered around this idea—less explicitly in Jane's, though the "helping" scenario is there.

Then there are the following dreams that dealt (as many of ours did) with our mutual best hopes for Jane's physical condition (my notes and Jane's both state that we didn't compare notes until the day after Jane's dream):

> From Jane's journals, Thursday, April 12, 1979:
>
> 1. I'm with a group of women, working in a department store selling stockings. All of a sudden I walk out, with no explanation. I hear one young woman say to another, "I guess she wants to take a walk herself instead of selling stockings."

2. I'm walking beautifully, a great stride, and am delighted and also wonder, how come? I see I have a short skirt on, and the dress has a high full bodice; I wonder if that's somehow responsible. Possibly as I'm walking along, a man or two gives me admiring glances.

From my dream notebook for Tuesday, April 10, 1979:

1. I see a friend from high school days, lying on his back on a beach. He is wearing short, flowery bathing trunks and his long, skinny legs are prominent.

2. I walk down West Water Street and into Jane and Rob's apartment at 458. Jane is walking around in shorts. Her thighs are fleshed out and firm, and she is walking in a marching step, so as to exercise her legs in particular. For a few minutes I don't remember that it's extraordinary that she should be walking; but then I remember and congratulate her. She says she's been walking for about three months but wanted to get good at it before she let others in on it.

The funny thing about these dreams, aside from the obvious similar themes of Jane walking (dreamed at a time when Jane wasn't walking much, and poorly) is the emphasis on clothing cut (shorts, a skirt) and the look of legs themselves. In my dream I see legs that are very thin (as Jane's were in reality), and fleshed out (as she and I both dream). And there's an air throughout, in her little dream scenes and mine, of bewildered (though pleased) surprise: When, and how, did Jane start walking? And I see her marching; in her dream, she's striding along . . .

"I think this dream means that I want to walk myself," Jane notes, "use my own legs now, instead of (just?) helping others by tending to their needs. . . In the second dream, I think my feminine aspects are depicted; as per the skirt, that I should express them more and that in the past I didn't, thinking that women were vulnerable."

Interesting that in my dream, my old friend (who was very thin in high school) is wearing flowery (i.e., "feminine") bathing shorts while lying (a vulnerable position) on a beach. Issues of gender and associated body condition—for both Jane and me?

Here, I picked a dream at random from Jane's notes—this one because it was recorded January 7, 1980, the day before my birthday. In part, it reads:

Outside in the back of 458 W. Water there were many trees. Groups of people, many old class members were tumbling in the treetops, rolling down them and out into space and back having a great time. Some, maybe Rob and Sue stood in Rob's old studio windows watching; and some sailed through the air from those windows to the treetops.

I look to see a small cruising cabin boat on some kind of swing, reaching from the rooftop next door, over to our old living room windows. It contains a small girl about 6, a woman, and a guy dressed as captain. The woman has told the kid this is too dangerous as they go swooping through the air and back. The girl's face is defiant and furious. She has short black hair and is thin. She says that she'll just do it herself.

Lots of my old students are around. One girl wonders if she wrote up a clear enough statement for a book I seem to be writing about class (though in actuality Sue Watkins is writing such a book). I ask the students to do a better job of their memoirs about class.

As in, who might that defiant and furious little girl be, Jane, insisting on "swooping through the air" all by herself?

So then I looked up my dream for January 7, 1980:

A very clear and moving dream. I am in a theater with a large crowd to see the movie that's been made out of *Conversations with Seth*. On screen is a close-up of Dan Stimmerman's lyrics to "Follow Yourself" [a song he composed on the dulcimer in class]. As the movie screen pans down the lyrics, a film chorus starts to sing the words, with Dan's voice and dulcimer leading.

All at once, the entire audience bursts into song, too. We are all moved deeply by the sense of camaraderie and ancient-yet-new purpose. Many old class members there.

[Then] a Dundee friend of mine and Jane and I are members of the crew of a fishing boat off the Florida coast. Jane tells me that she lost Rob at the last stop the boat made on shore—that they both got off, Rob went walking in another direction, and didn't return. Apparently she is looking for him among a group of islands we are approaching, as though searching for a love lost centuries ago.

But the song! The song is everything, ringing through me hours after I wake up . . .

Here in both groups of dreams lies that poignant air of fellowship contrasted with aloneness that Jane and I each felt so strongly in our lives, both privately and within the framework of our friendship. In my dream, even Rob has walked off "in another direction" and left Jane by herself (the stand she takes as a child in her dream; as we both did, in life, as children). And that telling detail of the ocean-going vessel in each dream, populated by a similar crew—though in Jane's version, the cruiser is swinging (perhaps dangerously, the woman admonishes) through the same "air space" where Jane's *Physical Universe as Idea Construction* experience—the beginnings of the Seth material—took place. And how interesting that in my dream, I'm part of the "crew" that's taking her to find Rob; helping her, in other words, the reverse of how we usually interacted (at least overtly).

So it would seem that even the method of our dreams correlated in much the same way our friendship did—similar themes and insights with different, though often parallel, details.

16

The Fortress of Food (Or No Food)

Jane and I had some hilarious conversations about food and how we utilized it. She suggested one afternoon that maybe she and I should switch diets. I pointed out that I'd probably manage to stay fat on what she consumed, which as far as I could tell consisted of coffee, cigarettes, corn bread, cereal, and peanut butter sandwiches; and she'd stay thin noshing quarts of ice cream and jellybeans all day, so what was the use? She agreed. "Goddamned beliefs anyway," she groused. But she didn't eat enough to sustain a canary, or so it looked to me whenever I had the opportunity to observe, which wasn't often. She was furtive about her eating habits, another characteristic we shared and never realized. She didn't like to eat in front of people, or be "caught" with food, as she puts it in her journals, and this was one reason she and Rob placed the bookcase divider in front of the apartment door—so nobody could walk in and catch her eating. She'd have time to—what? Throw her sandwich behind the couch? Yet I understand this secretiveness completely. I feel much the same, with opposite, yet analogous, results.

Jane looked down on food, or specifically, food intake, as an indulgence, "a goodie, a reward, and I didn't deserve it, just enough to stay alive," as she puts it in her journals, so she denied herself rigorously, even in private. Meanwhile, I'd typically eat tiny amounts in front of others and stuff myself the minute I was alone. Of course neither of us was fooling anybody. The problem was, we both thought Jane had the superior set of beliefs.

One of the things that had impressed her about Flood Man's "squab" dinner was how *much* food she claimed those birds gave. She told me that she and Rob ate the leftovers for three nights running. Well, that just mystified me—those were Rock Cornish hens, not thirty-pound turkeys. One hen made one meal for one person, as far as I was concerned. Similarly, Jane always made it a point at Thanksgiving time to tell me, and class, or the Friday night bunch, or all of them in succession, how she and Rob would buy "an ITTY-BITTY little chicken" to fix with corn bread stuffing, and how they'd eat the leftovers for days afterward. *Days* afterward? One bite per repast? But other than that, she didn't talk about food, except to mention her corn bread as a kitchen project—she made it often, even when doing anything at all represented a huge problem and she was more or less confined to her work-chair-on-wheels. It was simple, earthy and hearty, probably the most nutritious thing she ate. And she made it in the teeniest loaf pans you ever saw.

A typical meal at Jane and Rob's house if you were there around dinner time and they asked you to stay: a canned vegetable, usually peas, cooked in the can water, and served in it too; plain white bread on a plain white saucer; a petite hunk of meat loaf or a few cold cuts in tiny slices meant for all of you; milk, maybe some ketchup. Occasionally some store-bought cookies, of which Jane might eat a fragment. Coffee. The simple fare of people whose time and energies are centered on things other than shopping and cooking.

Once in a while one of the Friday night gang would bring some special treat—ice cream, maybe; a wedge of good cheese; maybe a home-made pie. Rob, who also ate sparingly, had nonetheless a homey appreciation for food, and enjoyed it, and the idea of it, though still in Lilliputian quantities; but Jane would get a certain *expression* on her face when you plunked anything like a *whole pie* down on the wooden-door coffee table, almost as if—not quite, but almost, I caught it flitting across her face—almost as if something smelled *really bad*. And sometimes we'd look at one another, and the whole thing would be right there, out in the open, and funny; we'd laugh, and the moment would pass us by. Only later, reading her journals, did it occur to me that Jane's childhood (unlike Rob's) had never included a single family moment centered on bounty, of meals or anything else; she'd spent her childhood cooking for, and serving, an invalid—not to mention that her own grandmother was hit by a car and killed while going to the store to buy Jane some Shredded Wheat! She had no associations whatsoever with food as tradition or kinship. Even drenched in all that alcohol and venom, my family had still shared something around the dinner table that I missed when it was gone.

Then there was the time we went to dinner at Clara and Brad's, old friends who'd opened the first organic food store in Elmira, possibly the world, in the early seventies. It's strange to think now that Jane and Rob actually accepted an invitation to dinner anywhere, but Clara and Brad wanted so much to please them and, I think, to try to raise Jane's consciousness about "health" food and maybe save her, as they saw it, nutritionally speaking.[1] They were into some Eastern guru-type religious phase at that time and in my private opinion had gone kind of loony over the whole thing, but they were exuberant, generous people, fun to be with, and Jane and Rob liked them immensely.

Jane and Rob and Maggie and Bill and I showed up for this feast, which was in Clara and Brad's second floor apartment over the store. We all dressed up for the occasion—I wore a billowy flowered pants suit that was too tight at the waist and about to get a lot tighter; Jane looked great in black slacks and a new print blouse with a stand-up collar, very flattering. She navigated the stairs without too much difficulty—in fact she did better than she had some years before, on those narrow steps at the Odessa grocery. Everyone was in a lively mood.

We took a quick tour of the apartment and crowded around the tiny dining table while Brad cooked barechested in Ali Baba-style pantaloons (Clara wore a matching outfit, with a halter top). They laid the dinner out before us in a buffet selection of food choices—piles of food, virtual mountains of it, dishes and dishes heaped full of it, pouring out of the kitchen. And every mushroom, cauliflower floret, tempeh ball—every single vegetable, every crumb—was deep-fried in some sort of oil that left a thick, rich golden crust on everything. You couldn't tell what anything was until you bit into it. We each had a finger bowl and cloth napkin to wash the grease off our fingers. "Health" food "diet," my respectable round behind.

I remember that Jane did her best to be a good sport and eat at least a bite of each tidbit put on her plate, and I remember her expression, which was what you would expect to see on the face of someone looking at a fresh dog turd. Of course, none of this stopped me from wolfing down plenty, an unusual lapse in my public eating behavior for which I paid big dues later, in the wee hours, by becoming hideously sick and throwing it all back up in violent, golden waves.

In the unfinished third-person point-of-view version of her journals that Jane called "The Bali Manuscript" (a "secret diary" she thought might become an autobiographical novel about her physical problems), she describes this dinner, and her perspective on food, in the kind of lush detail reminiscent of an Edgar Allen Poe story.

> They were . . . surrounded by what seemed to Bali to be mountains of food; three pots on the stove, steam rising, Brad stirring another like mad; piles of

fresh vegetables cut up in the tiniest of pieces and some unidentifiable chunks of stuff obviously food also. The kitchen was painstakingly old fashioned; no shining new appliances here; the stove second hand was the most ancient workable one they could find, for example, a big black one like those in somebody's great-grandmother's house. . . .

The dinner was delicious, prepared and served like a sacrament, lovingly lingered over, and Bali appreciated that angle; but watching people eat she thought; what a bunch of gluttons. And felt guilty because after all they were sharing the best—their best—the natural foods—and here she was being sarcastic or at least critical. Still, wouldn't they be better off eating like she and Rob did, a piece of meat, salad and a vegetable instead of piles and piles of stuff even if it was "natural."

Then she paused in thought: examining her own fine outrage against their "gluttony." Was this a shield; was she thin to a fault as some kind of badge of superiority . . . aestheticism?

Brilliantly clear in the writing, disconcertingly opaque in application, Jane's insights into her food beliefs, and how these might express themselves in other areas of her life, ran closely parallel to my own even in subliminal terms. In her unfinished "Aspects" manuscript for May 16, 1979, for example, Jane records this dream:

Sue Watkins, much fatter than she is *[great way to put it Jane!]*, sits with me on bed or couch; we talk lightly but she says something about my having great instincts for killing or some such. I laugh, wonder what would make her say a thing like that.

There are several women present . . . [they] are perfectly formed, but much shorter and smaller than I am. I say something about "little women" . . . so to them, I'm a giant, or some such.

Dream Interpretation [*according to Jane's notes*]: Sue being so overweight reminds me of my mother in retrospect; and I recall [Marie] saying I destroyed everyone I touched, and [her] saying I'd kill her if I ever got the chance. Sue is also a woman writer, with some of the same problems. I'd say here that the dream says that I'm afraid that if a woman uses power, it's bound to be destructive.[2]

The Little Woman thing is beautiful, combining a literary product by a woman with a literal interpretation . . . any artistic production by a woman is "little"/women are junior adults . . . and by those standards, any achievement by a woman is "giant-sized."

Compare this with the following dream from my notebooks for the same date, May 16, 1979:

> Barbara Coultry ["Bernice Zale" of *Conversations*, whom I met in college] and I are trying to get through a wooded area. We seem to be miniaturized, or else the woods are giant-sized. But there is a danger: Someone, or something, of gargantuan size, is picking people off the surface of the land and eating them like pretzels. We flounder along a river, sticking to the undergrowth to avoid being picked off and eaten.

Here, I'm with my friend Barbara, who is also a woman writer "with some of the same problems," as Jane puts it in her interpretation, and together we are trying to avoid destruction. To do so, we stay in the undergrowth (and are miniature, or "little women") so as not to be destroyed, by becoming some unseen giant's *snackfood* of all things (how demeaning!), an interesting dream-look at artistic confidence, and one that reflects exactly a certain shared idea about what happens to women who reveal themselves too much, or let loose their power, especially creative power, in the world.[3]

Thus I especially remember the time I watched Rob feed Jane. This was in their house, in late 1982, between her hospital stays (and around the time, as Rob later wrote in his notes, of what he calls her "natural death," interrupted, as it were, by medical intervention). It was a meal of pureed cereal and eggs, mixed, I recall.

She and I were sitting at her round work table, talking. She could still type with her long, elegant fingers; though not one joint moved on any of them, she could march them up and down on the electric typewriter keys—but she couldn't grasp a spoon, or raise her arms to feed herself. Now I could see how literally this mirrored her fierce ideas about what she was supposed to be doing, about the voice of her creative self as she spoke it: Writing, yes; anything else, no. For in fact she could do nothing else, could not move another part of her body—nothing except her typing fingers, her neck a little, and her mouth, to eat and talk.

Rob came out of his studio that day as if on cue—they must have set up a schedule—fixed the little bowl of food in the kitchen and brought it out to her. "This got much worse while she was in the hospital," he said to me. And I thought . . . then why go? Oh, Jane, why go in there, why not meet your fate here, among your cats and your manuscripts and paintings, with Rob, where you belong? I thought that she must feel some humiliation by my watching this scene—I know I would have—but they both treated it in a matter-of-fact way, with a certain air of astonishment on Jane's part, directed at Rob, as in—but this is what I thought we wanted! Something like that. The entire situation was filled with conflicts and terrors beyond my ken, including the end of their life as they had once known it.

Jane ate what I thought was a great deal that day, by the way, in comparison with what I'd seen her eat in the past. All the while, as Rob stood beside her and gently and carefully presented the spoon to Jane's mouth and she, bright-eyed as a nestling, accepted each portion, he kept up a smooth running dialogue with me about their beliefs, and Seth's comments, and the paradoxes and tradeoffs concerning the state of Jane's condition.

"It was all right there from the beginning," he said. "All of it, every choice we made along the way. Seth was absolutely correct from the get-go." Not speaking as if Jane weren't there, but with tender regard for her in that moment—she had to eat, and accomplish it in this fashion, and while he administered this necessity to her, we would all pass the time as we always had, talking about the mechanics of the universe, though Jane might not say much the while. I thought it was as intimate and loving a scene between them as I'd ever witnessed—and yet there was such unspoken anger and resignation in it that it seemed the air must fly out the window, to escape.

Later I was astounded to see six cookbooks, with Jane's handwritten notes in them, listed in the Yale archives repository—to me the most surprising of all that amazing stuff.

17

Jane in Class
A Portrait in Miniatures

The idea for Jane's ESP class was originally proposed by an Elmira kindergarten teacher, Florence MacIntyre,[1] in 1966, the same year Jane's *How to Develop Your ESP Power* was published. Florence met Jane and Rob through a fellow teacher who lived in one of the downstairs apartments at 458, and suggested right away that Jane start a "psychic" class.

"I didn't go for it," Jane said, "not then or later on when Seth said it was a good idea—I figured no damn ghost was going to tell me to start any 'ESP' class." But the notion kept rolling around in Jane's mind, and eventually she ran an ad in the Elmira newspaper to see what would happen. About half a dozen people (including Florence) responded, and so Jane's weekly ESP classes began in September of 1967 and lasted until she and Rob bought their new house in 1975 (with a few spontaneous "un-classes" held through 1979).

Much of what class was about has been recounted in *Conversations with Seth*, and its portrayals and memories of Jane are so woven through its context that it would be impossible, and impractical, to excerpt them all here. Still, the passage of years creates its own landscape. Little scenes emerge, voices murmur, things once considered to be of no importance take on the significance of irretrievable time.

* * *

IN MANY RESPECTS, JANE WAS A different person in class—she had a keener overt energy, for one thing, and only later would I understand that it was the one place she let herself run with it openly, as it were. (By 1972, she probably was moving around physically in class more than anywhere else, too.) Here we all were, packed in the living room of her *home*, the same room that for years (until they rented the adjacent apartment) had been Jane's writing space, filling it up with more and more noise, chairs, cigarette debris and smoke, and a virtual weekly explosion of animated opinion about everything. She not only dealt with the ongoing, frequently heated dialogues and debates on the usual conversational levels plus the underlying ones among anywhere from ten to thirty or forty people without missing a nuance—or forgetting to call bathroom breaks—she also went in and out of various states of consciousness (including Seth, Sumari, Seth II, and others) while maintaining her own lively equilibrium at all times, no small feat.

Class also provided a forum for Seth to interact with people on a regular basis, something Jane didn't otherwise seek—she didn't do Seth tours, for example, and their Monday and Wednesday night book production sessions were almost always accomplished in private. As she put it herself, "Class is as far as I go besides the books. Whatever Seth has to offer, it's in very personal terms, and the same goes for me. I'm not going to be a Seth missionary for mass audiences." Thus among other things, it gave Jane positive feedback in developing her confidence and abilities. You could tell she loved the give-and-take, and her perfectly balanced command of it, especially with the arrival of the Boys from New York.

This group of men and women from New York City started coming to class in January of 1972. Somehow they managed to persuade Jane that it was no bother, really, to drive five hundred miles round trip to Elmira and back every Tuesday to attend the four- to five-hour meeting (she extracted promises that they'd all get up the next morning and go to their jobs no matter what). So they would stuff themselves into somebody's car or van and make the trip every week, whatever the weather, wrangling and arguing all the way. "As it ended up," remembers Rich Kendall, who was one of this group, "the crew from New York was usually the first to arrive, even though the others at the time were mainly from the Elmira area. Once there was a very bad snowstorm all along the east coast, and we went up anyway. When we walked in everybody was amazed we showed up, and I believe it actually made Jane feel pretty good."

"Greater enthusiasm than that is hard to find," Jane said about them more than once, and the truth was that she loved those guys. She identified with their rambunctiousness—I didn't realize how much so until I read her journals, and understood her powerful cautiousness about "acting up" or "moving too fast," being too loud, saying too much. And she yearned, I think, sometimes, to be in their shoes—twenty-five years old, driving along a midnight highway in a car full of people, laughing and hollering all the way to the moon.[2]

"In general, we were rather unruly," Rich admits, "but Jane used to take it all in stride, and never demanded an official kind of respect that certain teachers, 'spiritual' or otherwise, might demand."

The only time I remember Jane taking real offense to something in class was March 12, 1974, when in the midst of a lively discussion of the "streaking" craze and one member's recent sprint down her street thus unattired, artist George Rhoads doodled a hasty cartoon of a remarkably endowed gentleman dashing nakedly across the landscape on wingèd heels, dubbed it "Seth Streaks," and passed it around. George filled several sketchpads with his unique doodles and drawings during class years (some of which appear in *Conversations*), but this one was especially outrageous, or anyway so we thought at the time. I know the date because George drew the thing on the back of the previous week's Seth transcript, which as I look back on this incident was probably as much the source of Jane's reaction as anything else. The drawing was handed to her last. Everybody was roaring with laughter.

Jane stared at it for a long time. She didn't laugh. In fact I thought she was going to cry.

She looked up from the drawing. "You people," she said, in a serious tone that shut everyone up immediately, "you people come here, and you come into my living room, and you forget—it's a privilege for you to be here." Without changing her expression, she handed the paper back to George and shrugged. "I don't know, George—I just don't know what to say. It just seems—I don't know, something. Disrespectful." Then she looked around at all of us, called for a break, got up out of her chair with somewhat more alacrity than usual, and left the room.

I for one was floored. I simply could not believe that Jane, of all people, could be so offended over a *drawing*. Sure, it was irreverent, but Jane was one of the most irreverent people I ever knew—in fact she thrived on that element of her personality, and her work, especially the Seth material, essentially sprang from it, as does any artist's. But disrespectful? Since when were any of us supposed to "pay respect" to any of this?

Not that Jane didn't get her back up about certain attitudes—she was especially incensed when anyone expected her to conform to some sort of spiritual chastity, especially in response to her smoking habits—and she did (privately) ask a few members to leave class, over what I'm not sure even today, except that it involved some ongoing belligerence that rose up out of the reincarnational mini-dramas that the participants refused to let go, even weeks afterward, and move on to other questions about its meaning.

Only after reading her journals and notes did I see how thoroughly Jane's irreverence ran alongside an equally powerful veneration for art, and its sources, that in its depth left her vulnerable to deep fears about being labeled a fraud, or made fun of; something many creative people secretly nurture, and hide. At the time I didn't understand this, either about Jane or myself, or anyone else of similar mien. Maybe some of my shrieking hilarity over this drawing came from this source; maybe all of us, George included, were venting our discomforts about a lot of things (there was certainly a strong element of wicked glee in our reactions). Or maybe none of that applies at all. It's hard to say—I remember only my chagrin. George dismissed the whole thing with a sigh and a shake of his head. (I still think the drawing is funny, however.)

Jane didn't say another word about it when she returned from break, or ever again, though later in that class, Seth had this to say:

> The truths are written in the pupils of your eyes and the cells of your being, and in your own vitality and joy. The truth is not in any book. It is in your living being and the vitality of your own breath. If, after many years, I can convince you of that truth, if you will forgive the term, then will you understand how the universe is always created, how it expands constantly from your own thought, and how you are the fountain of truth after which you search with such diligence.
>
> You create it now. You are it now. The streaker creates it now . . . Seth streaks, indeed, and so do all of you!

With that, Jane came out of trance and the discussion turned to other subjects and everything went on as usual—or as usual as that bunch ever managed to be. But as I look back on that incident, I wonder how close Jane came to ending class that night, on the spot.

"Jane said it shocked people that she questioned Seth's material," Rich remembers, "but that the idea was to try it out, test it out—but when we made fun of Seth to show we weren't putting him on a pedestal, we were really making fun of portions of ourselves. And then she'd say, 'Seth is not just another member of class.'"

* * *

SNIPPET: THE ARTFULLY PLACED QUOTES from the Seth material hanging on the walls of Jane and Rob's bathroom. I especially remember "You get what you concentrate on" positioned for viewing while sitting on the toilet.

* * *

SNIPPET: IN CLASS, MAY 1973, IN the middle of a discussion on consciousness, Jane turns to me and says, "I'm picking up something about Sean." She tells me that I've been instilling defiance in him and "encouraging brattiness" so he can act as a sort of spokesman for my own unexpressed feelings, especially toward my father. Sean is three years old at the time. At first I think, oh, shit, she's right, and momentarily feel wretched; but later I think, but don't say, yeah Jane, what do you know about it? Now, looking back on this, I think that "defiance" was a much more loaded subject for Jane, and for me, than either of us cared to realize—having nothing to do with Sean at all.

And then, of course, on the subject of children, there was the chasm of Jane's own background, as in the night she lit into Harold Wiles, of all people, for his casual mention of chauffeuring his sons to school sports functions. Jane went on at length in a disapproving tone about "overindulging kids," and when Harold replied that he didn't mind driving them and enjoyed watching the games, Jane seemed to disapprove even more. Listening, I thought she was making an issue out of nothing; that a parent's willingness to accommodate a few car trips to school events was a normal part of the deal, forgetting that Jane had nothing at all with which to compare.

* * *

SNIPPET: THE NIGHT IN 1972 WHEN author Richard Bach came to class. He'd been visiting Jane and Rob that day, with an editor friend, having run across the Seth books and recognizing a certain kinship with the origins of his best-seller, *Jonathan Livingston Seagull*.

I walk into the living room at 458 and take one look at Bach and nearly pass out on the floor. He's the most handsome man I've ever laid eyes on, and seems to me to be sitting in an aura of golden light, like a fairy-tale lion king, or something as mythic. Everything else in the room disappears. We talk, and he gives me some pertinent advice about being true to my writing. "Your art is meant to take care of you in the world," he says. I look over at Jane, who says to me, "Now, there is a *real* man, Sue-Belle," which should embarrass me, though it doesn't. Bach just laughs. When Jane calls a break I leave class and run all the way to my apartment, grab my copy of *Seagull*, and run all the way back so Bach can autograph it.

Later I find out that Jane was pretty smitten with the man herself—at least until a *Time* cover story on him hits the stands that fall. In that piece Bach spoke at length about Jane's work, but his (possibly edited) description of her as "a small middle-aged woman in a rocking chair," sends her into a tizzy for days. It's the "middle-aged" part that she complains about—she was forty-three at the time—but I think now that the vague hint of decrepitude in the rocking-chair allusion was really behind her reaction. "I mean, Jesus Christ, RICH-ARD!" she bellowed half (and only half) humorously. Though she treated her own reaction with some amusement, she was obviously hurt, and brought it up several times. (In her journal notes for November, 1972, she admits that this response colored her other ideas about the article, and outweighed the positive aspects of it.) So much for the state of smittenhood, I told her.[3]

* * *

BUT THERE ARE SO MANY SNIPPETS from those days—no book could hold them all. Carroll Stamp (a.k.a. "Mary Strand" in *Conversations With Seth*) sent me a manila envelope stuffed with her memories of Jane. She and her sister "Jean" attended class from May of 1973 until it officially ended in 1975. Carroll was also part of Jane's Wednesday afternoon writing class, of which this essay combines both settings:

> I was thirty-three years old, mother of four, a registered nurse, relief night supervisor in the labor/delivery unit, a born and bred Catholic and married eleven years . . . I was in cahoots with the part of society that was perpetuating the medical beliefs that we are helpless victims of disease and could only get well and stay well by the good grace of doctors, hospitals, medicine, surgery,

and following directions. I had already lost faith in this system because I was on the inside.

When I [first] arrived, class was in full swing. By class standards I was an esoteric bumpkin. The rest of [them] all seemed to know the latest guru's philosophies, state of the art books and practices; while I was just digesting reincarnation. George sat in full lotus position for three hours; I didn't even know it was called that but it looked mighty uncomfortable. The Boys from New York were only in their late teens or early twenties but somehow seemed older than I. They figuratively threw paper wads and airplanes while our accepted valedictorian Sue frowned and sighed. [My sister and I] made disparaging remarks *sotto voce* about her budging in to sit at the right hand of god . . .

We would walk in to find Jane ensconced in her rocker most of the time. She was usually barefoot with her feet propped up on the long coffee table in front of the couch, flashing her peacock-blue or cat-black toenails. Jane could pull off things like that—violet toes and emerald fingers, and it never seemed to occur to her that this was in any way outlandish. She was an original, all right.

She would have been in her forties then, with black hair she was always trying to decide whether to cut or let grow. Hence she found a way to compromise: the back was longish and the front shortish. She would have weighed between eighty and ninety pounds but she always said she was heavier, just as I always said I was lighter. When talking, trying to make her point, she would pick up one of her Pall Malls and stick it in the side of her mouth and hold a match in readiness for some distant moment when she would actually light it. The cigarette bobbed up and down as she continued talking.

At first I found her thought construction so abstract that mere social conversation seemed literally impossible. She listened intently but somehow I was never able to bounce off her. Her sense of humor was to me one of the most important facets of her personality. She viewed her work seriously but maintained a light-hearted attitude that diluted the heavy concepts. Her deliberate earthy language dispelled any spiritual aura that threatened to permeate the atmosphere. Others would have made a sacred cow of her had she not consistently defecated on the project. A certain amount of student-teacher respect she accepted graciously, but if the respect began to assume an obeisant posture, she would mentally goose the genuflection, shattering the illusion. This talent she had perfected to an art form.

In many ways she was as predictable and ritualistic as the birds she so loved to watch. In physical reality she clung to familiar routine patterns, which was rather a paradox since she explored non-physical reality with an abandon that seemed to contradict her physical existence. As I think of it now, she had many birdlike qualities, not only in size and gait, but she gestured quickly with her hands and moved her head in a graceful yet stilted manner that was somehow reminiscent of birds. Her eyes were dark and expressive and they darted like a hawk's, collecting massive physical and nonphysical data. She loved to pick up unspoken reactions, so her eyes would often dart away from the speaker, to check out the effect of his/her words on the rest of the group. I delighted in this when it involved others but found it quite irritating when she did it to me.

I never quite knew whether she was a sparrow pretending to be an eagle or an eagle pretending to be a sparrow. In any case she flew, even then I understood that much. Now I feel she was both, pretending to be Jane.

* * *

AND THEN RICH KENDALL, WHO WROTE down some of the remarks Jane made in class, sent me this collection of snippet gems:[4]

> I asked her what was happening in Elmira these days, and she said, "Everything."
>
> When people told Jane about staying home and experimenting with psychic experience, she would ask them if they were working, had a job. I think she felt it was important for people to be dealing with the world, and that they couldn't use psychic exploration as an excuse to not work with the world at large.
>
> Jane said that she let new people in class so we didn't get to be some kind of closed cult, where we couldn't stand hearing other people's beliefs, especially differing ones. She used to caution us about seeing people as beliefs. Yet she said that during some social gathering someplace, she was terrified to go into the back yard with the doctors' and lawyers' wives and that they thought she was a snob when she was actually just terrified—she didn't look at people as individuals, but made divisions, social and economic.
>
> "I don't mind being forty-six," she said once, "but I don't want to be forty-six and stupid."
>
> In response to hearing a tape of herself singing Sumari, she said, "If it's possible to go through five corners of a four-cornered universe, I've done it."
>
> She charged a few dollars per class, $2.50 when it began and later $3.50. When her books started selling well, she stopped charging, and she never charged for personal sessions. She kept a basket in class where you were supposed to put the money. There were many times people just didn't pay. Even I may have

"forgotten" a time or two, or three, and Jane used to get a bit annoyed at this. She never singled anyone out, and I don't think it was the actual money she was mad about, but the fact that we had agreed to this and then were not keeping our end of the deal and not saying anything as well.

She told us about the time when Seth had said that a certain person would show up in class, I think on a particular night, and when this guy didn't show, Jane got upset and thought that since Seth was wrong about that, maybe it was all bullshit and that she was distorting everything.

Jane spoke of the neighbor who was shooting pigeons on the roof near Jane's apartment, and she wondered why the pigeons kept coming back to the roof. The pigeons, she pointed out, never took up arms to try to shoot the men. Jane said, we are a species that is not pure beast or pure god, but perfect in its own way, though at times it was hard for her to see that.

I recall a conversation during a visit to her house that made a strong impression on me because it made me realize a major misconception I held of her and her life. I can only paraphrase the exchange, but I think the exact words are less important than the essence of it. I was telling Jane how I hoped to be able to create my life so that my days were filled with joy after joy, high after high, with peak experiences of consciousness filling my every day. I didn't say to Jane, "like your life," but it was implied. Without putting down my intent in any way, she explained to me that while she had her highs, her life was not an endless series of peak experiences, but filled with the same emotions and ups and downs that all of us grappled with. As naïve as this conception of Jane may seem today, my experience of her was basically once a week on Tuesday nights, when the magic of the universe poured into her living room at 458, and at the time I had only that context from which to establish a viewpoint.

I told Jane I saw eternity while I was on acid, and she said she did also, without it. She said, if you want to get stoned, get stoned on timelessness. I talked about taking drugs to find peace, and she said she never searched for peace.

There was a point shortly before classes officially ended when a lot of visitors came each week, necessitating the covering of the same ground we had been through years before, which led us to begin to feel a bit bored, something we never would have imagined could happen in Jane's classes. These feelings got back to Jane in the form of a comment one day, and Seth came through and said something to the effect that those who were bored need not feel obligated to come there any more. I feel that our attitude must have upset Jane, but I'm purely speculating on that. I personally believe that covering the same old ground was just the surface of the situation. We had reached a natural turning point, where it was time to get more into the world and use these ideas in our lives in a way that many of us had avoided.

Before she died, Jane said to Rob, "Don't let them make a god out of me."

And I remember the class when Jane asked everyone to go around the room and spontaneously say something to each person. When I got to Jane I told her I felt I would have a stronger connection with her in death than in life. She didn't say anything but kissed me on the cheek.

18

Put off, Piqued And Otherwise Perturbed

My mother was reading my copy of *The Seth Material*. I could tell by the look on her face that it was not going well. This was 1972 or thereabouts; our big arguments on the subject were yet to come. She skimmed the pages rapidly, as was her habit, and finished it, or was at least done with it, in a couple of hours.

I said, "So whad'ja think?" Her lips were tight enough to cut fishing line, so I really should have left it alone.

She shook her head. "Makes me afraid to go down cellar," she said. I laughed, but she wasn't joking. In fact all at once she was glaring with fury, pointing at me in full lecture mode. "Jane and Rob are a couple of *con artists*!" she hissed. "They've got a real racket going there, and you refuse to see it." She stepped closer, prodding my shoulder at every word. "They want something from you, *and don't you ever forget it*!"

Naively, perhaps, I was shocked. I knew she'd probably be suspicious of the Seth voice, but I'd imagined she would respond to the ideas—they were basically in the same ballpark as her own, albeit more focused on specifics. I expected some sort of debate with her about it all, some dissective argument, maybe even a wider discussion about dreams, coincidence, funny little instances of ESP—all of which we had talked about before, without rancor. Of course I already understood that she was put off by my friendship with Jane; but this was a *book* we were discussing, and I'd thought she would respond from a bookish point of view, rather than a personal one.

However opaque this little fiction, it rose out of the underlying regard that my mother and I did have for one another, despite our differences. So her con-artist invective was like a slap in the face: My own mother thought I was an idiot! But I said nothing. I'd asked for it; she had a right to her opinion. I swallowed mine and left it there to simmer away on its own.

Because a little voice—tiny, sarcastic, wearing my mother's eyes—asked me later, in the dark, *Well? What is she getting at?*

I never for a second thought Jane and Rob were con artists, or that they "wanted" anything from me (other than my own best efforts for myself). The accusation was so absurd on so many levels and for so many reasons that arguing it was plain futile. You liked the ideas or you didn't, you bought the books or got them free at the library, and beyond that, what? Nothing. Period. So what was this about? Was it about Jane's definitive, unapologetic way of expressing herself? Except that was a trait that my mother usually *admired.*

Some of it might have been a question of association, with which I sympathize completely. From the start it was intensely off-putting to me, and certainly to Jane, to see her work dumped into the "new age" category, which employs little common sense or quality judgments on the content of works so defined. Given my mother's opinions about religion in particular and her belief in the ubiquity of bullshit in general, I have to guess that she could not separate Jane's work, and ultimately, Jane, from her deep distrust of sales pitches, into which she included, with no small justification, anything smacking of organized metaphysical anything (though up to this point, she'd always been unfailingly kind toward the people involved).

That is a guess, though, and doesn't begin to take into account the darker worries that exist more or less as a natural undercurrent in any parent's heart, or the even more enigmatic possibilities of multidimensional relationship factors—maybe. It all surfaced again, with far greater antipathy, in the house-buying incident described earlier (as I must have known it would—how could I have imagined otherwise?). Only long after both my mother and Jane were dead was I able to sort through any of this enough to resolve some of my visceral reaction to it (I absolutely never mentioned any of it to Jane). Too bad they couldn't have hashed it out together; they had similar literary backgrounds, and Jane might have appreciated my mother's take on the world, coming as it did from someone whose past was more like hers than, say, my own was.

I ran into similar sentiments again, much later—first in 1994, when in searching out the thread of how I'd met Jane, I called an old friend from high school days, now a professional photographer I'll call Gary, to check on the sequence of how-we-met-Jane events as told to me some years before by Dan Stimmerman: That Gary had accidentally hit Jane's cat while driving along West Water Street in Elmira, had ended up taking her and the cat to a local veterinarian's office where the cat died, Jane had felt sorry for Gary and invited him over that Friday, Gary had asked Dan to go along, and so the thread wove on, as I remembered the story. As it turned out, Gary's recollections differed somewhat (though the cat still died),[1] but far more surprising to me was his response when I asked for his memories of Jane.

"About Jane?" Gary said. "Well, I liked her but I thought she was a total phony from the word go. I thought, Jesus Christ, what a scam. I mean, we got religions a thousand years old with this kinda stuff and here she's got this crock'a shit. I was at a table-lifting thing—me, Dan, the Grangers—and everybody was all googah and I thought, suuuure. I said something to Rob like, well, it sells books, doesn't it, to raise tables off the floor? I forget what Rob said, but he was polite.

"I was pretty polite myself, about my feelings about her, though—I don't think she knew. [*I bet, I thought to myself, taking notes.*] What comes to my mind about her is an analogy with the faith healer who admitted to Randi, the magician, that he was confused and probably fell in love with his own ideas. I mean, I think that's what Jane was really doing."

I said, "Well, if each of us isn't in love with our own ideas, whoever else will be?"

"Oh, I suppose," he said dismissively, and I thought, hey, poop on you, pal—though Gary has always cultivated a sardonic air, and it's hard to figure exactly what he does like, if anything.[2] But my main reaction to his comments was something like, jeeze, this was how you really felt, and you kept going over to her house, drinking her wine, being "polite?" I hate to shoot back the word hypocrite, but . . .

Psychic charlatans exist, of course. A few purport to speak for Seth or Jane, and have published books based on this claim, sometimes taking on the role in great detail (one "Seth" couple even uses Rob's note-taking format, with times and side comments logged about bathroom breaks, barking dogs, ringing phones, etc.). No intrinsic harm in any of this as a means of insight and discovery, but beyond that—well, it's one thing to copy masters' paintings as part of the learning process, but to pretend that the copy is an actual da Vinci is forgery. *This* is what a con artist does.[3]

I've never had much interest in "proving" Jane's work or motives any more than I would, say, Ray Bradbury's (you might not like Bradbury's outlook but I doubt you'd accuse him of faking the stories). Again, the ideas either intrigue you or they don't. Jane's unique combination of intuitive agility and common sense either sparks something in you or it doesn't—same as with any work of art.

Aside from that, and ironically, it was Jane's intense focus on her work and insistence on effort that sometimes made her not the easiest person to be around. Whenever I told her about a writing project I'd started, be it story or novel, her first and often only question was, "How many pages have you got?" There were never enough. At the time I took this as a rebuke, letting it obscure her encouragement, and so after a while I pretty much stopped telling her about things I was working on (though the truth was, as Jane well knew, most of my writing projects fell by the wayside unfinished). As a student who went to two of Jane's writing classes remembered it, "She decided out loud that I wasn't working enough, so that was why a piece was either bad or less good than it should be, never that it might be more or less close to what it was trying to be." And she could indeed be "prickly," as Debbie Harris puts it in her journals, about odd things like worldly travels;[4] and heaven help you if you admitted that you'd ever in your life shelled out the bucks for a Scientology mind-sweep, or handed yourself over to some guru, or something of that nature, not that I blamed Jane for her through-the-roof reaction to this sort of claptrap.

"The hell of it is," Jane said often enough, "I tell people to do their own thing and then I get upset when they do!" In fact her instant indignation over such topics was probably the source of my friend Tim's assessment of her—"I thought she was intolerant of other peoples' opinions," he told me one day many years after her death, and I understand how he might think so, as Jane liked to initiate debate, always cut to the chase, and accepted nothing at face value.

I didn't think Jane was intolerant—she naturally connected with the heart of hearts in people, and focused on it, even if she didn't especially like them—but she could be dismissive, and furthermore had a habit of interrupting other peoples' narratives with "Yeah, that reminds me of the time when Rob and I—" and off she'd go on her own, frequently unrelated, storyline! This was very annoying, of course, not to mention deflating, even though you could see she meant no harm by it and in ESP class at least, everybody interrupted everybody else all the time, with gusto. Conversational formalities weren't exactly the norm. However it's more than possible that some of her social mannerisms grew from simple impatience with the undertone of neediness, or press for approbation (or a word from Seth), that more or less oozed from people around her (me included). This became an almost inescapable element in anyone's relationship with her, with few exceptions—the Grangers, for example, or ESP class member Frank "Fred Lorton" Longwell, who were friends with Jane in a way that didn't expect, or yearn for, metaphysical feedback. As Debbie Harris admits in her journal entries, "When I tell [Jane] my [travel] experiences, I expect some sort of positive reinforcement . . . but she doesn't give it and this makes me wonder why not." Then Debbie observes, "People like Jane, people in her position, aren't necessarily going to react the way one would expect them to . . . I suppose."

All of that is fairly ordinary human give-and-take, though, whatever the unspoken hopes of those in Jane's company might have been (or that she did in fact enjoy helping people whenever she could). Thus I was surprised (though again, more intrigued than offended) when in late 1999 my writer friend, Susan Thornton, told me, in describing her memory of the one time she met Jane, that she "kind of thought [Jane] was a fraud too." I knew it took some courage on Susan's part to tell me this, and for this and other reasons, including our long-standing friendship, I asked her to elaborate.

Susan and I met in 1978 at the Dundee *Observer* office, when she came in to renew a subscription for her parents, who had a cottage on nearby Seneca Lake. At the time she was living in Cambridge, Massachusetts, and had read several of Jane's books, but was not so much interested in Seth as she was in simply meeting another writer. So I took her with me to Jane and Rob's place one day that November. As it happened, two former ESP class members had also stopped by, to say goodbye before moving out West. We all sat around Jane's round work table in the living room, talking about this and that.

Susan writes:

> As the six of us sat [there], I became aware that something unusual was about to happen. Jane was sitting to my right. I became aware of a change in the atmosphere in the room, as if something were speeding up, and in a moment Jane took off her glasses, cast them to the table, and began to speak in an entirely different voice. Her usual voice was husky and high pitched, spiced with an occasional nervous laugh; this new voice was deep, sonorous, confident. Jane's eyes grew deeper and darker, more intent. I realized Seth had "come through," and I was part of an impromptu "Seth session" such as I had read about in several published volumes . . . As soon as Jane had taken off her glasses Sue had the presence of mind to switch on an old portable tape recorder that was sitting on a nearby bookcase.
>
> Seth spoke at length to the couple who were moving away, and then began to speak about the importance of imagination and the creative life . . . Then I

had the opportunity to ask a question. "But what about the ego?" I asked. I had been reading Freud, Jung, Adler, Perls, I was keenly interested in psychotherapy, in various theories.

According to the transcript of this session, Susan at this point suggested "that the ego is a real psychological structure that can be frightened of the insights offered in the dream state." She writes, "Jane [then] turned her dark, different, suddenly intense eyes on me. Which personality was it that was staring at me from her face? Was it hers? Or was it some 'other?'"

Susan and Seth then exchanged these remarks:

SETH: My dear friend, what is the ego? Is it a part of you who does not want to do what you want to do? Is it a part of you that mitigates against what you are? Is it a part of you who is an enemy? Is it a part of you who does not understand your intuition? Is it a part of you you want to put down?

SUSAN: I think it's a different thing for each person. I think in general for some people it becomes the part of them that doesn't listen to dreams. It becomes the voice that says, "This is reality, there can't be any other like this," that says, "this is a table." So when a person who has this kind of idea about the ego has a dream where the table looks differently, then the ego gets frightened.

SETH: What is your ego?

SUSAN: I don't know if I can answer that. It's a hard question for me to answer.

SETH: [*With gentle amusement:*] That is a very good answer.

"Fraud is an interesting, and loaded word," Susan acknowledged in her reply to my questions about her remark:

In one way I was jealous of Jane. Especially at the time I met her I was sort of floundering as a writer, whereas she was much more dedicated. I mean, look how dedicated [Jane and Rob] were, gosh.

I admired her fiction, for example *The Education of Oversoul Seven*, I liked it a lot; that I thought was a genuine imaginative effort, and I respected it and found it clear, engaging, well written. Jane's poetry I thought sucked and that she showed incredible balls to include it at such length in her published works. At times I thought someone at Prentice had a screw loose to keep sending her contracts. The books, while I loved *Seth Speaks*, tended to get long winded and repetitious . . . I kind of thought, who is Jane kidding?

Then when I met her at her place and saw the entire phenomenon, I didn't know what to think, but I wasn't entirely convinced. If I'd been at a session once or twice a week for years as you were I might have been more of a believer. . . .

But somehow it seemed too easy to me. I think I thought Jane's role was too easy, just to be a conduit for another voice, and so even when I saw it happen, I still on one level didn't want to believe it. In a way I wanted to be a believer, or at least be more of a witness than I was. The single encounter I had was so sort of mystifying and strange I wanted more . . .

So as I keep turning it over in my mind I'm still kind of baffled. I certainly don't think Jane was a fraud in the sense that she wanted others to believe in or "buy" a religion. That was quite clear. And the last book, *The Way Toward Health*, is very difficult to read as it's quite obvious she couldn't use the Seth material to help her own physical disabilities. And that is very poignant and sad . . .

I guess I did tend to think that just to dictate a book to her husband and have the typed-up manuscript accepted for publication was too "easy" in a way. However, now that I think about why I thought that, I have to realize there is jealousy in that thought. To sit and dictate is hard enough, and I've always had a struggle with making myself sit and write. And in some respects Jane was braver than I, more willing to face the unknown, or she just had a more comfortable feeling about it. . . .

So on reflection, back to Jane, I think on the one hand, that on one level I did think, yes, she is pretending to be Seth to get book contracts. It seemed "easier" to me than all the "hard" work I wasn't doing, i.e., creating fictional manuscripts from scratch. Also, I was caught up in the Bread Loaf [writers' conference] mindset at the time, which was that "artists" started from nothing, and pulled whole books out of themselves. Which wasn't what Jane was doing. And which was also a misconception.

And so there it is, I mused, reading Susan's remarks—the impossible burden all of us seem so driven to place upon ourselves, and especially on creative aspirations. In that, Jane's life experience was universal, exaggerated only by degree. At the time of this email exchange, Susan had just finished seven grueling years of work on a memoir of her love affair with the hugely prolific novelist and medieval scholar John Gardner, who was killed in a motorcycle accident in 1982, four days before they were to be married.[5] Like Jane, Gardner had a powerful, all-inclusive work ethic about writing, an equally powerful expectation of the same from students, and an accruing physical condition (in his case, alcoholism) that would eventually erode his life and lead to his death. And like Jane, Gardner affected a young neophyte writer so profoundly that her life's work from then on essentially springs from that encounter.[6]

There are many parallels between Susan and me, and the mentors each of us discovered, and the layers of beliefs therein about creative ease, or the lack of it as a virtue. A gifted teacher of writing technique, Gardner nonetheless virtually canonized its difficulty; only through endless revisions over months, perhaps years, he believed, does one even begin to approach a finished product. Jane on the other hand accomplished much of her writing in states of consciousness where the material was just *there*, basically waiting for her to come pick it up, a sensation she once described to me (with accompanying gestures) as "like each project somehow has a place—like over here is a line-up of *Oversoul Sevens* and over there is Seth's book dictation all ready to go, and behind that is his *next* book, and over *there* is another book on aspects . . . and all I have to do, and I know this is tricky as hell, is focus on one and it opens up . . ."

Obviously, this was an astounding facility, though perhaps, again, only unusual by degree—most writers have had a story or two drop fully formed into their heads on occasion. But Jane's abilities accelerated that process, especially in voicing the Seth material. Fundamentally, her genius lay in the method as much as in any of its products, perhaps more so. She demonstrated for one thing the limitless elasticity of the conscious mind, of conscious knowing—of information itself, for that matter. As Rob later remarked, "Her artistry in speaking for Seth, without hesitation or revision, without ever referring to notes or losing her way during a delivery, no matter how long it lasted, was a very creative manifestation of a most unusual phenomenon."[7] No wonder, then, the other side of it, her endless self-questioning, the physical problems that held her back and eventually immobilized her.[8]

Thus I appreciate Susan's suspicions about Jane's ease in "just [being] a conduit for another voice" because in its way this reflects not only Jane's own trepidations but mine, and yours as well. For if an endeavor is easy (or at least appears that way to others), then what is its worth? Contrarily, if it's a struggle—if enormous obstacles have to be overcome to achieve a thing—what then is its worth? Is it automatically more valuable, or valid?

And if so, how do you hold yourself back to insure it?

19

The Symptoms And How They Grew

She was in a playground the first time it happened, Jane told me. "I started to climb up on the monkey bars and I . . . hesitated," she said. "Something just . . . stopped." It was 1965, not long after a humiliating incident at a hypnosis symposium, in which a young psychologist had declared that Jane must be schizophrenic, using the Seth sessions to dominate Rob; she was thirty-six years old. Though she'd experienced whispers of such symptoms before, including bouts with an underactive thyroid, it was this incident that stood out in her mind and amended her self-assessment. "My first feeling of physical insecurity," as she recalls in her journals later, in 1972.

From that point on—from stiffness noticed in her neck and shoulders, then in her hands, some trouble walking—Jane's physical problems began to accumulate, slowly at first, with intervals of normalcy; in my early memories of her, she is slender but robust and nimble, the only giveaway (in my mind's eye) the prominent knuckles on her somewhat frozen-looking fingers. But by the time of the flood in 1972, things were clamping down on her in earnest. Overnight, it seemed, she was getting up from her rocker as if she were grinding through badly-meshed gears. In class she'd wait until break time, when the room was chaotic with people going in and out of the bathroom, push herself into a half-crouch, hesitate, turn slowly, and walk from the living room to the second apartment across the hall in the same half-sitting, bent-over position, one careful step at a time, every footfall as carefully placed as if on ice. She stopped wearing slacks or short skirts and leotards to class and instead wore flowered "muumuu" dresses that covered her to her ankles—except in trance, when as Seth she'd hike the skirt to her knees and plop her foot up on the coffee table while expounding.

She rarely broached the subject of her physical difficulties, and when she did, it was always in the most superficial of terms, as "the symptoms," never a name, or a label. For one thing she was ashamed of the condition and for another, it was really nobody's business. Besides which, she was wary of medical labels and the negative connotations implied. She was formidable about this, though never overtly—you just knew she didn't want to talk about it (she didn't discuss it in print until writing *The God of Jane* in 1979). So we all became practiced at not noticing, not looking, certainly not mentioning—though it was plenty obvious that she wasn't half as impaired while she was speaking for Seth, or singing Sumari (during which she would gesture with her arms, shoulders, head, and upper body in almost ballet-like, really quite beautiful theatrical expression). That contrast we dared point out to her, but her reaction was subdued, usually nothing more than a "No kidding?" and a shrug. Now I wonder if this didn't simply serve to humiliate her even more—a goddamned ghost could make her body work better than she could, for chrissakes, what was the matter with *her*?

So nobody said much of anything to her face. We knew that her dignity pretty much depended on figuring this business out for herself.

And sometimes it seemed that she had figured it out—or anyway that some physical release was going on; she'd walk straighter, or move a little better, or she'd flex her fingers for us in triumph (and then go on to other subjects). Sometimes she'd lose herself in the conversation at hand and just let go, and her constrictions would *become* less, at least in the moment. And other than that—an enormous "other," really—she seemed healthy, if thin; not perfect by any means (who was?), but certainly not the grotesque figure that her own journal notes from those days portray so poignantly. On March 9, 1973, she wrote in the "Bali" manuscript:

> She got up, bent over, grabbing the door support, hunched; aware of it, and fixed dinner . . . Earlier she'd looked into the mirror, closing the bathroom door so that the full length door mirror faced her room. And frowned. There she stood, frontward, not at all bad really if you didn't look too close, good face, great wide eyes glasses or no; jeans, shirt; from the front good enough shape, and obvious vitality.
>
> The side view was another matter; the legs showed; not straight at all, and the shoulders, and all together funny, misshapen; at least now, the jeans looked baggy; she wanted to cry at the side view . . .

I'd like to think that my natural exuberance and good health helped Jane in some way when I was right there with her, laughing and joking, Sean with me sometimes, all happy and new. On the other hand, maybe I exacerbated her fears in that regard, as an example of what happens when you're able to do anything you want to do—you run around pissing your time away because you *can*. But I always made sure I told her that she was looking good, or perky, or energetic, or something, even if she wasn't looking much of any of those things.

After a while, if she talked to me at all about the physical troubles she was having—which wasn't often—I'd make suggestions that I knew were somewhat scandalous to her, such as, "Oh, what the hell, why not just find out what medical treatments are available and worry about the ramifications of it all afterward, when you're not in pain?" or "Why not hire a yoga instructor or a physical therapist to come in a couple times a week and do range-of-motion rehabilitation, it brings back joints and muscles in people who've been lying in bed a long time, why not try it?" She'd brighten up, ask me questions, get enthusiastic, and when Rob would come in the room she'd repeat these remarks to him. But he never acted especially enthusiastic in return, and you could see the air deflate right out of her.

I have to be careful here—my memories are probably colored by the fact that I was sixteen years younger than Jane and could not grasp why she just didn't *make* herself walk. Also, I had an athletic background from high school and college that Jane did not, and in reading her journal notes about her efforts to exercise, I got the impression that for one thing she didn't understand that resulting muscle soreness, for example, is not only natural but indicative of progress—she seems to take it as a sign of worsening conditions rather than its possible opposite. But this was the seventies, and there were no fitness gurus for women in the way there are today. And, she might not have been talking about ordinary aches and pains.

Probably my suggestions were undoable, or maybe she and Rob had explored these avenues by then, to no avail, or maybe they'd fundamentally given up, I don't know. (Their friend Frank Longwell, who'd once been a chiropractor, did stop by regularly and do some adjustments and motion therapy, I found out later.) I was hardly an expert in the realm of physical challenges, as for one thing I had none, and so I just let it go. Jane would work this out in her own way or she wouldn't. And that was in fact what I hoped she could and should do: Work it out on her own. Or not.

Which was glib of me, without doubt.

I remember the day Jane told me her mother had died, in a Saratoga area nursing home, on May 10, 1972—two days after Jane's forty-third birthday. She hadn't seen or spoken with Marie for something like fifteen years, and given what little I knew of her childhood, Jane's distance from her mother seemed perfectly appropriate to me. Yet she seemed shell-shocked by the news—almost frightened. "I used to be afraid she'd haunt me when she was alive, let alone after she was dead," Jane said, but she didn't laugh. In a way, her mother had managed to do just that.

In her journals after Marie's death, Jane writes:

> I was afraid—magically—I'd turn into her (and she'd go free) so my own symptoms terrified me . . . I can still hear her raging bitch bitch screaming at me through the night . . . the spitting—the hair-pulling—the threat of killing both of us—the letter saying I'd murdered her she threatened to mail—She's haunted me through the nights and days—consciously in the past; probably unconsciously now through habits built up—shadows of attempts to protect myself . . .
>
> What about this new present with its ghosts rising into time that is now—my time? Her bones are fused from the arthritis; I feel furious at that I guess; that she'd allow it and bring it into my experience—as years ago I felt furious with grandfather for dying and bringing that into my experience.[1]

Eventually, Jane's remissions won her less ground and the reemergence of symptoms lost her more. In her journals throughout 1972, she is congratulating herself for making it up and down a long series of stairs at Mansfield University, in Pennsylvania, where she gives a speech before 400 students: ". . . more stairs than I've seen for god's sake in years, stacks and stacks all over . . . Gave myself suggestions which worked like magic—and was in silent tears my knees hurt so much by the time we got home." Three years later, as she and Rob move to their new house, her difficulties are settling in on her with a vengeance. She spends a few minutes a day walking around the living room with the aid of a wheeled typing table, carefully noting the time spent and any "progress" made. "She can now take, say, ten steps at a time," Rob notes on August 25, 1980, "leaning on her typing table, instead of the one or two previously possible. But we've also grown careless again: She walks but once a day, instead of the twice I suggested recently, and which she agreed to, and which Seth seconded in a recent session. Still we're very pleased with her progress . . ."[2] But after a while she stays put in her wheeled office chair and pushes herself around, if at all, in that.

Sometime in the late seventies, her eyes began to protrude, at first just noticeably and then, again seemingly overnight, rather alarmingly—they bulged right out of the sockets, as if they were going to explode. The first time I saw this, I was horrified—and repelled. To me it seemed that in a span of mere days, surely no more than a couple of weeks, something dreadful had happened here. Could she see anything? I found it hard to believe that she could. (According to her journal notes, her vision is affected to varying degrees, sometimes a great deal and sometimes not much at all.) She seemed not to focus on me as we talked (later I found out that her hearing was also affected), and her eyes had a rubbery appearance resembling—I couldn't stop thinking of this—the opaque eyes of dead animals. And she was so thin; when I (very gently) put my arm around her shoulders, her bones felt like toothpicks. Yet I didn't want to hurt her feelings or humiliate her; she and Rob must have some sort of handle on this, I thought—so I said nothing. And neither did she, nor Rob. We yakked on as if everything were perfectly normal. And in many ways, this was true—she was producing terrific Seth sessions as usual, working on her own book projects and poetry, albeit slowly, fixing dinner—including her beloved cornbread—as she could, seeing fans and friends, answering mail, meeting every day with all the optimism she could muster. Writing in her journal, she says, "I have been wise, I believe, not seeing a doctor these years. But I still have to put the whole thing together. The distrust we've built up over the body and its processes is terribly unfortunate so I have to combat that . . . relax and quit stewing and let the healing processes work."

* * *

CHRISTMAS EVE, 1977: I GO OVER to Jane and Rob's for the evening; Maggie and Bill Granger are already there. I take a camera with me for the first and only time, and snap photos of everybody as we open presents. When I get the pictures back, I see that in every one of them, Jane is looking down at the floor to minimize the appearance of her balloon-like eyes. By mid-1978, she can no longer close her lids completely, nor are her eyes tracking in synch. A photo taken of Jane and Rob in the summer of 1978 for a *Village Voice* article captures her situation in shocking, pitiless close-up (probably the reason the cynical bastards chose to use it, I thought).[3] In another photo taken in December, 1978, Jane's entire face looks artificial; her wide-open eyes could be fixed in place, without lids at all, if one did not know otherwise.

Somewhere in here she loses a front tooth; it just fell out, she says, undecayed, a casualty of receding gums. Yet in the fall of 1980, she perked up enough to throw an author's party for me when *Conversations* came out—in fact she seemed to be in better shape than I'd seen in a long time, that old ESP class effect. (She even talked again that day about starting a small, maybe monthly class). Even more astonishing (and to me, now, humbling) in this time period, she agreed to see me and my new husband, who was openly hostile toward her, and had demanded to meet this Seth person—which didn't happen, which I understand completely. I remember little of what she said to us during that visit, except that she spoke to him in a companionable, direct tone, addressing his dignity and talking about the "natural mysticism" that everyone experiences and even her appreciation of skepticism, as she so kindly called it. And she was in very poor shape by then, obviously in pain—but she did this for me, to try to help me resolve yet another unresolvable moment in my life, and she did it with exquisite graciousness and sympathy.

By 1982 her speech had begun to sound slurred, as if her tongue were too thick in her mouth. For some reason (childhood associations, probably) this upset me more than any of the rest of it; I wrote a panicky, half-angry letter to Jane's editor about it and he replied in kind, as worried as I was. It took her forever to answer the phone, he said, and when she did get to it she sounded half asleep, and spoke as if her mouth were full of marbles. And her hearing, once so acute, was terrible, he added. She'd had to call Rob to help her out.

But neither of us said anything to Jane or Rob.

I hid my discomfort about all of this with a smile and a good word, for what else was one to say? Rob was right there; he wasn't blind or stupid, so I stayed out of it. And Jane didn't offer to confide in me about it, either. As far as I know, only Carroll Stamp's sister Pat ("Jean Strand" from ESP class days) dared to bring it up, and tentatively at that. In a Bali-like third-person point of view ("I was practicing using dialogue and the complicated punctuation it required"), Carroll describes that scene, and a rather unnerving precognitive experience that preceded it, so vividly that it's a little difficult to read, even today (she uses the pseudonyms I gave her and Pat in *Conversations with Seth*):

> So [sometime in 1974], Mary is treated to a shaking experience. Accidentally glancing at the back cover of one of Jane's Seth books, upside down,

> Mary sees at first the typical back flap photo of the author. Then as she blinks, her eyes slide slightly out of focus, and a face appears out of part of the inverted features. Startled, not only because she sees it but because it is frightening. Protruding eyeballs aiming in different directions jump out of a skeleton like head. The mouth shapes a soft, sad . . . *oh*. Not quite human but a face nonetheless.
>
> "Optical illusion," she says aloud to herself. She walks away with heart pounding and after a few minutes when composure returns so does she. "Nothing but an upside down paperback book," she thinks, relieved. Then . . . again the lopsided features appear.
>
> Over and over, she [walks away] and returns and so does the face. A few years before, the incident would have been noted, scientifically rationalized, categorized and promptly forgotten, but now reality has begun to assume new dimensions. Coincidence and emotional reactions are no longer taken for granted.
>
> Time must pass . . . So it comes to pass just like the picture. Mary and Jean visit Jane and the face is there. Everyone [in the living room] is stilted and repressed. Mary and Jean smile, smile, even laugh, tight stomachs trying to digest the rage [they feel].
>
> "Your eyes are bugged, Jane," Jean offers cheerfully, always the braver of the two. A ridiculous understatement considering the Marty Feldman look. The left eyeball continues to look at the ceiling while the right stares at Jean defiantly.
>
> "They're much better now," Jane says, with false enthusiasm. "I can almost close them, see?"
>
> She could not, of course, because the lids were far too short to stretch around the globes. Mary and Jean don't argue. Jane's unblinking eye holds them fast.

Carroll adds, "This is all true. [After this visit] we went directly to a doctor friend's and described what we saw. He agreed it appeared to be hyperactive thyroid. I've since felt that the thyroid was so out of control that it just stopped altogether.

"Jane called a few months later. I went over and figured out how to get her to the hospital [for the first of two lengthy stays]. They admitted her and the rest is history with a lot left unsaid."

Carroll was exactly correct, of course; many of the problems Jane had been dealing with—including ear and sinus fullness, sleepiness, and depression—were the result of a severely underactive thyroid. And still, Jane was determined to figure it out on her own, separate in a way even from the continuous volumes of analysis and insight directed to her from Seth. On May 3, 1972, she writes in her journal:

We do quite simply choose, say, a physical illness, instead of a conscious problem . . . the illness becomes the battleground, and the battle itself goes underground. Part of the decision itself is the agreement to "forget it" consciously, close it out of our thoughts, and not confront the beliefs or series of beliefs that have given us trouble. So the first step to health is to actively seek out the beliefs and to be willing to tackle them on a conscious level.

The idea that we can't get better is part of the defense mechanism we've [set] up ourselves, of course . . . It came to me quite clearly that we do have *conscious* control over our bodies and our health. Somehow as I write this, I do so with a sense of shock. *Conscious control*? Yes. Why have I been giving all the wrong directions?

Why am I saying, I feel so badly, I hurt, my feet hurt, I'm so slow? Constantly? Of course to now, all those things in my physical reality are true. *Because those are the directions I have been giving constantly and my body has been carrying them out with fantastic loyal obedience.*

Yet the condition itself cries out to be alleviated. So that even in following my conscious directions, the body still by its actions and feelings shouts out that there is a problem that should be solved. The warning—that something has gone underground . . .

. . . If I'm supposedly getting so much . . . so many benefits . . . why the hell aren't I content? Am I? Hardly. It hurts to hold back. Some part of my body always hurts; except when I'm concentrating working—say in class or in a good session or writing. I used to love to clean house, arrange furniture, it was fun and now (ha, see, all the energy I wasted, banging around, when I should have been writing . . . that's what came to mind . . .).

Of all the questions that people ask me about Jane, the most frequent is why Jane didn't "use the Seth material to get well." It's a complicated question to answer, in large measure because it overlooks the specific role Jane had in its creation; but also because it rises from an erroneous assumption about the material itself.

While they were producing the material, Jane and Rob didn't have the same perspective, let alone the time, that readers of the Seth books enjoy. Unless Rob read back to her from his handwritten notes whenever they took breaks during Seth sessions, Jane usually didn't have any conscious idea what had been said (though often she was aware of the concepts). So she'd have to wait for Rob's typed copies if she wanted to study them—and meanwhile, there were years and notebooks full of other sessions to read and digest.

Moreover, the material was not put together and presented as an instant infomercial to success—it isn't a "read it, and Ye shall have it all" body of work. It *is* a kind of schematic of the workings of the physical universe—primarily, that your beliefs form the reality you experience. To change the experience, you have to change the beliefs. The material gives specific exercises and techniques for doing this (asking for information in dreams is particularly fruitful), but there is no stairway to perfection. "Perfection" isn't even the goal. In fact, there *is* no "goal," or any "answers" as such; the answers, as Jane and Seth would say ad infinitum, are within yourself. Pay attention to the contents of your conscious mind, Seth would say. Therein lies your world.

Jane understood this about the material from the start. "Rob and I look to these ideas to solve problems of ours," she remarks in her journals, "but at least we expect to have to *use* the ideas, not just have the information given to us." And she studied herself, and her problems, relentlessly. Throughout her journals, she writes keen, perceptive essays on the subject of her physical hassles, and these are breathtaking in their honesty and perception of beliefs and reasons behind her plight. She rails against the idea that she is somehow supposed to provide the perfect example for her own work—"Carl Jones [from ESP class days] said something about my old students thinking I should have no physical hassles at all, 'being the channel' for all those great goodies and I suppose the remark and implications made me mad; the dumb bastards I think, feeling instantly guilty"[4]—a standard never imposed on novelists, for example, or other artists, where so-called imperfections are viewed as natural elements of a creative mind. And yet ultimately, Jane cannot shirk from asking herself those same questions: How could she, who was coming up with this fascinating stuff, not get it? Not be able to apply it? What was wrong with her, anyway?[5]

Well, nothing was "wrong" with her at all, in that respect. Her symptoms and ultimate end mirrored to perfection her beliefs and fears, about herself, her gifts, and what she was supposed to be doing in the world; and she followed those beliefs with an intractable, indomitable will. It wasn't that Jane didn't understand the roots of her problems—in fact she, not to mention Seth, had dissected them quite well over the years. And it wasn't that she couldn't "use" her own ideas to get well. Simply put, she did not dare let go of her physical restraints. She never quite made it out of the thicket of her own beliefs, which served not only Jane, but Jane and Rob as a couple. Difficult to say, but true—and they knew it.

One of the most compelling sessions in the immensely affecting Deleted material (which is almost entirely devoted to Jane's symptoms) is not a Seth session at all. Rather, it is another voice that Jane expresses on that evening, February 19, 1972, in their motel room in the Florida Keys. It is, as the voice itself puts it, the voice of her own creative self, or "Creator," that speaks out in the warm Florida night, and as such, it expresses Jane's beliefs in explicit, frightening absolutes. The entire session took place on two consecutive nights, and is far too long to reproduce here, but some of it, excerpted for emphasis, will amply demonstrate the point. "It must be remembered," Rob says in his notes, "that at the start of this experiment, neither of us knew what would develop."

All right [Jane said], call me the Creator, this part of me that's talking. We're using it to designate what I am.

I'm composed of your strong drives for creativity. My purpose is to protect and direct your energies specifically in the areas of writing and painting. I'll state what I think simply. *I* want this dialogue because my purposes are not being met. My efforts have obviously worked against themselves.

Strong moral ideas welded what I am together—welded the creative drives like glue. Part of me was born in Ruburt's childhood. This part was strengthened by your [Rob's] own ideas of work and creativity. You became the policeman. I relied on you to see that Ruburt's creativity was channeled and used, protected, but most of all not frittered away.

I believe that you both must write and paint a reasonable amount of time daily. I was always against any jobs that would divert you as long as you were not in dire need, in which case I was willing to suspend my judgment.

You began to change your ideas. I expected them to be unswerving. When it seemed you would not police the two of you with the *intense fervor* necessary, I began to do so, and took upon myself all those attitudes that had been yours. It was easy. Ruburt is literal minded in many ways. He looked up to you.[6] The constant suggestions took root, and I used this for my purposes.

I am literal-minded, in that I believe you are meant to be creators, and I have done all in my power to see that you did not swerve.

There was difficulty with the books. My drive was being met, and yet the money was being used to support a status quo that I could condone only for the first few years in Elmira.

I do not want you to go hungry, or to be unhappy. I do not want you to be in want, but outside of that nothing else concerns me but your work.

My methods have not brought about what I wanted, however. Now you spend half of your time trying to figure them out, and what is wrong with Ruburt—time that you should be working. I do not care if both of you die poor, but I do demand that you live using your abilities. That purpose unites you, and when you are not tuned to it completely you are unhappy or sick, one or the other. I am protective because I know that this is so. It is the purpose that gives everything else in your lives meaning.

I go along with the psychic development, as long as it adds to your work and influences it. I am suspicious of it if it prevents you [Rob] from painting, because of notes, but this does not bother me when you are painting also.

My demands, to me, are simple and reasonable. More than that, I see no others worthwhile. All you have to do to please me is work a reasonable amount of hours daily; then I do not care what you do. But I expect that purpose to govern and direct your lives, to be the focus about which all other events happen, not a sideline.

I accept no substitutes, and in that respect I am like a jealous god. I am also somewhat like a computer gone amok, however, if my methods do not meet my ends. I want the main energizing portion of you directed into your work, both of you. Now they have been directed toward Ruburt's condition. The condition will vanish automatically if these ends are met. They are side effects.

I have tried to have him sit and write books, chained to his chair, don't you see. The purpose is twofold—to see that he worked creatively himself, *and could not have a job*, and to have money so that you could paint full time.

I am tired. I have done my best. I have worked long and hard for you; though it *seems* that I have been a tyrant, I have always tried to be the servant of your own abilities. I am dismayed. I did not think Ruburt would work unless he was chained to his chair, so I chained him, both to do his own work and to force you to do yours. Then you both fought *me*. He did not like working chained, and I tried to make the chains appear as natural as I could.

He is not physically harmed to any great degree, or maimed. I can say however that for some time I did not care if he was, if these purposes were met. I see now that they would not be, that instead all your time would be spent concentrating upon the condition that was meant as a protection, until no work was done. Hence my dismay.

I was not appreciated, though I did my best for you.

Friday, November 13, 1981: One of the last times Jane and I sat around and talked, like the old days. It's also one of the few times I typed up parts of our conversation—two days afterward, according to my notes. By that October I'd left my second husband and Sean and I and our two cats were living in a tiny efficiency apartment in Dundee, and I was feeling balance, not to mention serenity, seeping back into my life. My friendship with Jane was never quite the same after this marriage—not that I blame her; I had been something of a mess for a while, and not at all fun to be around, or listen to. But that evening, the old magic seemed to be rustling around in the corners of her living room again; for once I had no interest in Seth coming through. I wanted only to talk with Jane, my old friend.

"Just me there," my notes say about that Friday evening:

> Rob went into his studio so I talked mostly with Jane, who admitted that she's delving deeper into her physical problems but doesn't seem to have much grip on them—in fact, she's getting worse, with occasional spells of improvement. She's stiff all over, no longer walks around, has very protuberant eyes, and is presently stuffed up to the point where her hearing (always excellent) is affected.
>
> We talked quite a while about this. I suggested [not for the first time]—why not just go to the damn doctors and get some relief, even if it's only for a little while, get some distance? Jane said that Frank Longwell and Rob nearly bundled her in the car to go to the Robert Packer Hospital in Sayre, Pennsylvania recently. "Rob threatens to take me there, imposes a deadline, and I always manage to get just a little bit better," Jane said.
>
> I told her that I consider the Seth material to [represent] the emergence of a new species of consciousness.
>
> "Yes, it's the search for God, or new gods," Jane said. "But five years ago I couldn't have said that—it would have been too terrible." She said that she sometimes gets the feeling that because of her increasing physical difficulties, she's therefore just leading people down the same path—into the same type of trouble. "But then Rob tells me that's pretty egotistical," she said, laughing uneasily.
>
> "But," I said, "maybe this is the way that you showed your humanness—that you felt you had to deal with some large question within the material; to have something major to answer to, or it would all have been too glib. As in, who am I to talk—I have *no* problems?"
>
> "Yeah, I suppose," Jane said. "Of course it's never just one thing. But you can get into the situation where you identify with your pain instead of with your joy—"
>
> "Sure," I said, "because when you feel the need to justify what you do, you have to demonstrate how difficult it is; *you* know, like, say, having a child, being a single parent, getting involved in messy personal stuff . . . "
>
> We both laughed. "Or this," Jane said, gesturing at herself.
>
> I told her that my mother had been getting some relief with cortisone treatments for [lupus-related] arthritis. "Sounds pretty damn good to me," Jane said. So I encouraged her to go ahead and try it—means a hospital stay for tests and all, "but what the hell?" I said. "Why suffer? Why not use medical assistance when you have to? Certainly I have, often enough . . . "

This is where my notes stop, though Jane and I talked way into the wee hours. I remember that she used nasal spray quite a bit, the strong stuff, every ten minutes or so; I described my horrendous experience with such sprays, which have a bounce-back effect on the mucous membranes (as I told her) and eventually make you more stuffed up than ever. I'd had to quit cold turkey, as it were, and besides stuffing up for days to the point of choking, I'd suffered awful nosebleeds; a doctor I finally consulted in the local clinic told me the inside of my nasal passages resembled a cocaine addict's. "Some suggestion," Jane sneered, picking up the spray . . .

She told me that she often felt blue and weepy, and "nostalgic, as if this were all in some distant past"; I reminded her, plaintively, of all the times I'd called her up because I'd felt so depressed. "Something's wrong," I remembered saying to her, "I feel down all the time. I just can't get out of it." At the time, Jane had advised me to "go out into nature" as a way of finding relief, I reminded her. "I took a lot of long walks, but it didn't seem to help much," I said. "Nothing helped."

"Yeah, I'd say something was wrong," Jane acknowledged, looking as if she knew exactly what I was talking about. "What'dya finally do about it?"

"I went nuts and got married," I said, and we both sniggered nastily, and I wanted to say, so what do *you* do about it, Jane, no walks in the woods for you, no nothing—what do you do about it? Sit here and examine, and examine, and examine? What are you going to do about it?

But I said nothing, and as we did so often, we just let it go.

* * *

I AM HAUNTED BY A MEMORY OF something that couldn't have happened.

I see a long dimly-lit corridor with an uncovered light bulb set in the high ceiling. This could be the hallway that ran between the two apartments at 458, but it seems to be the wrong color paint on the walls. Jane and I are standing at one end of this corridor, talking about the poet T. S. Eliot. She is wearing a black turtleneck, short black and white plaid skirt, black tights, worn brown loafers. She tells me that Eliot had a profound effect on her when she was younger, but later in life, she was more drawn to e. e. cummings. In a sudden burst of exuberance, she skips down the hallway ahead of me yelling lines from Eliot's *The Wasteland*, leaps into the air, and whacks the light bulb with the tips of her fingers—in this memory I clearly see her black nail polish—as she yells out, "In the room the

WOMen come and GO/Talking of MichaelANGELO!" She lands gracefully on her feet, and we laugh.

The Jane I knew could never have done this, but the memory is not made up, or a dream, at least as far as I can tell. Her journals from the fifties mention reading aloud from *The Wasteland* "before breakfast" on at least one occasion, but . . .

I must have her mixed up with someone else, but who would that be, exactly? And when?

20

The Hospital and Beyond

Dream, May 19, 1982: Jane and Rob have a house in the woods. She and I are sitting together talking, when she interrupts our conversation to tell me that she hears Rob calling to her from upstairs. She says she has a mental image of him opening a door, calling to her, then closing the door—open and close, open and close.

I half see this image myself . . . it seems to me it's a call from another dimension, or a voice from a far-away world, beckoning to her.

Then I see the two of them walk out the door. Jane is shaky and her legs aren't working quite right, but she's walking nonetheless. As she leaves, she turns to me and says that she has to go somewhere, but that I should carry on.

All very strange and haunting . . .

* * *

I DIDN'T BOTHER STOPPING AT THE desk on my first visit with Jane in the hospital—this was in the fall of 1982, after she'd been admitted for the second time. She'd developed terrible bedsores, Rob told me, and septicemia as a result, and some other problems. On this occasion Rob had called me; before, earlier that spring, I hadn't even known she was in there until she was about to come home.

I found the elevators and punched in the floor number, feeling like a conspirator. Somehow I was sure that if I checked in at the main desk they wouldn't let me see her. I don't know why I had this feeling. Maybe it had something to do with what I encountered when I stepped off the elevator.

The antiseptic hospital stink filled my nose as I walked along the corridor, searching out door numbers. Up ahead, in a room near the nurses' station, someone was howling in pain. The sound rose and fell without letup, a terrible shrilling wail punctuated with strings of unintelligible words and disjointed sobs. For the luvva god, I thought to myself, why doesn't somebody go in there and *do* something for that person? The nurses' station was deserted. No one else was in the hallway.

Suddenly the wailing, unintelligible words cut through the air with awful concision: "GODDAMNIT FUCKIN' HELL FUCK!" the voice screamed, "GET ME THE FUCKIN' CHRIST OUTTA HERE!" Then the cries broke into miserable, hopeless sobs.

The room, and the voice, were Jane's.

I almost turned around and left. I'm ashamed to admit it, but I hesitated at the edge of the doorway, thinking I could just go away and come back another time, or maybe never, and nobody would know. Surely there must be a nurse or doctor in there with her—surely there had to be. But there wasn't. When I screwed up my courage and walked into the room, I saw that she was alone.

"Sue-Belle!" Jane cried, "Sue-Belle, Sue-Belle, help me, do something, talk to me, tell me somethin'." She was lying on her back with her arms folded across her chest in the posture of death. But her shoulders, elbows, and wrists were so stiff that her arms weren't resting in that position—they were fixed rigidly, like a marionette's, hovering just above the sheet. Pillows sandbagged her on either side and under her upper arms. Up on the wall, a television soap opera mumbled on and on.

I said something like, do you want me to go get somebody? No, she said, sit here and talk to me, talk to me—She was breathless with pain, straining with the effort not to scream in front of me. Sweat ran down her forehead and into her eyes.

I went in the bathroom, ran a washcloth under cool water, and sat on the bed and wiped her forehead and face with it while I blabbed about something, I don't remember what—Sean, my cats, whatever came to mind. Her natural hair color had started to grow in; it was a nice silvery-black, thick and wild. I rubbed her head a little. "What the hell's going on here?" I asked, finally. She told me she was having a reaction to medicine they were giving her to clear her lungs—something like that; I remember the lungs part. She said she'd been like this for—did she say hours? Hours alone, like this? How could it have been hours? I told her I would go find a doctor and drag him in there by the balls if I had to, but she said no, don't go, stay here with me, keep talking to me about something, anything.

Then she gritted her teeth and let loose another groaning sob. "My elbows, do somethin', do somethin', goddamnit *goddamnit*!" she gasped.

I dropped the washcloth and cupped her elbows in my hands—it was all I could think to do. She let out a sigh, so that must have helped, maybe just by shifting the position of her shoulder joints a tiny bit, I don't know. Then I imagined (as we'd done in those alpha experiments back there a couple million years ago) that my hands were heating pads, radiating a healing fire into her elbows, heating them right up and melting them into soft pleasant sunny-warm silly-putty. I imagined this as clearly as I could, trying to override the shock and fear whanging away in my heart. And something actually seemed to happen. Jane whimpered, panting, but she relaxed—just a bit. Just a teeny, tiny bit.

"You're okay," I soothed, illogically. "You're okay now."

"I don't want to live like this, Sue-Belle," she said. Her voice was driven, desperate. "I can't; I don't want to. I just can't do it anymore."

"Well, you don't have to," I said. "You know that." I smiled at her; she nodded. Our faces were inches apart; I could feel her breath on my cheeks. Sweat trickled down her temples, but I let it go, kept my hands on her elbows. "But you know the choice isn't living like this or dying," I told her. "You can live differently."

"I don't know," Jane said. "I don't know if I can. I got myself in too deep—I went way too far. I don't think I can get back."

"Yeah, you're in pretty deep," I acknowledged, "but nothing's writ in stone." Then I said something to the effect that she could pick a middle ground someplace; the choice wasn't between complete perfection or complete decrepitude; she could find a place in there where she could live as well as possible, maybe not running around, maybe in a wheel chair, "but you could watch the birds out the window, play with the cats, be with Rob, write," I coaxed.

"I don't know," she whimpered. "Maybe I can't do it all—the Seth stuff, the books."

"Then fuck the Seth stuff," I said. "Just write novels or poetry, or whatever you want. I'll type up the manuscripts for you, come on, what the hell, it'll be fun."

She said, "Yeah, that's what Rob says," and at that moment, Rob walked in the room.

"What's this?" he said. His face was expressionless; his tone, aggrieved.

"Boy, am I glad to see you," I said, standing up. I explained the situation as I'd found it: Jane in horrific pain, left alone in the room to suffer. But instead of the incendiary reaction from him I'd anticipated, Rob merely stood there, arms folded in front of him, face set. "Yeah, that's happened before," he said when I finished. "There's not a lot they can do about it." Then he gave me a look that clearly told me I should leave; so I did.

I was shaken to my bones and furious with Rob—why wasn't he out at the nurses' station, ripping someone a new alimentary canal? Only years later, after I had seen my parents through their own hospital trials and deaths, would I understand Rob's reaction and the sheer hopeless exhaustion that lay beneath it, like the weight of an endless ocean.[1]

* * *

THREE YEARS LATER, LATE SUMMER, 1985: I'm changing the sheet on the sofa where my mother likes to doze, in the room with all the big windows, where she can watch the birds. She is gravely ill with lupus and liver cancer, thin as a shadow, her eyes huge and dark. As I'm helping her back on the couch, she says to me, "I don't want to live like this. I've gone too far to come back."

I stare at her in surprise. We've never discussed the obvious fact of her pending death. I say, "You could still get better," though I know she won't.

"I guess I'd rather be with him," she says, meaning my father, who died in 1983.

I look her in the eye. "Then make up your mind," I say. "Do what you want to do, make up your mind and do one or the other, but don't go on torturing yourself. You can get better if you really want to, but it's all right to leave." And a few weeks later, she does.

How odd, and ironic, and yet how appropriate, that I would have the same conversation with each of them, Jane and my mother, near the end of their lives—the women on either side of me so unremittingly apart, who would each die of autoimmune diseases gone unremittingly awry. Whose own mothers had each died of the same.

* * *

JULY, 1982: JANE HAS BEEN HOME from her first hospital stay for a few weeks. Briefly, she seems hopeful, upbeat; looks forward to working on her next *Oversoul Seven* project. In her journals for July 6, she writes,

". . . now that I'm able to type even this well—very slowly, finger at a time, dodging bedsores on my backside—but determined to make it—I don't know really where to begin. I *am* doing far better than I thought I could though . . .

"Both the fingers on my left hand were too sore—a condition now improving by leaps and bounds. Anyway this means I can type daily notes or poetry or whatever, doing the best I can each day . . . I feel as if a year has vanished during the entire experience, one spent in minor agonies—mostly of bedsores, humiliations of smarting skin and punctuated now and then by the dreadful negative projections of the medical profession . . ."

As she has so many times in the past, she shows small but definite improvements. Rob sets up a typing table for her in the converted breezeway off the kitchen. "Trying to get comfortable so I can type longer," she notes. ". . . fingers are stronger on the keys and I know it'll be okay . . . Am typing a bit faster." She records dreams, writes some poetry. "Still doze off at certain times," she adds, due to thyroid medication adjustments.

But gradually, then swiftly, she begins to lose ground. She has trouble putting the paper in the typewriter; then her journal entries become almost illegible for the typos. Her last typewritten journal entry is made on July 15, 1982:

> Reading more of Rob's notes and doing a little work on *Seven*; it's a start. The last few days have been quite humid and warm, Frank dropped in briefly, Margaret . . . 8 [sic] a few times briefly, eyes seemed to read better.

Two handwritten pages follow. They are smeared and difficult to read. They are her last journal entries, made in August of 1982, as follows:

Oh thy voice
is so familiar.
Where have I
heard it before
in dreams
or tiny lullabies
or glittering
waterfalls
at noon,

Counterpart
companion

There is a
summer
band
in a secret
glen

What mysterious voices
speak

---

soon Sue

Attached to this is a page entitled, "The Idiot Flower." It's a brief excerpt from *Conversations with Seth*, a soliloquy about trusting one's innate vitality. "Goodness is as natural as a flower that grows," it begins.

* * *

SHE REENTERS THE HOSPITAL THAT fall, and stays there through the following January, 1983. She returns to the hospital that April and stays there until she dies on September 5, 1984, of complications from soft-tissue infection, arising out of the rheumatoid arthritis she'd suffered from for so long.

I didn't visit Jane very often while she was hospitalized—three, possibly four times at most, including the last time, three days before she died. I have no excuse for this; doing more was simply and utterly beyond me. I had my hands full driving back and forth between Dundee and Elmira, trying to manage my mother's rapidly deteriorating condition and the wrenching, conflicting, and too often unsympathetic opinions of her doctors. So I wrote Jane letters and sent funny cards, kept in touch with Rob by phone, and told myself that having a lot of visitors would just intrude on Jane anyway—for, miraculously, throughout her long and often painful stay, interrupted constantly by hospital personnel and procedures, bombarded with pessimistic suggestions and dire predictions, uncomfortable physically and who knows how despairing, she continued to produce her work by dictating to Rob (who missed only one day's visit in all that time) not only poems, dreams, notes and analysis of her situation, but a series of dialogues on art and related matters, a four-month group of short, mostly personal Seth sessions, and in January of 1984 began her last Seth book, *The Way Toward Health*, which she delivered steadily to the last, six days before her death.

Debbie Harris, however, who had once sought Jane out as a fan, went to see Jane at least several times a week over the course of nearly three years in what became a role of adopted companion. At some point Rob had asked her if she could drop by the hospital now and then and help Jane pass the time when he couldn't be there, and so Debbie did just that, without any apparent self-consciousness about it at all. In her journal notes from that time, in themselves a riveting memoir, Debbie recounts not only the progression of Jane's decline (even then, with startling if small remissions: "August 12, 1984: Jane got her right knee, which the doctors told her would never move again, to move again"), but of an unusual friendship in microcosm, pieced together out of Debbie's good will and Jane's need for company and diversion, and which despite the setting and circumstances carried with it—how could it not, I suppose—all the same elements that were so indelibly woven into Jane's relationships with almost everyone.[2] Great conversations about the nature of reality. Funny comments and insights. Discussion and interpretations of dreams. And the inevitable requests for help with personal matters—relatives in trouble, awry love affairs, the eternal Boyfriend question; a suicide attempt by Debbie's sister in the fall of 1983.

"Saw Jane tonight," Debbie notes, "asked her to use her sources to see what she comes up with [about this]." And a few days later, "Talked with Jane about my two most recent dreams, and she agreed that the abortion element in one of them probably referred to my sister's 'aborted' suicide attempt; and that the dreams appeared to be quite positive, at least in terms of another attempt not occurring in the future [which it didn't]. . ." In other visits, Debbie describes her latest romance: "Talked everything out with Jane about my love affair with C., and feel a little better. She told me that she thought my relationship with C. involves an alternate probability where most of the relationship is occurring, with occasional dips or spillovers or bleedthroughs into this probability. She thought it involved neurological crossovers . . . 'Well, you're in love,' Jane said. 'It's nice to be in love.'"

Years later, while copying these pages for me, Debbie wrote, "Boy, Sue, I'll tell you, reading those notes over again after all these years is pretty harrowing. Now I really regret bringing Jane all my problems, considering her condition. She really didn't need them on top of her own." A hindsight regret I certainly share, arising to some extent out of the uncomfortable impression that nobody ever had anything of similar bearing to give back to Jane.

As to this, Debbie's journals include a dream that Jane described to her on June 23, 1984: "Jane is in Saratoga Springs, in her house passing out plates and plates of food to an endless supply of hungry people. Then she is in [her Elmira] house bustling about fixing herself something to eat. This fades or dissolves back to her hospital room as she realizes she can't fix herself anything to eat because she's in the hospital."

Debbie continues, "We had been talking about the way dreams incorporate elements of physical reality for their own purposes, and she gave this as an example. But it was an example with a twist: She'd fallen asleep late at night with the TV turned on. The program schedule listed a certain show for a certain time, and she woke up from the above dream to find that the program in question had been changed to one of those by a relief organization showing starving people in different parts of the world.

"Her dream reminded me," Debbie added, "of a conversation we had once not too long before—after the New Year—about food in physical reality, and spiritual food. And she stated that there is no basic difference between them. Quite a dream, eh?"

Still and all, Debbie was helping Jane through some lonely hours, trying to find subjects about something in the world outside the hospital walls. And in that, Debbie manages with great unaffected aplomb. "After a bit of casting about [for something we hadn't talked about before]," she writes in July of 1984, "we finally hit on something—apartments we've lived in, a detailed description of my apartment, apartments and dwellings that appealed to us like geodesics and underground houses, and modern appropriate-technology forms of energy for heating, etc., like solar or wind power. This got us going, and 9 P.M. came quickly. Jane was pleased with herself, getting out of mental ruts, and I was pleased she [felt] so much better so quickly and said, 'I'll look for further improvement next time.'" During another visit, Jane comes up with the idea of resuming her unfinished autobiography, *From This Rich Bed*, by dictating it to Debbie to take down in longhand. "Somehow," Debbie remarks, "I doubt that the 'bed' she had in mind is the bed she is now more or less confined to. Just the same, that title seems *telling*; she started working on it at least ten years ago." Though she never followed through on this, Jane did manage to recite a few paragraphs of personal background, which Debbie transcribed as follows:

Jane told me, "I always knew I'd be a famous writer."

She said that she was technically a virgin when she married Rob. That after she and Walt were married, when they first came to making love and she caught sight of his penis, she'd cracked up, because it was so big and she couldn't see how in hell they'd manage it. She never said in so many words, "I never had sexual intercourse with Walt," e.g. But when I asked her, "So you were technically a virgin when you married Rob" (words to this effect), she said yes.

She said that whenever she and Rob made love before a Seth session, or before a class session, that the results for the ensuing session were spectacular. And that sometimes she and Rob would make love for the sake of these results in a session. She said that Walt . . . had beautiful eyes and no chin and that she romanticized him.

She said that she met Rob when she was on the point of leaving Walt, that Rob could come with her or not as he chose. They [she and Rob] wound up living together for some time—like a year or more—before they finally got married, primarily for the sake of appearances in the eyes of his family. They met in Saratoga Springs, New York.

She said that when she reached her teenage years she began to sneak out on her mother, who by now was bedridden. This had to do with getting out of the house in the evenings to meet girl or boy friends. She would make up some plausible excuse and then leave. I asked her if she felt justified in doing this. She said she felt entirely justified.

Somewhere in the midst of all of this, possibly in the fall of 1983, Maggie Granger calls me from the hospital after her own visit with Jane. Maggie is beside herself, understandably. She asks me to talk Jane into "dropping the Seth ideas" and submitting to medical procedure without argument—apparently Jane has been arguing plenty about it, though it seems to me she's submitted to a lot, too. (At one point, according to Rob's notes in volume 1 of *Dreams, Evolution, and Value Fulfillment*, doctors had proposed as many as six major-joint replacement operations, with no guarantees as to quality of results. "Even if Jane had all of those operations," Rob writes, "even if she ended up able to walk after a fashion, she'd still have arthritis. She was suffused with it. Our beliefs said so. So did her body, as anyone could see . . . And Jane, trying to protect herself from the negative suggestions that had been administered to her like psychic hammer blows, ever since she'd entered the hospital, could only weakly demur on the subject of operations.").

But I would read those notes of Rob's much later. Unfortunately, on the phone in 1983, rather than just telling Maggie that I'll talk to Jane, or some innocuous lie to that effect, I say something like, Well you know, Maggie, Jane has the right to make her own decisions about herself based on anything she wants to base it on. We all do.

Maggie blows her stack and has at me for several minutes, something about how I'm a fool, that something has to be done, that Jane is just being stubborn, hanging on to all these ideas. I begin to get pretty heated myself and we accomplish nothing. Finally she bangs the phone down and I stand there in my living room thinking: *What if she's right?* What if none of us knows anything about who we are? What if we're really at the mercy of the universe? How do we ever really know? I realize I'm not angry with Maggie—what the hell, she's terrified and sick over her friend's condition—but what was I supposed to say? That I'd rush to the hospital and talk Jane into repudiating who she is? This is supposed to save her?

It's the last conversation I ever have with Maggie. Years afterward, in 1995 or thereabouts, I'm clerking behind the register in a friend's antiques store in Watkins Glen when Maggie comes in, shopping for collectibles. I've lost a lot of weight by then, so I'm not surprised when she doesn't recognize me right away. No, the interesting thing is that when I identify myself to her, she still has no idea who I am.

"Sue . . . Watkins? Watkins?" she says, groping. Yeah, I say, remember all those Friday nights at Jane and Rob's, all those Christmas Eve parties, the time the cat jumped on your lap, the bars we used to go to, the stories . . .

She has no memory of me whatsoever. It's as if I'd never existed in her reality at all. She excuses herself and leaves the store.

A year or two after that, I run into Bill Granger at the local mall, and the same thing happens. Bill goes along with my greetings and subsequent exchange of *bon mots* in his familiar jolly style, so it's several minutes before I realize that he doesn't have a clue about who I am. So again, I explain ("Jane and Rob's house . . . parties . . . bars . . . stories . . ."), and again . . . he apparently has no memory of me at all. He nods, smiling, friendly, utterly perplexed.

As if it had all been . . . a dream?

Because in the end, the inevitable curtain falls. "Wednesday, September 5, 1984, 11:50 A.M.," Debbie writes in her journals, "Jane died 2 A.M. this morning. Just phoned Rob to see if he was there or had gone down to the hospital. To my surprise he answered, and then he told me. So it's over. Mostly I feel relieved on Jane's account: glad she is suffering no longer. Hope she's having a good time, hope she's working out her hang-ups better now, hope she's OK." Debbie then calls me. The news is no surprise after my visit with Jane three days before. In fact, my first thought is something like, well, if anybody can report back on what it's like out there, Jane can; wonder if she'll be in touch? Not so off the wall my conversation to come with the woman in Watkins Glen, then, about voices, and where they've gone, and how they might return to speak to us once more. Of all the mysteries reality encompasses, death is the only one confirmed by silence.[3]

* * *

OCTOBER, 1984, DUNDEE: A GORGEOUS autumn afternoon, a month or so after Jane's death. I invite Debbie Harris and our friend Bart to come over to my house and watch *The Seth Video* for the first time.

Originally taped at 458 on June 4, 1974, by a New York film crew for a television special, *The Seth Video* is in two parts—an interview with Jane and Rob by Harold Channer, the television show's producer; and filmed excerpts from that evening's ESP class, including what would turn out to be the only visual record ever made of Jane speaking for Seth.

I had known Jane for sixteen years and would one day discover how little I'd understood about who she really was; Debbie had visited Jane all those days in the hospital, but never witnessed a Seth session; Bart, who had lived around the corner from 458 during class years and later read all the books, never met Jane at all. So there we were, the three of us, sitting side by side on the couch with the drapes drawn, on a perfectly beautiful autumn day, watching this video for the first time, and we all started crying. We made no sound, we said nothing. We just sat there the entire time, tears rolling down our faces, each of us crying for something that has been and something that had vanished—Debbie for the person she knew so briefly and the phenomenon she never got to see; Bart for the person he respected and never had a chance to meet; and me for all of it, for the loss of a friend and mentor, and something else, something enigmatic and almost inexplicable—the loss of a part of me, too; of the person who understood my peculiar combination of characteristics and insisted that I learn to cherish them; and for days gone by that, as with all days gone by too soon, will never come again in this life as we know it, except in dreams—and memoir.

* * *

OR MAYBE THOSE DAYS ARE closer than I think. Consider this: My present house is surrounded by a large yard and numerous garden plots, which worry me, *sotto voce*, in the back of my mind, as I sit at my desk writing. They need my time. So I go outside and while weeding and mowing I worry about my writing. Ideas come to me. They need recording. I need to get back to it. It needs—my time. Never mind that I turned the outdoor work into a humorous gardening column for the Dundee *Observer* and later a book.[4] Or that I enjoy the physical exertion, and the knowledge that I can deal with machinery and chores, like a pretend farmer without the real hassles. No, I'm still plagued by the unrelenting feeling that I'm *wasting my time*. I might better have an apartment with no lawn to tend, no gardens to distract me—right, Jane?

Eventually I let most of the gardens go, and start buying vegetables from local roadside stands. Winter brings respite from the lawn. And while I sit and write, I yearn to be outdoors. Then in January, 1998, while hiking with Sean near Phoenix, Arizona, my boot crimps and injures my left Achilles tendon. This never quite heals, and over the next year and a half it becomes chronic; sometimes better, sometimes worse. It hinders my walking, and I notice, moreover, some subtle changes in how I assess my capabilities. Up to this point I had a habit of walking two to five miles a day with longer weekend treks, eight or ten miles at a clip, my dog trotting along beside me. Now when I think about walking anywhere, I automatically consider how far the hike is and whether or not I can make it without the tendon swelling and throbbing and maybe rupturing like a violin string? I have started to abridge my imagination, in other words. Like Jane, wondering if she can make it downstairs to the mailbox—an ordinary thing no one thinks twice about doing . . .

Suddenly, I can no longer run around the goddamned block.

Never before in my life have I ever, for one second, doubted my ability to walk anywhere, play sports, or do anything requiring physical effort. Even more interesting, I notice that the tendon swells up and aches if I *sit at my desk* for hours at a time, hurting as badly as if I'd been stomping along the trail or driving a shovel into the ground all day.

Mental exercise: I sit on the couch with my feet up, ankles touching, imagining the right Achilles tendon speaking to the left, imparting its perfect physical condition to its partner in empathic exchange, like old friends—or counterparts, perhaps.

I mean, really, what is this—the voice of a shared belief? A ghostly kick in the head? I could of course have the tendon surgically repaired, but if I also did not resolve the underlying conundrum—what then? What might happen next to get my attention, do you suppose?

Endnotes

Introduction: Memories, Memoirs And Something in the Middle

1. Original hardcover published by Contemporary Books, Chicago, Illinois, 1988.

2. The "class" referred to here is the somewhat misnamed weekly ESP class Jane held in her apartment on Tuesday nights from 1966 through 1975 (with a few informal class meetings held after that).

3. *The Seth Material* (Englewood Cliffs, NJ: Prentice-Hall, 1970; reprint, Cutchogue, NY: Buccaneer Books, 1995), p. 10 (all page references will be to the Prentice-Hall edition). Seth is the name applied to the "energy essence personality" for whom Jane spoke in book dictation sessions and in spontaneous give-and-take dialogues from early 1964 through August of 1984, just days before she died.

4. Later I briefly toyed with the idea of writing a formal biography of Jane, as opposed to a memoir, and even went so far as to submit a thirty-page proposal to half a dozen publishers, all of whom turned it down, despite some initial interest. And, really, this was a good thing: Biography is a specialty unto itself, and to do one of Jane would require a multi-volume, gargantuan effort of focus and perseverance that I simply didn't want to apply. (Other writers have approached Rob about doing such a biography, but for various reasons, including Rob's own natural hesitations, this didn't materialize.) Besides, a memoir allowed me to explore Jane's impact on my life as metaphor; not possible in the confines of the biographical framework.

5. *The "Unknown" Reality*, volumes 1 and 2 (Englewood Cliffs, NY: Prentice-Hall, 1979; reprint, San Rafael, CA: Amber-Allen, 1997). In volume 2, of that work, Seth says, in part, of counterparts:

> Time expands in all directions, and away from any given point. The past is never finished, and the future is never completely formed. You choose to experience certain versions of events. You then organize these, nibbling at them, so to speak, a bit "at a time."
>
> The creativity of any given entity is endless, and yet all of the potentials for experience will be explored . . . You follow in terms of continuity one version of yourself at any given "time" . . .
>
> Quite literally, you live more than one life at a time. You do not experience your century simply from one separate vantage point, and the individuals alive in any given century have far deeper connections than you realize. You do not experience your space-time world, then, from one but from many viewpoints (pp. 462–63).

I address the issue of counterparts in *Conversations with Seth* (originally published in two volumes in 1980 and 1981 by Prentice-Hall; new revised, combined volume edition published by Moment Point Press in 1999). The discussion includes examples that were given by Seth in ESP class (see chapter 18), including other supposed counterparts of Jane's and mine.

6. I plan to donate all the papers, materials, and letters contributed so generously to me for this project to the Jane Roberts archives at Yale University, where they will be available to researchers in their entirety.

1 Nobody Ever Asks Me This

1. However, I still appreciate the *tone* implied in one of Jane's earliest sessions, for January 29, 1964, in which she, speaking slowly and deliberately in her own uninflected voice for Seth, says, "I do not want this material to be considered any sort of mumbo jumbo. It is not a cult in the terms that people often consider material that seems to come from a source beyond the individual who gives it.

"The designations spirit, and medium, and so forth, are ridiculous to begin with. You are simply using inner senses. These senses are not magical, they certainly are not religious in any sense of the word, and I am not some degenerated secondary personality of Ruburt's. Nor will I be compared with some long-bearded, beady-eyed spirit sitting on cloud nine" (from *The Early Sessions, Book 1 of The Seth Material* [Manhasset, NY: New Awareness Network, 1997], p. 143).

2 A Life of the Mind

1. Interview in the Elmira *Star-Gazette*, 1973.

2. Walt was absolutely correct in his surmise: There were indeed "sexual overtones" to these visits, and according to Rob's notes in *The Way Toward Health* (San Rafael, CA: Amber-Allen, 1997), it began when Jane was a small child. "We talked a lot about the priests in her life," Rob writes for May 18, 1984—just four months before Jane's death. "She described again those visits from Father Trenton. She talked about how the one priest who put her to bed when she was but three or four years old would 'play' with her sexually, and how Marie [Jane's mother] finally figured that out. This was the one who called her up while we lived together; he was old and living in a retirement home . . . She described how Father Trenton sat with his back to Marie when he was mad at the mother, and how Father Rakin [who also burned some of Jane's books] made advances to her . . . The first time they met, Jane said Father Rakin said to her when she was but thirteen: 'You're just too forward.' A nice greeting, and one Jane obviously still remembers" (p. 222).

Jane never said much about this to me, and the few comments she did make, about a priest who "chased her around the bed," were delivered casually in group settings, with deprecating humor, no hint of the frightening child-molesting scenario or later sexual browbeating that Rob's notes make plain. I had my own childhood experience with such matters, involving an orthodontist who preyed on a number of his young clients, as we all discovered later when one of these girls—not me—finally told her parents. Such things were not openly acknowledged or discussed in those days, and thus I didn't (or wouldn't) recognize the iceberg beneath Jane's remarks, even when she read aloud portions of her unfinished autobiography, *From This Rich Bed*, in which she describes the "advances" made to her by priests when she was a young adult. No mention made, in those readings at least, of the childhood incidents.

And incidentally, Walt Zeh died on November 11, 1999, while I was writing this memoir—in fact I had composed a letter to him in early November, telling him about this work, though for some reason I never sent it. For weeks I kept wondering if Walt were still alive; I'd never met him, but thoughts of him kept drifting through my mind. Then in late November my research assistant Mary Dillman traveled to Saratoga Springs and discovered the fact of Walt's death.

3. Sue Reeves Williams, whose father was the American Lit professor of this transcript, sent me a tidbit about Mr. Reeves's memory of Jane in academia: "Unfortunately," Sue wrote, "I didn't get to ask him about Jane until after he'd had a stroke (in his early 80s). He seemed to have lost his sense of humor. He said he did remember Jane, sniffed, and said, 'She fancied herself a poet.' With pleasure I informed him that Jane had published (at the time) seventeen books of poetry, fiction, and nonfiction. He harumphed and changed the subject—he never could stand to be contradicted."

4. Another person from Saratoga days who remembers Jane vividly is Agnes O'Connor Hamberger, who as a child lived near Jane and Marie on Middle Avenue. Agnes took the time to send me this essay of her memories, which I've edited slightly here:

> My recollection of Janie, as she was known in the neighborhood of Saratoga Springs on Middle Avenue: She was my first hero! I waited on our front porch almost every day the summer before I went to kindergarten, and many summers after that for a glimpse of her so I could approach her and probably be a pesky little kid that was starved for her company.
>
> There was a magic about her—she was different in ways I am not able to really articulate but she took an interest in me, at least that is what I perceived, and paid attention to me. Our street was inhabited by "older people"—she was the only young person living on our block that I was intrigued by and when she was able to spend time outside of her home she did come over to our large front porch, set up a chalk board occasionally and teach (must emphasize "teach") me the alphabet, and draw pictures for me. I never got enough of her company.
>
> As time went by she graduated to filling my head (and some neighborhood kids that would occasionally come by) with dreams of putting on a

play (drama) in our garage. She as leader and my little playmates along with brothers, Joe and John—(talking now about when I was six or seven years old) with her help started to "rehearse a play" but it never got off the ground—many endless days we'd wait in our garage for her to come over and start our rehearsals—she did come over and "work" on an idea or two but never had the time to spend with us that we, I, wanted so badly.

I remember posting one of the younger children at the front door of the garage to look out for her approach as I sat inside and tried to arrange things so she'd be interested in what she'd find available for scenery. The garage had an upstairs that we were forbidden to investigate but of course we did. Up there were odds and ends—most intriguing of which was some old clothes and costume jewelry packed away that had belonged to a great aunt of mine. Our play never did materialize, though Jane did put on a play with (other) youngsters that I didn't know in a loft of a building around the corner and again in the loft of a building down on the extension of Middle Avenue, not on our block. I am sorry to say though I was part of the invited (paying perhaps two cents for the privilege) audience, I don't remember the content of the performances probably because of my young age. But I'm pretty sure she was the author and director rather than the performer.

Janie was for many years the only caregiver in evidence for her bedridden mother, Marie Roberts (nee Burdick). Marie's hand is evident in a picture of me as an infant in my baby carriage—my mother told me that the day the picture was taken was one of the last days Marie was able to walk outside of her home. Marie was a beautiful woman who was confined to bed because of a very debilitating form of rheumatoid arthritis. She was well loved by Janie and because she was admired for her spirit and loving nature gained support from her doctors and Catholic priests who visited her regularly.

Those were the days when doctors made house calls and I doubt that they charged for their services in Marie's case. This was a time when one got by as best they could. In this day and age, some bureaucracy probably would have found Marie incapable of being a good mother and Janie could have been taken from her. But . . . they "made it" on their own with support from caring people.

Marie was given the job of answering several doctors' after-hours phones. I visited Marie with my mother once in a while in the evening after supper and saw her answer those calls. Her hands ravaged by arthritis were more like claws but she managed to pick up the receiver and answer the calls with great efficiency, and write a message legibly; she had the sweetest voice you'd ever want to hear. On those visits Marie was always in a perfectly lovely bed jacket—usually a pale pink or peach colored satin—gifts from her friends of which she seemed to have had many. I'm sure that Janie's mother was a recipient of what we nowadays would call welfare. I don't know how else they could have survived.

Janie had her hands full at an age when no child ever should have to be called upon for so much effort. She prepared their meals, cleaned the house and took care of her mother to the best of her ability. Every memory I have of Janie and her mother's interaction was beautiful, and uncomplicated. Mother was in charge but was to my knowledge not overbearing.

Please note—I was in that home infrequently—there may have been more help involved (in later years there was a series of caregivers) but I remember being there when Marie would ask Janie for something or other—and kept her up to speed as far as housekeeping goes.

I remember *one* time when I thought I'd have some time with Janie but Marie was really pulling the mother thing on Janie—telling her to clean up her room which was on the second floor. Janie cleaned it up all right—she threw scads of clothing out her second floor bedroom window. I'll never forget seeing the most gorgeous sun hat (pink and white gingham) flying out of Janie's bedroom window, and thinking, why would she want to throw that away? Well, she wasn't throwing it away—she eventually scooped it up along with everything else she tossed out the window and took it back from the lawn to her room—it was just her way of cleaning up her room—throw it out and get it back!!—perhaps in better order.

Most of my memories of Janie took place in the summer but I remember her coming over to our house a few times during the winter to talk to my father—very much zoning in on begging him to draw her portrait (she must have been twelve or thirteen). He always declined. He was a talented artist but never thought he was good enough to do any subject justice. When she came over on those occasions she wasn't interested in me or anyone else other than our dad. Looking back I realize she most likely was looking for a "father figure"—someone who would notice her.

Janie became acquainted with my mother and father well before I was born so felt at ease with them. I truly think Jane had a child's version of a "crush" on my father; he allowed her to call him by his first name, Kearney, and she called my mother by her first name also when she was very young so in doing that she probably felt special. I understand that when I was a baby (a novelty on our street) she and another neighbor girl would take turns holding me on their laps and taking me for walks in my carriage—Jane was only seven or eight years old when I was in my first year of life but times were simple and our neighborhood was sheltered and safe.

Jane brought me into her home only a few times—once to share a drink she made out of those wax bottles with a little sugar water in them—they were colored but all tasted the same. I remember standing at the kitchen sink in her kitchen and tasting the concoction she made of that little vial and about eight ounces of water and complaining that it tasted just like water. The wax bottles cost a penny and Jane was going to make a great drink out of that penny's worth of sugar water. That particular day we went

> out to the side yard and we came across a young cat—it wasn't her cat but she knew how it would track a moving object—in this case a large blade of grass—it was my first introduction to interacting with animals. I just never forgot that. We didn't have a pet and no one that I knew had one.
>
> When Jane went to high school she had a job after school—I didn't know that till I read Robert's notes in one of her books. That would explain why we didn't see her around very much during that period. She did attract friends and several would congregate on her front porch in the early evening—boys and girls—just hanging out talking etc. . . . When they were approaching being "too noisy" her mother would call to Jane to put an end to the meetings. Later, she [went to] Skidmore College, so was again not around much. She did have a boyfriend with a motorcycle (Walter Zeh) and the two of them conjuring up all kinds of gossip took a trip to California to visit her father, who as I heard from gossip as a youngster, deserted his wife and child when Marie became ill.
>
> I just thought she was great—so daring—she's the only person I ever knew who used a large scarf as a backless blouse. We all know that is pretty risqué—but she was fearless.

Indeed, Jane apparently made an impression on people who knew her but casually, though perhaps not always the one she might have preferred. In 1989, I sold a copy of my book, *Dreaming Myself, Dreaming a Town* to an older couple who lived near Dundee, New York, who up until then had expressed to me no interest whatsoever in the subject matter—yet they greeted the prospect of reading my book with exuberant enthusiasm. As it turned out, the woman had grown up in Saratoga Springs. "Sure, I knew Jane years ago, when we were kids," she told me. "She was that real skinny one who smoked all the time and wore black!"

5. *Reality Change* (Eugene, OR: SethNet Publishing, fall 1994).

6. *The Seth Phenomena*, video (Jeffersonville, PA: Bob Terrio Creations, 1993).

7. In his notes for *The "Unknown" Reality*, volume 1, p. 41.

8. And in fact it was during a conference of science-fiction writers in 1956 that Jane spontaneously went into a Seth-like trance in a setting reminiscent of later ESP class days. As the writer A. J. Budrys recalled in a 1977 interview for KPFA Radio, Berkeley, California:

> At the first [Milford] conference, Cyril Kornbluth turned up with this thin, intense, raven-haired, bird-like woman named Jane Roberts. Cyril was living in Waverly, New York, which is near [Sayre], Pennsylvania, and somehow or the other, Jane Roberts and he had gotten in contact.
>
> Now, Jane's ambition at that point was to become a free-lance writer, fiction writer. More specifically, fantasy or science fiction. At the time her

interest in the occult was way in the back—way in the background. She was presented to us as somebody who wanted to learn how to write this stuff, period, and she was no loonier than anybody else in that [crowd].

And we all snickered behind our hands at Cyril and this protégée because, well, we were like high school boys at a prom about the entire question of sex, and at the time the whole community was so straight and so naive, that we assumed that of course she was Cyril's ha ha ha protégée, and then we didn't know what to do with that information. We did a lot of daydreaming, I guess. And Jane was not what you'd call a sex object, but she was an extremely striking personality.

And somehow it happened that Cyril and [writers] James Blish and Damon Knight and I got to talking with Jane, and developed what you might call a contact high—I don't know what else to call it. But we were all telling each other how great we were, and we had gone off by ourselves—we were sitting in I guess it was Jane's hotel room, which was up in an attic somewhere in the third most luxurious hotel in Milford, Pennsylvania—and we got to talking about writing and releasing your emotions and the next thing we knew, one of us had started to cry and everybody was extremely tensed up, and Jane suddenly began prophesying . . . she just suddenly slipped into this mediumistic mode and began talking the kind of open-ended thing that I guess mediums talk that can be interpreted any number of ways, in this heightened voice and in this tense situation. [So] I began replying to her in exactly the same style, and this was not a conscious satirical move—I don't think it was even an unconscious satirical move. It was that something in my fatigued and excited brain—I was only about twenty-three, twenty-four, at the time—responded to this and something switched over and said okay, we're gonna do this—we're gonna do this. And Jane and I began to converse in this manner. It was response and antiphon, actually, it was . . . it was a very strange feeling. At the end of which time we were kind of bonded into this tight little group of people. We began telling each other things we never told anybody. We had somehow released the barriers that exist between all people and certainly between all adults. We began talking about things that were important to us—it was I guess what you might call a spontaneous group therapy session at that point.

And we never got into the occult or the mystical again. Jane did not say, you know, we have evoked certain spirits—she did not identify our past lives—this was long before she wrote things like *Seth Speaks* or any of that. She was—she was a young kid too. And whatever it was that she was in the grip of was something that she hadn't gotten familiar with and hadn't yet learned to manipulate.

Manipulate is maybe an invidious word; all I meant by it was put her hands on it and guide it and direct it—I meant manipulate literally. . . .

> In any case, we were all you know, really loosened up by the . . . events at Milford, and to have this Jane Roberts thing superimposed on it hit the five of us like a ton of bricks, and we—we were brothers and sister. We did not have to finish sentences. We were really, you know, the classic contact high. And I drove Jane home and I drove Cyril home and I never laid eyes on Jane again. All further contacts were by phone or by mail—that I can recall. I'm pretty sure that that's exactly right. We all corresponded—we had a great round-robin correspondence going for a while. . . .
>
> Jane must have been a very gratifying person to know if you were in the right frame of mind, and there was no malice in her—there was not a bit of malice or avarice that I was ever able to detect. What she did, she did out of all sincerity, whatever it was.

Damon Knight also recounted this scene of Jane in trance in his book *The Futurians: The Story of the Science Fiction "Family" of the 30s that Produced Today's Top SF Writers and Editors* (New York: John Day, 1977). "It seemed to me," he says, "that . . . we made up a unity of some kind, composed of two pairs—Cyril the dark analog of Budrys, I the blonde analog of Blish—around the central figure of Jane" (p. 205).

9. *The Seth Material*, p. 10.
10. *The Seth Phenomena*, video.
11. *The Seth Material*, p. 14.
12. Ibid., p. 15.
13. *The Early Sessions: Book 1 of the Seth Material*, p. 20.
14. *The Seth Material*, pp. 16–17.
15. *The Seth Material*, p. 19.
16. On the "spirit guide" question, Jane told her ESP class on June 20, 1972:

> I consider the Seth material as evidence of other aspects of the multidimensional personality. I expect it to lead me to still further insights. To label Seth as a spirit guide is to limit an understanding of what he is . . . The minute I found out after my first book was published that this automatically put me in what people call the psychic field . . . I was so humiliated I could hardly hold my head up . . .
>
> I'm using my writing [and] my life to transform intuitive, sometimes revelationary material into art, where it can be enjoyed, understood to varying degrees, and stand free of the stupid interpretations . . . The whole psychic bit as it is, is intellectually and morally and psychologically outrageous as far as I'm concerned and I want no part of it or the vocabulary or the ideas.
>
> Even if and when our scientists prove telepathy and clairvoyance, this will certainly help our ideas of personality and reality; but the nature of

> our existence and reality and the scope of that reality cannot be proven in those terms. You cannot put them down as fact in that particular context.
>
> This meant personally that I was regarded as having the truth and a spirit guide . . . by spiritualists and those in the field, or being a fraud or psychologically disturbed at the other end, and in that frame of reference there is no in-between. Either I was looked up to . . . not as myself, but because of Seth, or I was thought of as a nut and disturbed. And I refused the entire framework.

17. Jane developed her aspect psychology theory in her two books: *Adventures in Consciousness* and *Psychic Politics* (originally published by Prentice-Hall 1975 and 1976, respectively; both books have been reprinted by Moment Point Press, 1999 and 2000, respectively).

18. The Deleted material, mentioned in Rob's notes throughout the published Seth books, refers to the sessions directed to private matters in Jane and Rob's life, or, on occasion, to friends and others who asked for advice. Rob excised these sessions from the ongoing body of material and placed them in their own notebooks, and as such they form a powerful, intimate examination of the *joint* reality (as Seth often phrased it) created and lived by one couple—Jane and Rob—and thus demonstrate how each of us does the same.

One small example of the volumes of Deleted material observations directed toward Jane comes from a December 18, 1974 session, in which Seth, referring to Jane by her male entity name, "Ruburt," notes:

> In order to fear the opinions of others, particularly the opinion of those in authority, you must first to some extent respect those in authority, and hold some faith in their ideas. You are taught to respect such authorities, and as mentioned [previously], while Ruburt defied authority as a child he was still dependent upon authority's welfare.
>
> Now he has fear that if the "authority," the people, do not like what he says, then they will not buy his books, and deny him that "welfare." At the same time he has been determined to go ahead. Instead of the people giving him handouts as a child, where he had to be careful of what he did and said, he saw them as contributing to his welfare through buying his books, and if he went too far and offended them, they would stop.
>
> None of this ever had to do with Ruburt privately, but with Ruburt and his contact with the world. None of our sessions, or his own natural development would ever bother him. The question was how these could be related to the world, how people would interpret or misinterpret, or how he would be regarded—for he took it for granted that anyone offering revolutionary ideas would be punished or ostracized.

Because of these feelings he was afraid of setting himself up as a new authority for people to follow blindly. This problem also vanishes when he realizes, as he does, that there literally are no authorities. There are only people.

3 *None of That Girl Stuff Allowed*

1. "Ned" is the pseudonym—first name only, for obvious reasons—that I gave Sean's father in *Conversations with Seth*.

2. Many others wrote to me about the help Jane gave to them over the years, both in the usual conversational sense and in other ways—including the dream state. For example, "Priscilla Lantini" of *Conversations*, wrote:

> Once during class days when I was in need of direction I took some jewelry of my husband's to Jane for her impressions. She thoughtfully wrote out for me his beliefs and even a few of mine that I wasn't aware of. This was very helpful in saving my marriage. Both my husband and myself have great lessons to learn from each other.
>
> One particular dream of Jane comes to mind. It happened shortly after her death. I remember thinking when she died that it was on the same day [September 5] kids went back to school here and that Jane was beginning a whole new learning experience, and how appropriate. Then one night in my dream state she and I met in a classroom in the basement of a school. She looked wonderful; very strong and healthy. We talked and hugged each other and then headed for the elevator to go up. I never remembered the dialogue, I'm sorry, it seemed enough in my mind that I had seen her again and I felt that I also was embarking on a new adventure in consciousness.

Carla, "Priscilla's" daughter, sent this:

> My first introduction to Jane came via my mother through her discussions of her weekly group meetings at Jane's house. I was around fourteen at that time. I really didn't pay a lot of attention to it. I was naturally curious. I digested some and disregarded the rest until one night when something very frightening happened to me. It was very late and I fell asleep on the couch. I was alone. Everyone else was upstairs asleep. All of a sudden I was conscious of this extremely loud buzzing, kind of like being under wires on a utility pole. It of course scared me and I remember opening my eyes to see myself below. I could see me covered in a blanket. My cat was curled up on my feet. He started to stretch. Well let me tell you I was having heart palpitations. I don't ever remember being so scared in my life.

> I woke up and ran upstairs to mom's room. I was crying. She calmly sat me down and explained out-of-body experiences to me. The next morning she called Jane and I talked to her on the phone. She put it into perspective so that I could understand this and to not be frightened but instead enjoy the experience and flow with it and play with it. She said most people never get the thrill of an out-of-body experience. I must say to this day I still have these experiences and when it happens I can still hear her voice in my head telling me to have fun with this.
>
> Another time in my life Jane was to play an important role was when I was seventeen. I found myself in a situation of being pregnant. I was madly in love with this person; unfortunately this was not my dream of the future. I was in utter panic [and] with lots of thought I decided to have an abortion. I had such guilt. I felt like a murderer.
>
> I couldn't seem to get past this. My mother thought that maybe I should talk to Jane, that she could give me a different perspective on this. I called her and she was wonderful, so understanding. In her own view she explained how this was a life experience of mutual agreement, meaning that this fetus knew that it would never be born but wanted to experience this reality just so far. It may have been a friend in another reality or life, perhaps this experience had been reversed in another lifetime. She told me to hold no guilt. Whatever the reason this was a mutual agreement. She also told me that if I had the question then I had the answer as well. She had an impact on my life that unfortunately she may or may not have known.

Richard Kendall, one of the Boys from New York from ESP class days, now a literary agent and aspiring author himself, remembers this:

> In 1981, although Jane's own health was in difficulty, the following incident occurred. I was experiencing some health problems which manifested in severe bleeding from my nose. One day it was so bad I decided to call Jane to ask for help, which I rarely did during all the years I knew her. I might call her occasionally to share some news or some thoughts, but rarely ever called to ask for help. Rob answered and said he would relay the message.
>
> I then took the train into Manhattan and about three o'clock in the afternoon while walking I felt this wave of incredibly calm energy encircle my body. This energy was quite tangible, and I could feel my entire body super-relaxing, for lack of a better description. I did not know what to attribute these feelings to, and did not think of connecting them to my phone call to Jane, because I hadn't spoken with her directly.
>
> Jane called me about seven P.M. She told me she had tried to reach me by phone numerous times during the afternoon, and when unsuccessful, had concentrated on sending me energy, imagining it all over my body. She then went on to discuss some of the reasons she was picking up that were behind

my health problems, and was quite supportive and concerned. Here is a paraphrase of some of what she said:

> You have a characteristic of being very expressive with your energy and then clamping down on it by tightening your muscles, which is part of the problem. Don't be afraid of this characteristic, but be aware that when you feel panicky, you are not using your energy easily.
>
> The problems are also connected to your life situation . . . realize that taking care of yourself in the world is natural, and don't let your age make you ashamed of working in whatever job you have, be it at a factory, or whatever *[Rich was thirty-one at the time]*. Our society is based on the idea that everything that can go wrong will go wrong, so tell yourself that things will work out in their own way. But if your fear of going to a doctor is so great and keeps building up, then that will just aggravate the symptoms, so you'd be better off going to a doctor.

She then told me to imagine a doll in my own image, a smaller version of myself, and talk to it, tell it that everything will be all right; to tell it that it's a good doll, that I'll protect it—and to give myself a break, and love it.

Rich also noted this dream from September of 1990, six years after Jane's death: "I was visiting Jane and Rob and was alone in Jane's room with her. She came up to me and said, 'You haven't been feeling well, have you?' and I started to cry and said, 'No, I haven't.' She put her hands on either side of my face and said she would have a session for me, and disappeared . . . Then I hear her singing Sumari [her poetic trance "language"], but she was still invisible—then I noticed that the rug was forming an outline of a woman, of Jane, and the tufts of the rug began to move as if the wind were blowing over it, which I knew was Jane's energy even though she didn't materialize."

It's interesting how much this dream of Rich's is like one of Jane's, about me, that she recorded in her journals ten years before, on May 7 (which happens to be Rich's birthday), 1980: "As soon as I closed my eyes last PM in bed, I had a vivid brief experience in which I was couching Sue Watkins' head in my arms and comforting her. She was crying—not about anything new—but everything—I told her I got depressed too—everyone did—I was looking down at her head."

And the thing is that I was very depressed around that time over many things obvious and not so obvious, and on the previous Sunday, May 4, of 1980, in an eerie foreshadow of Jane's dream—of which I knew nothing before I read her journals for this memoir—I'd started crying in front of my mother as I sat on the bed in my old room (so she must have been looking down at my head); I remember secretly wishing that she'd sit down and hold me, but she didn't—after a few minutes she just left the room, thinking, I'm sure, that I wanted to be left alone. So Jane's dream was about the mothering I'd wanted, much as Rich's dream expressed.

5 Going Back

1. This dream is described in detail in chapter 1 of *Conversations with Seth*. "All the details of the night were clear to me," it says in part. "I leaped out the window and flew into the night; down past the sailboats moored in the sound; down through the dark water . . . up out of the warm, thick sea into the air and past the gray-shingled houses lining the West Chop beaches . . . And except for the ecstatic, perfect freedom of flight, I could have been walking the streets of Vineyard Haven on any fog-shrouded summer night."

2. Of course I wasn't the only neophyte writer Jane encouraged, or impressed with her work habits. As ESP class member Vickie Smith, who attended ESP class for several years until mid-1972 while she was a student at nearby Corning Community College, recalls:

> Jane was so much more for me as a teacher-of-finding my own voice and even believing I could have one. In class one time we did a psy-time exercise and wrote about the experience, handed it to her, and took a break.
>
> My [essay] was a description of crouching in the hedges between our house and a neighbor's, and looking out at the world through the framework of the interwoven roots and branches. [As I sat there] I suddenly became aware that Jane was reading mine, because I sensed somehow that she felt or "saw" the moment I described. It was such a rich experience because it had scent and I could feel the warmth of the sun . . .
>
> I came over to her and sat on the floor and she said quietly, "You should be writing . . . I like how you've described this, it has a sense of presence." Then she started talking about the writing class (which I knew there was no way I could do), but the blood was roaring in my ears so loudly I just kept nodding at her . . . Jane knew that [for me] writing was more than scritch-scratch on a page and I knew that she knew in that moment [that] we were warmed by the same patch of sun.

Also remembering Jane's encouragement of his writing abilities (and his secret hopes for a private word with Seth) is Richard Wolinski, a.k.a. "Will Petrosky" of *Conversations with Seth*. "Jane was one of the most supportive people I ever knew," Richard wrote to me:

> She encouraged me to write at every opportunity. It was Jane who said she needed help with answering her letters—which I did for a number of months in 1974 and 1975. One weekend, I drove to a wedding in Rochester, New York, and decided to come to Elmira on Monday, the day before the

class. I called Jane and headed over to the house on Water Street. Rob was busy painting, and Jane was working in the private living room on one of her books. She gave me some correspondence and I spent the afternoon answering letters. I asked if I could sit in on that night's book session, and at first she said no, that it was too boring.

I said that I didn't mind—actually, I had two thoughts at the time. One was that this was my chance for a private session with Seth, the other was that I'd have something over the other boys from New York. Hey, what the hell, I was twenty-three. After a while, she called out from the other apartment that I could stay for dinner and then the session.

Dinner consisted of broiled frankfurters, and then we sat down for the book. Rob and I sat in the sofa across from Jane, who closed her eyes and went into trance after a moment—not suddenly, as in the class sessions. Seth spoke in a monotone, picking up exactly where he left off.

After a while, I grew bored. It was very hard to follow Seth. There was no life in his voice, no changed intonations. When he said "Dictation" prior to starting a book session, he was completely correct. It was as if Seth were reading from a manuscript located in another dimension, and relaying it to Rob at a pace suitable for transcription. When volume 2 of *The "Unknown" Reality* came out, the session was virtually unedited—a couple of words were changed here or there, and my pseudonym was added. A pun involving my name "Rich" was changed to a new pun based on my alter ego, "Will."

Following the session, Rob relayed what Seth had said to Jane, and Jane spoke a little about the sequence of material in the book.

"Pretty boring, huh?" she asked me.

I nodded yes, but told her that I wouldn't have missed it for the world.

Jane was always supportive about my writing, encouraging me to set my thoughts on paper. I think because we both wrote, there were elements of identification between us. I wish, though, I'd been able to stay still at my typewriter and put things down on paper, instead of saving my best lines for phone conversations, or my best paragraphs for reveries in the shower. I wish I could send Jane some of the material I wrote during the years I edited the KPFA Radio magazine [in Berkeley, California], or the mystery novel I recently completed (which now sits and sits and sits on an editor's desk, waiting to be perused). I was such a kid then, not knowing what I wanted, my consciousness flying in all different directions like a top spinning out of control. My insecurity was laid out on a table for all to see—especially Jane who, I think, was able to look past it into the heart of my being.

Her autograph in *Oversoul Seven*: Rich—You Wave Your Lives Like Banners. Adindo, Jane. In *Psychic Politics*—Dear Rich—No one named or nicknamed Rich can be poor in spirit. And if you ever think you are, you need spiritual glasses! Love, Jane.

And my favorite, in my copy of *Dialogues*:

Dear Paranoid Friend:
Ashes to Ashes
Lust to Lust
Use It Well
So It Don't Rust
Cheers, Jane

The last time I saw Jane was during the 1980 Olympics (January or February) when I drove down from Lake Placid and stopped in Elmira. I was hoping for a last glimpse of Seth, but he never put in an appearance. Jane looked well, though she did not once move from her chair.

It's now been fifteen years since then, and I think of her often, and I suppose she looks in on me from time to time, as she must do on all the class members. I hope that next time a class reunion comes about in the dream state, that I could switch gears into full waking consciousness and say hi to everyone. Hey, Sue!!!!

6 *The Strange Case of The Chestnut Beads*

1. *The Chestnut Beads* and its sequel, *Bundu*—originally one novella—were both published in *Fantasy and Science Fiction* magazine, in October, 1957, and March, 1958, respectively; *Beads* was reprinted in 1963 in a Rod Serling anthology by Bantam Books, which is where I read the story in the fall of 1963. (In her journals for August 8, 1963, Jane writes, "Letter from Rod Serling—said *Bundu* damned good story, handsomely written! Too adult for TV though—[Serling] will read *Rebellers* as soon as possible!")

2. These kernels are by no means static, however, as I discovered while writing my article on *Chestnut Beads* in 1994: The act itself seemed to create even more interconnections with the story than the ones originally in it—but in *my* present as it continued to evolve.

It was late November, 1994. I worked on my article all morning and took a break at lunchtime to drive into the nearby village of Watkins Glen and visit Linda, manager of the antiques and collectibles co-op where I had a small booth of goodies for sale, mostly rummage sale culls; I was hoping she had some money for me. When I arrived, Linda was busy sorting out an enormous collection of old postcards that she'd purchased that morning, a couple thousand of them, stacked everywhere. She was arranging them by subject in notebook sleeves and shoeboxes, and pricing each of them for sale, a huge job.

Usually I'm not much interested in old postcards, but these were exceptionally beautiful ones from the turn of the century. Completely at random, I picked up a notebook full of them and opened it. The first postcard I saw was a scene near the Chemung River in Elmira. Next to it—and I nearly missed it because the photo looked so new—*was a postcard of the apartment building at 458 West Water Street* where Jane and Rob had lived during all of the events I'd been writing about that morning.

The photo had been taken from the intersection of West Water and Walnut, specifically showing the apartment's kitchen and big bay windows (as well as a very young red maple tree in the front yard). I pulled the postcard out of its sleeve and turned it over.

The card was postmarked from Dundee, and had been sent by someone named "Lillian" to a "Mrs. Parker" in Beaver Dams, New York (a hamlet near Watkins Glen). The postmark was August 10, though the year was faint and obscure. Of course, Dundee is where I was living when I wrote *Conversations with Seth* in 1979, the year Jane's editor had discovered the "Sue Watkins" tidbit in *The Chestnut Beads*—as I'd been describing a mere half-hour before.

Linda, the co-op manager, lives in Beaver Dams.

Sean's paternal grandmother's first name was Lillian—another funny connection with the Watkins name. (The village of Watkins Glen, by the way, is not named for Ned's family.)

And that Mrs. Parker person . . . gee, just the day before this I'd been reading *Last Train to Memphis*, Peter Guralnick's biography of Elvis Presley, in which Colonel *Parker*, Elvis's famous promoter, is of course prominent. Some of my interest in Elvis's life comes from the simple fact that he and I share the same birth date, January 8. Standing there in the co-op, I recalled that Jane's birth date is *May* 8, in 1929.

I said to Linda, "I have to have this card!" (It was $2.00.) Linda told me that she had ten others just like it, though uncanceled (unused), in a shoebox that was out on the counter. I gave these a quick look-see but for some reason decided that I didn't want them. Then I came back home, stopping at the foot of my driveway to pick a bunch of mail out of the mailbox.

And here is what I found there:

(1) A reply from the man who had once lived in the first-floor apartment at 458, as shown on the postcard, during the years of Jane's ESP class. Leonard was responding to a letter I'd sent him on November 5, asking if he had any memories of Jane that he'd like to share for my memoir. His card featured a sketch of a lighthouse and seaside-cottage style hotel, identified as one located in North Truro, on Cape Cod. Inside, Leonard had written that he would put some material together for me and that I could drop in any time.

(2) A reply card from the artist George Rhoads, also responding to my November 5 inquiry about Jane-memories, also saying he'd gather up some material for me. Included with this note was a postcard of one of George's paintings, a cartoon-like scene entitled "Labyrinth of Proverbs." A labyrinth is right!

Because . . . earlier that morning I'd been looking through my dream journals and had come across some records I'd set aside a while before, on "dreams and the mail" coincidences. The *specific incident* in those records had occurred in 1987, when I'd received a *postcard* (waggishly addressed to "Oranda," incidentally) from George while he was visiting Martha's Vineyard (off the Cape Cod coast); his card had arrived the same day as that week's *New Yorker* magazine, in which a cartoon appeared with exactly the same scene of two women walking in front of a row of seaside-cottage style houses as depicted on George's card! And on that 1987 postcard, George writes that while on the Vineyard, he had met the novelist Phil Dyer, "whose great-grandfather is depicted on a local *postcard* standing next to a 350-pound halibut" (George's words). And I'd been going over all of this just that morning, in 1994.

(3) Also in my mailbox was a newsletter from the Newhouse School of Journalism at Syracuse University . . . where I was a student when I first read *The Chestnut Beads*. And the thing is, this was the Spring 1994 edition of that newsletter. What was it doing, just getting to me then, in November?

(4) And finally, there was a letter from *Amazing Stories* (a magazine similar to *Fantasy and Science Fiction* in form and content) rejecting my short story, "Rummage Sale of the Gods," whose main (female) character is a collectibles dealer—a funny connection to the antiques co-op where I'd just picked up the postcard.

I thought, this is too much! And then I went into the house and got out my stamp magnifier (which brings tiny paper fibers into clear focus) and looked at the cancellation on the postcard of 458 . . . and the year was . . .

1929—the year Jane was born.

It's also interesting to note that I'm not the only one who read, and recalled, this old novella of Jane's. Mae Lou of Maple Valley, Washington, wrote me a lengthy letter describing the impact Jane's books have effected in her life, and added this: "I have read science fiction since I was six years old and I learned to read from my brothers' Jules Verne books. It's all I've ever read for enjoyment. Having three older brothers buying every edition of *Fantasy and Science Fiction* helped. When *Reality Change* published two of Jane's stories I got a big shock, as I remembered them from my childhood, the same with *The Chestnut Beads*—you described."

7 *Really Great for Any Age at All*

1. As to her early literary ambitions and yearning for recognition therein, Jane wrote the following passage, which essentially sums up my own parallel feelings, in her journals for January 13, 1977:

> Was reading an article on [the American poet and novelist Robert Penn] Warren, and the awards given him. He's an elderly man now and I was thinking when I'm old, they won't give me awards; or I won't be a respected

elder writer or statesman (stateswoman?) of the soul. An old attitude of mine, yet I thought that doing comparable work in, say, the world of novels or literary conventional poetry—I'd receive recognition, but my books aren't reviewed as books in the *Times* or other such places, but are put in the psychic field. There's no doubt that I don't really like being considered in that field; I don't respect the people in it; and from calls and letters it sometimes seems, at least, that [those] readers are nuttier than most other people—which is saying a lot—and probably an exaggeration on my part. I'm probably ashamed of the field and being allied with it . . . in terms of what? My own conventional thoughts about it.

This is old stuff; but as a kid I must have latched on literary success as the answer to all of my problems; and *that* involved a certain amount of intellectual snobbery; it also implied though I didn't know it, a strong desire for recognition and respectability . . . in a . . . restricted but "superior" group.

To be a writer meant the solution of all problems. I don't think at the time I thought in terms of great mass acceptance, but I'm not sure here.

My own natural abilities kept pushing me elsewhere, though. The poetry was acceptable in my eyes, but wouldn't provide any money at all and I thought . . . that I had to make my creativity pay. I sold my science fiction which I enjoyed writing very much; but then after the conference decided that it was too . . . pulpish a field . . . By then in my thirties I was upset—a writer was supposed to have published a book by then . . . In the meantime, *The Physical Universe As Idea Construction* came along, and the ESP book.

I thought, and I was right, that [the ESP] book contained some of my best writing to date; and the subject grabbed my interest and abilities; the whole thing was new; I had no idea that a "field" was built up about it—or that others—nuts, some charlatans—were also involved in matters I found so absorbing and unique. I was afraid that the psychic interest would lead me astray as a writer, though, since the ESP book wasn't fiction or poetry—to me then the only artistic expressions. Non-fiction I thought was for journalists.

I began to have psychic experiences only when they could be firmly tied to writing and firmly tied to "my next book," and with *Adventures* particularly. I disapproved of some of my own student's experiences in class, and some of my own I suppose—because they sounded so like those reported by people I thought were off base at best. At the same time I was intuitively attracted to the questions and experiences themselves, and when I left myself alone would find myself initiating more—even in my writing class, which wasn't supposed to be a psychic one.

Some of those events were terrific; I *did* appreciate them—but also because they were mine, rather than reported to me by others. They threw me back into that "psychic field" again, though.

> I'm not sure but I think I stopped going dancing [at bars] when people [there] began to ask me questions, etc. . . .

As to her feelings about the Seth experience along these lines, Jane writes in her unfinished "Magical Approach" manuscript, "I consider Seth as a creative psychological [manifestation] of the highest order—a mystery—that I may or may not one day unravel. But he bears an indelible stamp of authenticity and integrity that I recognized at once."

8 *Friday Night Get-Togethers And Other Fun Times, More or Less*

1. This episode is recounted fully in chapter 6 of *Conversations with Seth*.

9 *The Meat Market Marriage*

1. Equally prophetically, the JP's unusual last name was the same (with a slightly different spelling) as that of my second husband (though they weren't related), whom I wouldn't meet for another six years (again, echoes of names). My second marriage would last exactly as long as the first one—eighteen months. "Well, at least you know your limits," Jane chortled, years later.
2. The full session is included in appendix 3 of *Conversations with Seth*.

10 *The Seat of the (Somewhat) Unconscious*

1. Interesting that, unlike true girl friends, Jane and I could not confide comfortably in one another about such things as "female problems"; yet it was precisely that distance between us, the center around which we operated, that allowed this rather astonishing episode to happen in the first place.
2. For some reason I find it evocative that nearly two years after Jane set fire to her blouse, I recorded a dream on March 17, 1975, about Jane setting herself on fire. "She is in bed but okay," my dream notes state, adding that this was in fact the day that Bill Granger went into a local hospital for surgical evaluation of his stomach ulcer. Of course in 1975 I knew about the blouse incident and Jane's self-healing aftermath, so this dream isn't precognitive in the usual sense—except for its connection with our alpha efforts as directed toward Bill, and the healing possibilities implied. Unfortunately, I didn't record the outcome of Bill's evaluation, though I do recall that at some point, possibly at a later date, a portion of his stomach was removed in an effort to cure the ulcer (nowadays, antibiotic therapy is frequently used instead). It's the juxtaposition of this dream and the real-life incidents, with Jane at the center, that gives the dream its precognitive flavor.

3. "The Magical Approach," is an unfinished manuscript that Jane wrote in a journal-like style and includes excerpts from the Seth material. It was posthumously edited and published by Amber-Allen in 1995.

4. As reflected by the many remissions and temporary improvements she experienced later, when she was in terrible physical condition—remissions that frequently defied doctors' assessments of what was possible.

II *The Honest Appraisal (Yowch!) And Similar Tales Close to the Bone*

1. See chapter 4 in *Conversations with Seth.*

2. This had to be demeaning, though in a 1977 interview with Lawrence Davidson for Radio KPFA in Berkeley, Jane insisted that she couldn't recall her reaction to Boucher's words. "[As a writer] I just thought of that [sort of thing] as one of the particular problems that I had, like if you had trouble with poor composition or something," she said. "It was a game."

> At the time, I wasn't overly bothered, mostly because I thought of myself as a writer first. But I did go to a science-fiction writers' conference where I was asked whose wife I was, and that made me utterly furious. I mean, I was furious, and I swore up and down the line, you know? [Laughs.] But at that time, at least, I thought that if you were a good-looking woman, you had to play it dead cool and I guess I grew up believing that.
>
> As far as my writing was concerned, I thought that I did a great job, I really did [laugh] and I still do, with male characters and female characters as well, and I thought that a lot of the male writers did a lousy job when they were portraying women and that a good writer could identify with either sex and learn human motivation regardless of, you know, what sex was involved.
>
> I never thought of myself as anything in those terms. I thought of myself as a writer. Although it is true that when I wrote stories I had to make sure in a lot of cases that the male hero came out on top. My market at that time was *Fantasy and Science Fiction* magazine. Some of the other science-fiction magazines were men's markets. Slicks were just below that. And in those magazines, the male had to win. But in *Fantasy and Science Fiction* you really had quite a bit more freedom. As long as it was a good story they didn't hassle you that way and at least one of my stories was based on the idea of a nun who talked a war overlord from another planet out of invading the earth—and she was a heroine!
>
> But I didn't think of myself as stating a cause so much as writing the kind of story I was interested in with characters that ran true and I did wonder, of course, in many different ways, what women would do if they ran the world or if they took over and this kind of thing. And that was what *Chestnut Beads* of course was all about.

[At one point Cyril Kornbluth helped Jane get her first story published in *Fantasy and Science Fiction.*] I had read Cyril's stories and he was probably, I don't know, ten or fifteen years older than I was, but I discovered that he lived not too far away. And I was in my mid-twenties. So I wrote him a note that *Fantasy and Science Fiction* had had my first story for months, and Cyril asked my husband and me to see him. We later became great friends, but that afternoon he snapped a photograph of me—I had shorts on, it was in the summer—and [I took] sort of a sexy pose in this great big huge chair—and later I found out that he sent this photograph to [Anthony] Boucher, who was the editor of *Fantasy and Science Fiction* magazine, with some kind of a little note—this cute brunette has written a story, etc., and anyway they picked the story. And again, at the time, I don't know what my reaction was to that. I just can't remember.

I mean, I know I was glad the story was picked. But again, as far as the sexism angle is concerned, I was one of the very few science-fiction women writers then, and most of them were men and had their own families. And maybe that did have something to do with it, I don't know. [At the time] I wrote *Chestnut Beads*, I do know that I wasn't sure that if women did have the opportunity to take the world over—if they would fall into the same errors that I believe the males have made, and I think I tried to point that out. And then too, at the time, part of that was pretty real to me because I did really think that I might not live to be forty, that the world would be destroyed, that nuclear destruction would go on. I grew up with that idea, really, and the story is based on the concept that it did, and the women took over—the few that were left—and tried to run things. . . .

3. In her journals, Jane records this advance amount as both $2,500 and as $3,500; possibly the final figure was different from the one she'd been offered at the time of this little wing-ding.

4. Though of course I hold, it should go without saying, no grudge toward Jane for having such feelings, however fleeting they might have been. In *The Way Toward Health*, Rob notes for May 18, 1984: "Jane was terrified a couple of times that she might be pregnant by me. Yet except for one time in a passionate moment she never had any urge to have a child. 'But I certainly felt the feminine part of you was the part you couldn't trust,' she said . . . [In Jane's younger years] she was very afraid [of getting] pregnant, and never fooled around. After our marriage she was afraid . . . it would wreck our careers. I reminded her that when she did get pregnant, I hadn't been terribly upset, and accepted it" (p. 221). Jane miscarried the pregnancy.

"It's true I had no urge for parenthood," Rob writes in an earlier note for *The Way Toward Health*, "but I didn't think [in terms] of betrayal, or bargains. Jane was afraid getting pregnant would ruin my career because I'd have to work full time. I could have reacted better than that, I'm sure" (pp. 191–92).

12 *The Flood, and What Washed Up There*

1. Later I thought that Jane must have had a strong feeling of nostalgia for that old bike of mine, harking back to her days in Sayre with Rob when she had a part-time job selling Avon products and kitchen knives, going door to door by bicycle along the streets and byways of rural Pennsylvania . . .

2. In fact, every one of Elmira's bridges was ruined beyond use and required repair, and several others north and south of the city were also washed away. The National Guard put up a temporary pontoon-type bridge for emergency use—Elmira's southside had been cut off from the two local hospitals—but the only way for me to get to my parents' house at that point would have involved a lengthy drive of possibly a day or two (no one knew for sure) far upstream to find a safe place to cross. I was on my own, at least for a while.

13 *After the Flood and Into the Soup*

1. *Dreaming Myself, Dreaming a Town* (New York: Kendall and Delisle Books, 1989).

2. As explained in the Seth material, the name "Sumari" refers to a type of psychological alliance, or "family" of consciousness, existing among various levels of activity and inclination. In class, Jane often spoke or sang "in" Sumari, a kind of a cappella sound-language, and also wrote poetry in it, with "translations." While I intuitively connected with the family-of-consciousness idea, the Sumari songs and most of the poetry left me more or less in the dark. Still, it seemed the only possible title for this newsletter.

14 *"The Work" and Other Puzzles*

1. "Ruburt" refers here, of course, to Jane—the name Seth used for her throughout the dictated material. In a January, 1970, session, Seth explained: "I [speak] through the auspices of a woman of whom I have become quite fond. To others it seems strange that I address her as 'Ruburt,' and 'him,' but the fact is that I have known her in other times and places, by other names. She has been both a man and a woman, and the entire identity who has lived these separate lives can be designated by the name of Ruburt."

2. I wasn't the only one whose family looked askance on Jane, however. As Carroll "Mary Strand" Stamp writes, "Going to [ESP] class was probably the single most outrageous thing I had ever done in my life. My mother was scandalized; my husband was, if not supportive, at least tolerant . . . the rest of friends and family thought I had gone overboard. They cautioned me about cults and devils and hell but I merely ignored them and instead took up the anthem, 'You create your own reality.' Looking back, it's a wonder I survived the wrath I created."

3. I don't think my mother could have put her fears into words anyway—they were too amorphous, and sprang from many painful sources, including a difficult childhood with her own mother, who was a gifted poet and painter and a charming, mercurial alcoholic. Of course the one thing I'd done exactly right in my parents' eyes was to have Sean. No argument *there*—just a quiet sense of irony from my perspective now, looking back on all of this.

4. The chiropractor probably thought his advice was not untoward at all. To impart some idea of the enormous and almost Machiavellian social pressures that still pervaded the issue of having children in those years (and to some lesser extent today), consider this passage from Jane's unpublished "Magical Approach" manuscript, in which she describes going back to Rob's family physician after miscarrying to find out why her diaphragm had apparently failed. "It was he," Jane writes, "who had outfitted me with an ordinary diaphragm instead of one for a tipped uterus, which he knew I had, because as he told me with obvious relish, he thought Rob and I would make great parents no matter what we thought."

5. A factor in their lives that Jane and Rob understood also, of course. In Rob's notes for volume 2 of *Dreams, Evolution, and Value Fulfillment* (New York: Prentice-Hall, 1986; reprinted, San Rafael, CA: Amber-Allen, 1997; page numbers refer to original edition), Jane describes the effect of seeing four former ESP class members, who dropped by their house in the fall of 1981. "During their visit I noticed that my right leg, propped upon the coffee table, would suddenly fall very quickly and unexpectedly to the floor," Jane wrote in her journals. "When company had gone . . . my leg suddenly dropped and my entire body turned independently of my will or intent to the left. This happened several times. Then in a moment of dozing I suddenly found my body moving forward, half standing, with strong energy and more or less natural motion—all by itself. Effects continued [the next day] . . ." (pp. 489–90).

6. None of these book ideas panned out with Prentice, however.

15 *Cross-Corroborating Beliefs And Odd Stuff of Which Counterparts Might Be Made*

1. Spiritual Frontiers Fellowship International is a group whose mission, according to its web site, is to "illuminate, for all people, the reality of physical death." Jane didn't especially like the group's pretext ("I don't believe [there] are spirits in the terms meant," she remarked in the June 20, 1972, ESP class. "I think the whole concept [is] limiting and an inferior level of development if you will, and a definite hindrance to the search in which I'm involved and I hope you're involved in.") After much debate (and refusing to accept any fees in any case), Jane decided not to speak at the SFF New York chapter's meeting.

She had many other offers for speaking engagements and interviews, however, most of which she declined; all are interesting to contemplate. A short list of these through 1981 includes:

1960–64: Worked afternoons as a secretary and lecturer at the Arnot Art Gallery in Elmira.

1966: Publicity trip to New York City for *How to Develop Your ESP Power*.

1970, 1971: Two other invitations to be on the SFF program (declined).

1970: Turned down an offer to be on the Long John Knebel radio show in New York City.

1970, September 7–19: Jane and Rob do a ten-day, six-city book tour for *The Seth Material*, the only one she ever takes on for Prentice-Hall. During that tour she was interviewed by a reporter for the *Boston Herald Traveler* and appeared on the television show, *For Women Only*, WBZ-TV in Boston, during which Seth came through and spoke to viewers for twenty minutes. Rob made no notes.

1971: Spoke to an Elmira high school class on her book, *How to Develop Your ESP Power*.

1972: Spoke to four hundred psychology students at Mansfield University, Mansfield, Pennsylvania. Refused a second invitation four years later.

1975: Jane is interviewed by Ed Busch of KNBR radio, San Francisco.

1977: Brad Steiger asks Jane to speak at a "psychic thing," according to her notes, in place of Peter Hurkos, the Dutch psychic. She says no.

1977: Hunter College, in Pennsylvania, invites Jane to speak (Jane's notes don't mention the format, and say nothing about accepting, so she probably declined).

1977: Jane is interviewed by former ESP class member Lawrence Davidson for his show, *Probabilities*, on radio KPFA, Berkeley, California.

1978: Jane and Rob interviewed for a two-part article in *The Village Voice* (see endnote 3, chapter 19).

1979: A Hollywood agent writes expressing interest in representing Jane for movie adaptations of her life and the Seth material. Turns out this agent had worked with Dick Bach on the film adaptation of *Jonathan Livingston Seagull*. Later that year, a production company writes to ask about optioning her life story for a possible movie for television. Jane and Rob spend a fun evening speculating on who would be cast in the various roles. However, nothing comes of either contact.

1979: A reporter from a New Jersey radio station comes to Jane and Rob's house to tape a two-hour interview, during which Seth comes through.

1981: Jane sends a letter to Meredith Wheeler of ABC news, turning down a second invitation to be on that show. Same day, a British journalist at CBS in New York contacts Jane to ask for an interview for a newspaper article, but Jane declines.

2. That Jane was almost morbidly sensitive to ridicule should have been obvious to me, given the fact of her upbringing, though it was not, particularly. Since most of

us experience and hate the sting of derision in our lives, I didn't give a lot of thought about it—plus, she seemed to handle so well what incidents of it I observed. Then in May of 1984, while Jane was hospitalized and only a few months before she died, I decided to respond to an insulting article about her that appeared in an Ithaca weekly paper. I sent a copy of the article and my reply to Rob, who reacted by telling me in no uncertain terms not to mention the offending piece to Jane (which I never did) and advising me not to reply to it (which I did anyway). "She doesn't need that, and it's pointless," he told me. The paper in question printed an abridged version of my letter and as far as I know, Jane never knew anything about it.

A more amusing example of this sort of thing happened to Debbie Harris in July of 1996, while she was moving to a town in Florida. She was driving a U-Haul full of her household goods, and towing her car, when the front end of the truck began to shake alarmingly. So she pulled off the highway at the next exit and stopped at the first pay phone she could find to call the U-Haul service center. Lying on the phone booth shelf was a small comic-like booklet, which turned out to be a fundamentalist Christian tract warning people specifically about Seth and Jane! "Seth is a demon," the tract's cartoon angel-figure states, without qualification. Exactly the sort of thing that made Jane furious—and secretly hurt her.

A complete accident that Debbie just happened to stop at that phone booth, of course.

3. Somewhat nostalgically, I thought again of Jane's potbellied rich man appraisal while reading Rob's essay for April 20, 1982, in volume 1 of *Dreams, Evolution, and Value Fulfillment* (New York: Prentice-Hall, 1986; reprint, San Rafael, CA: Amber-Allen, 1997; page numbers refer to original edition), in which Jane dictates her justifiably indignant response to the doctors who were probing, examining, and discussing her difficulties. "Some of them talked about her right in front of her as though she weren't there," Rob notes. He quotes Jane as saying, "The particular group of young doctors I saw, the specialists, were probably the finest-looking dandies that Elmira has known. They were superlative-looking young men, dressed in the latest of fashions, and even in the hospital it was apparent that they were properly clothed in the finest of *social mores* as well. They were in their collective way like magicians, producing wonders out of the clear air, stunning you with their charming smiles and manners, trying to win you over to some strange cause. In this case it was the *operation* cause . . ." (p. 50).

Not that I disagree with Jane's assessment, exactly—it's just that I would never have thought to apply the image of *dandies*. To me such outfits were merely, well, professional work clothes, and not overdressed at all!

16 *The Fortress of Food (Or No Food)*

1. Though in her early journals, Jane notes that she's been reading some books on nutrition, and makes a list of vitamins and their various attributes and

effects. She makes no further notes along these lines after the Seth sessions begin (however, she did continue to take a selection of daily vitamins).

2. I didn't think of it until I came across these dreams, but I also have to wonder about subliminal associations I might have made between Jane and *my* mother, who was small and slender, and held back her considerable creative abilities (she was a gifted writer, particularly of humor) in a mix of fears and furies about the limits of being female, as she saw it. And so I wonder: was the enormous rage my mother felt toward Jane in part an expression of something that all *four* of us (including Marie) shared, in some sort of counterpart exchange, in which each of us acted out beliefs in a dangerous world?

3. Jane's dream and mine correlate even further than that, in an almost dizzying array of connections, none of which I knew a thing about until I compared the two while writing this memoir. In mine, Barbara and I find a place of safety in "our" grandmother's house by the riverbank (we are not biologically related). As I noted at the time I recorded the dream, this grandmother figure was a person from an actual photograph I'd seen the day before at a Dundee crafts show, where a dollmaker had demonstrated how she made doll-duplicates of people in ancestor photos. The figure who appeared in my dream was from one of these photos, a Mormon woman from the late 1800s. The dollmaker herself, my notes say, was a girl of about twenty who somewhat resembled me physically; her dolls were exquisitely rendered.

So here is the same element of "little women" as in Jane's dream, as well as the configuration that Jane objects to in her interpretation, of women being "made" into "junior adults" as she puts it (like dolls?). Except that in my dream, my writer friend Barbara and I find *safety* in the house of this "made into a doll" woman—a Mormon woman at that (implying a strict female role), and in my dream a "common ancestor," not biologically, but culturally—who offers us a refuge.

In Jane's dream, she and the "little women" find themselves in an apartment with two men, one of whom is "boorish" and mean to the women while the other reads poetry. In my dream, Barbara and I find ourselves in a gym (dream-pun?) standing near a man I knew from Dundee, a musician who used to cheerfully brag about the number of women he could "chalk up," as he put it, in get-togethers after his music gigs. So in both dreams, there's a shared element about men being "mean" as well as embodying art (poetry and music) as a male quality and using it to put women down—make them "small" (though it should be noted that Jane's dream touches on the actual meanness and psychological damage wrought by her *mother*).

Jane notes in her dream's interpretation, "So the dream shows me the sex beliefs involving creativity that have been bothering me (*Little Women* also had a young girl writer as character. Soupy!) . . . I see that I equated spontaneity with being 'a hysterical female'—and if <u>that</u> underlay my work—then I was open to ridicule and pretending to be something I wasn't." Well, "pretending to be something I wasn't" is a fear that powerfully underlies my own creative work, and thus in my dream, I look for refuge from danger—retribution for showing myself?—in a house of traditional (though here kindly) female roles. However, the grandmother thus depicted has been lovingly made into a doll in my time, and by a young girl who resembles me, no less. So perhaps the dream is showing me that I can turn traditional roles into a symbolic object that offers psychological comfort when I choose to use it. (All of which would apply to Barbara, too.)

17 *Jane in Class: A Portrait in Miniatures*

1. "Florence MacIntyre" (a pseudonym) is a featured character in *Conversations with Seth.* She often served as devil's advocate to many of the more liberal viewpoints expressed in ESP class.

2. As to this image, I very much enjoyed a dream about Jane sent to me by Anthony of Greensboro, North Carolina, who came across the Seth books in 1987 [and thus never met Jane], at about the same time he was diagnosed with thyroid cancer (from which he made a full recovery). Anthony writes, "I was curious about Jane's own thyroid problems and wondered to myself if that area of the body somehow signaled a problem with communication—a blockage of energy of some sort.

> One night I had my one and only [out-of-body]—I floated downstairs with this silver umbilical cord attached to me. I came back and observed my body on the bed and lay down into it. The entire time I felt a pulsating sensation in my forehead which vanished immediately upon re-entering my body.
>
> Then I had a long, uninterrupted dream about Jane. She was wearing a black turtleneck, looking very ebullient, healthful, carefree, and happy. We had a long discussion which took place in various locales. First, we were indoors in a living room, then in a sports car with the top down, and finally in the evening on the grass looking up at the stars.
>
> The complete message of that dream has left me now, though at the time I remember a distinct feeling of interconnectedness with all forms of life—the immensity of the universe and its beneficence overwhelmed me.

Anthony isn't the only one who dreamed of Jane wheeling around in a car (in actuality, she didn't drive, though it's an image that fits her), with all its attendant metaphors, including this one (slightly edited), from Robert Waggoner of Ames, Iowa. Robert also never met Jane (in physical reality anyway), but his dream captures something amusingly class-like about her personality:

> Dream of March 3, 1998: I'm sitting in the passenger seat of an older car (like a 1964 Ford Fairlane) that is being driven by a woman. I notice that

she is not a very good driver, as we careen over a curb heading into a parking lot. Suddenly, I notice that at the end of the parking space, we are headed for a statue of the Virgin Mary, and it looks like we are going to hit it! The driver puts on the brakes and we stop just inches short of a collision.

When I look over at the driver, I realize it's Jane Roberts, but then I think "it can't be, she's dead." Immediately I realize this is a dream. I turn to her and say, "Jane, do you know this is a lucid dream?" She smiles affirmatively. I couldn't help but notice that her front teeth were somewhat crooked.

I began to tell her how much I admired the Seth books, and how important they were and are. She talked a bit about that, but concluded with a statement that they weren't the end of the story, that there was more to it.

Suddenly I had a fantastic idea. I looked at her and asked if she could transmit the knowledge of Seth directly to me in this dream. She smiled, almost pityingly, and said it wasn't that simple; everyone had their own way, and that was the beauty of it all. I had to look within, and I'd find it there. I held her, and she told me that events interacted with different layers of time and space and lives, and in this incredible overlayment was a beautiful complexity and simplicity. I could feel the beauty of this concept.

[*Robert adds:*] I have a few comments about this lucid dream. First, "Jane" may have been a symbolic representation of my own creation, I just don't know. I thought it was hilarious on a symbolic level that her poor driving almost wiped out the statue of the Virgin Mary. In one way, I think that was a fear of her self, that she was usurping the "divine order" through the Seth material. Also, even though I'm not Catholic and the Virgin Mary has little interest for me, it does make me wonder if Jane Roberts represents for me the same idea of a female human-deity mixture, and in her driving, despoiler of the old order.

I was very much surprised by my request that she magically transfer the Seth knowledge to me in the dream. Upon awakening, that seemed totally farfetched on the one hand, and made me wonder at my sense of neediness on the other. But on another level, the request seemed like an acknowledgement of worldviews and their transference. When we talked about how time, events, space, lives, interacted and overlaid, it seemed to suggest that at certain points in life the bleedthroughs were more likely and possible, and they couldn't be easily forced. Things like that happened at their own pace and time.

I was surprised at her cool response to my praise of the Seth books. I can't remember her exact words, or if this was my succinct appraisal, but it was like she didn't think the books were the "end-all, be-all." Those are the words I recall.

And lastly, I was surprised that I didn't use this opportunity better, and instead let my lucid control/realization fade. As I went about my day, I thought of a number of things I could have done in that lucid moment.

Interestingly, about two hours after I woke up, I was driving across town looking at the street map, when I looked up and realized that all the cars had stopped except for mine—a dramatic braking stopped me from hitting a woman's car in front of me by mere inches—eerily reminiscent of the dream braking.

Well, there you have it. I really did get a good laugh out of Virgin Mary as potential road kill. Dreams are great.

3. Jane was of course pleased by the national-recognition aspect of Bach's accolades in *Time* magazine. Other mainstream publications weren't always as intelligent in their assessment of her. In her journals for August 20, 1980, Jane notes, "*Psychology Today* comes in mail with an article on *The* [*Course in*] *Miracles*—mention of me as a 'housewife in Elmira susceptible to trances.' Anyhow I've written a short enough reply. I was mad as hell after working my ass off all these years; housewife, ugh."

But other than this rocking-chair issue, I remember Jane later saying only this about Dick Bach himself, about his book, *Illusions: The Adventures of a Reluctant Messiah*, which she liked: "Just once," she remarked, "I'd like to see a story about somebody who realizes he's God and doesn't have to die for it—lives on to old age, has a riot, all kinds of sex, earthy fun, acts like he *enjoys* the goddamned place he comes to *save*."

4. Rich developed a friendship with Jane outside of class that in its way was as complex as mine. After her death, Rich served for a while as literary agent on Rob's behalf, clearing up several contract snafus from the past and researching numerous other legal matters. He also tracked down original TV and radio tapes that resulted in his publishing company's production of *The Seth Video;* and *Jane Roberts: The San Francisco Interview* (1988), from a 1975 KNBR radio program.

18 *Put Off, Piqued, and Otherwise Perturbed*

1. "Nah," Gary told me on the phone that day. "Here's the way it happened":

> I was driving down West Water Street and saw some woman hit this cat with her car. I stopped. I felt bad because this woman was so upset—it wasn't her fault; the cat ran out in the street. So I told the woman to go on. Jane came out of the house and she and I took the cat to the vet's, this in my car. We should have taken the woman [who hit the cat] with us—she wasn't fit to drive.
>
> But this was long after I'd first met Jane. I was in Corning Community College—this in 1967 or '68. [Local artist Bill Macdonell] was doing this mural and he invited me to take photos and make slides of the models posing for it. Jane and Rob posed against a white backdrop in [Bill's] studio. They were supposed to be among the disciples at the Last Supper! Ha. Bill

later projected the slides to outline his painting, which was on a wall at The Foundry, a bar in downtown Elmira. It was on the wall for many years [until the flood of '72 destroyed the bar], which I'm sure Bill got a lot of drinks for.

After that, Dan got to know Jane, maybe through [another friend]. He took me over to Jane's house later. It was a coincidence they knew each other, nothing to do with the cat.

2. All right, I'll tell you a secret: "Gary" is the father of my first child. This fact of our lives' connection (an inadvertent, rather than a romantic one), and the way his opinions dovetail with my mother's, strikes me as weirdly logical, and more than mere coincidence, in some ironic way I can't quite grasp—almost as if he and my mother were partly the same person, at least in regards to me, though this isn't exactly it either. And the nature of their objections is a mystery to me, for the most part—if this is trickery, where's the gain? If it's to sell books, there are rather more lucrative ways to do it than putting up with forty-some people crashing furniture around in your living room every Tuesday night at two dollars and fifty cents a head.

3. As to this whole issue of other-Seth claimants, Seth had this to say in a February 5, 1969, session:

> Now Ruburt's ego, so hard to win over, is now up in arms because it regards me as its exclusive property. It need not worry. It took me long enough in your terms to set up our communications, and our [reincarnational] relationships in the past helped in this behalf. It is quite natural that others in your acquaintanceship who are experimenting should go through a stage in which it seems to them that they are receiving information from me.
>
> Suggestion operates, and any trance deeper than ordinary for them can be interpreted in these terms . . . The material is like a touchstone from which other creations may flow.
>
> Thoughts and emotions form, of their own electromagnetic reality, vitalized products called atoms and molecules . . . To some very valid extent in our sessions, changes occur then within Ruburt's physical organism, for in responding to my communications, electromagnetic alterations are therefore inevitable. You have however more of a merging. I do not for example completely take over. There is a complimentary merging with my patterns, however, predominating mentally and psychically, and to a certain extent emotionally.
>
> On the one hand his personality is enlarged in that the self structure includes far more perceptions than ordinarily. Further actions are recognized and interpreted. The speaking systems, however, and mental faculties have to be trained to handle the additional data; this of course causing some distortions along the way. They are unavoidable. The emotional system of the

medium must also learn to handle further stimuli, and then also learn to do so in such a way that balance is maintained.

Another dimension in your terms is simply added, a more extensive one, and when this is done properly, as I have tried to do, then the medium's personality is not only strengthened but its abilities used far above the usual [norm]. The process however is highly involved with perception, and is largely a matter in learning to handle, recognize, and use constructively perceptions that other personalities are not equipped to handle.

When you see what Ruburt can do occasionally, and the troubles I can have with distortion, then you can be sure that I would not double or triple the chances for distortion by attempting to speak through anyone else. He need not worry. Besides, I like him too well.

There is also something else that he seems to have forgotten—that your own relationships, yours and Ruburt's, and the relationships between us in the [reincarnational] past, do much to make our communication possible. You transmit also, or rather you act as a transmitter whether you are at a session or not. So unless there is another *identical* Ruburt and Joseph combination, I am stuck with you.

On the same subject, in her "Magical Approach" manuscript for August 10, 1980, Jane writes:

[After a two-month session layoff] I was impressed anew by Seth's immediacy. Boom a lay boom a lay boomalay boom—there he was again, as clear as ever, as if there had been no break at all. And he was obviously ready with a new body of material, in another attempt to extend the framework of our understanding and perception. I thought of the many imitators (Seth mimics, I call them) who seemingly have sprung up in so many places. Then as well as now hardly a week's correspondence goes by without some contact from someone who "speaks for Seth" . . .

In *Adventures in Consciousness* I explained what I think happens in such cases and stressed the creativity of such episodes—as the psyche personifies itself, using Seth as a symbol. But the difference in quality of material is so drastic (at least according to what I have seen or heard) that Seth's originality has come home to me in an even clearer fashion.

Then too, sometimes chicanery *is* involved by people with some psychic ability who haven't the knack of originality and who aren't honest with themselves. Today, again . . . I think of the tape of "Seth on Death" that a fan just sent me: an embarrassing display by a trance personality who pretends he's my Seth—and gives seminars at 45 dollars a head. These people who have "great respect" for me, use Seth's name, identify him as the writer of our books, then say that people will have to make up their own minds about the issue. They *don't* mention that I've informed them that "their

Seth isn't mine," but their material is so mediocre that I'm astonished they find anyone to listen.

4. And Debbie had some out-of-the-ordinary travel tales to tell. Among other adventures, Debbie sailed with a friend around the Mediterranean to ports in Sicily, Greece, Crete, Turkey, Cyprus, Syria, Lebanon, and Egypt; met the poet Robert Graves in Majorca; taught school in Chiang Mai, Thailand; and backpacked her way through Burma, India, and Kathmandu, as well as many other countries and hair-raising odysseys. A student of esoteric literature, t'ai chi, and astrology, Debbie looked up Jane's books after two friends on separate occasions said to her, "If you like Don Juan, you'll *love* Seth."

5. *On Broken Glass: Loving and Losing John Gardner* (New York: Carroll and Graf, 2000).

6. Susan notes in her memoir: "I loved it that [John] was interested in psychic phenomena and ESP. For several years I'd kept a dream notebook, writing down my dreams each morning. When [John and I] got to know each other better he looked at me with that piercing gaze and scolded: 'A waste of a great artistic intelligence.'" (Ironically, when Gardner died in 1982, Jane said to me, "You know, he interested Rob and me a lot; my god, he had terrific output, though I thought he used his intuitions in a funny way, compartmentalizing them, or something like that.")

Susan adds, "I still kept track of my dreams, and that summer of 1979 recorded an odd one: 'Dreamed about John Gardner (this after following him around tongue-tied for four days [at Bread Loaf], wide-eyed and silent like a calf), [that] he looked right at me and said, 'Look here, Susan, it's all very well to be modest but you're boring as hell. Can't you just contradict me once in a while?'"

7. In *The Seth Phenomena* video, Rob says, "I calculated the hours that Seth actually spent dictating [*Seth Speaks*], and . . . it was something like two weeks' work to produce a book that, I believe, is between four and five hundred pages long. That shows you the command of the language and the clarity of thinking that Seth, speaking through Jane, could demonstrate, which is incredible. Because when Jane and I, either one of us wrote a manuscript, we slaved over it, you know, three or four drafts, or whatever it took to finish it. And here Seth would sit down, Jane would go into trance very easily, and he'd start dictating chapter whatever on that book, word for word, first draft—finished draft, and that was it."

Rob adds, "But we also used our critical judgment, and understood that he was saying some excellent things there. It just wasn't the speed and ease with which the book was being produced, it was what he was saying in the book that was so intriguing to us.

"We wanted to present the material as it happened, literally. We did not want to excise it from everything else in our lives, so that it was off to one side, and dry and unemotional. We wanted to show others, if they were at all interested, how this happened, and give some insight into why it happened and where it could lead. So putting in [my] notes was automatic right from the beginning. It involved a lot of research, which I usually did later. See. I might spend a year doing the research, Jane would produce the book in two weeks! How do you reconcile *that?*"

8. In her unfinished "Aspects" manuscript on August 5, 1975, Jane asks herself:

> Does [Seth] then represent the great portions of the psyche that we have hidden from ourselves as we pursued the one-line level of consciousness; because those portions were too big to fit our puny concepts of reality? Only now and then those portions emerge, take psychological form, and speak, and by their very existence point out the fact that we inhabit only the surfaces of ourselves, like tiny insects hovering above the great oceans of our own souls.
>
> Maybe I had to isolate Seth, for myself, but also for others; so that we could view our own greater dimensions . . . under conditions bizarre enough in themselves to mock our usual concepts of the self.

19 *The Symptoms and How They Grew*

1. As to the past influencing Jane's physical condition in later life, Jane herself understood, and agreed, that this wouldn't occur without her consent. About this, Rob says in volume 1 of *Dreams, Evolution, and Value Fulfillment:*

> I think that Marie's domineering rage at the world (chosen by her, never forget) deeply penetrated Jane's developing psyche and . . . caused her to set up repressive, protective inner barriers that could be activated and transformed into physical signs at any time, under certain circumstances. Out of many possibilities, [Jane's] conditioning was psychically chosen and accepted, and through that focus she meant to interact with the mother's behavior. This . . . is an example of the way a course of probable activity can be agreed upon by all involved.
>
> In Framework 2 [a reference to inner reality, the creative source from which we form all events], for example, Marie, pregnant with Jane, could have decided with her daughter-to-be upon certain sequences of action to be pursued during their lives. Or in Framework 2 the two of them could have cooperated upon such a decision before *Marie's* birth, even. If reincarnation is to be considered, their disturbed relationship this time might reflect past connections of a different yet analogous nature, and may also have important effects upon any future ones.
>
> Additionally, Jane could have chosen the present relationship to eventually help her temper her reception of and reaction to the Seth material, making her extra-cautious; this, even though she'd seen to it ahead of time

that she would be born with that certain combination of fortitude and innocence necessary for her to press on with her chosen abilities (pp. 76–78).

2. *The Magical Approach*, p. 59.

3. However discouraged Jane must have felt about her appearance, in this two-part article, published in the *Voice* October 9 and 10, 1978, she and Rob speak with gusto and affection about their life and work. At one point reporter Jim Poett asks Jane, "What does Seth think of you?"

> "Oh, he thinks I'm a nice kid. He thinks I'm gifted."
>
> "That's the good part," Rob said.
>
> "Otherwise, he thinks I'm very stubborn, have a lot to learn. I don't know, hon, what does he think of me?"
>
> "He thinks sometimes you choose to pay attention to what he says," Rob said, "and sometimes you don't."
>
> "If he didn't treat me with respect," Jane said, "that would [have been] it."

4. From Jane's journals, Saturday morning, June 26, 1976.

5. A number of people, most of whom had never met Jane, sent me copies of dreams in which they'd attempted to help her with her difficulties—a nice turnaround, to say the least. Many of these dreams contain details that appear to pick up on events both physical and psychological in Jane's life. For example, Shelly, a fan from the Midwest, wrote to me about this one from September of 1982 (the dream itself is undated):

> The first I remember of the dream is seeing a woman with light wavy hair well covered by a wide-brimmed straw hat identifying herself as your mother handing me a hardbound copy of your book, smiling and suggesting I look to the middle of the book where I could find your autograph. Imagine my surprise when I [later] read that you were selling autographed [copies of] *Conversations with Seth*, like the one I received in my dream.
>
> [Then] I saw Jane, but not as she looks in the pictures in her books but as a young boyish man with coal black hair [that was] short and coming to a point in the middle of his forehead. She had very large dark eyes, made up rather theatrically with black shading and with the expression of very intense and pointed concentration. She was dressed in a 20s or 30s lightly striped dark suit.
>
> I should interject here that I am in an automobile-related business so I believe [that is why] I used a car symbol in this dream. I was showing Jane the things to look for in buying a fine old Bentley automobile; particu-

> larly showing her that the door hinges were all outfitted with grease fittings so that the oil kept the doors swinging freely. When I read about Jane having trouble with her joints I saw the connection of the door hinges.
>
> I feel that perhaps Jane is feeling rather hemmed in by too much publicity and people leaning on her for more intellectual, spiritual, and psychic information, to the point that she feels like she is losing her freedom, and this is a reflection of that loss as well as a stubborn determination to produce what and when she wants. Not to be forced into creative endeavors. Too much to ask of an artist. Too much to ask of anyone! That is all, really; I don't spend much of my time thinking about other people's lives, and would not appreciate some unknown person to me examining my problems . . .

This dream-image of the oiled car door hinges is an interesting one, connecting as it does to the idea of freedom—of doors swinging freely open, of the implied freedom of the awaiting vehicle (similar to the other car dreams in previous endnotes). I also like Shelly's take on Jane as the young "boyish man" with pointy black hair and theatrical makeup—there's a certain psychological concision about that image, and a connection with the get-up she put on for the cross-dressing class, described in chapter 9, "The Naked and the Dread," of *Conversations*: "A black beret tilted jauntily on her dark hair, and all was topped off by a heavily drawn-on Vandyke beard that gave her the all-round appearance of a rakish Frenchman." Of course Shelly had read *Conversations* by the time of her dream, but it's an interesting, and subjectively accurate, use of imagery.

Also, her dream description of the woman she sees as my mother (who had dark hair) is, interestingly, a more accurate description of me, including the wide-brimmed straw hat, which I used to wear, at the time of this dream, while gardening.

6. "He" and "Ruburt " refer, again, to Jane. That this voice speaking for Jane's "strong drives for creativity" also referred to her as "him," as did Seth, seems to me indicative of the central wellspring, or focus, from which she derived her powerful and diverse abilities.

20 *The Hospital and Beyond*

1. As Rob admits in his notes for *The Way Toward Health*. "I was evidently so numb," he writes on August 30, 1984, "from repeated doses of fear and concern and negativity and Jane's worsening situation daily, that I couldn't react [to Jane's assertion that she wasn't going to die yet]. I didn't believe or disbelieve it. I was afraid to hope, perhaps" (p. 359).

2. Debbie's journal notes of her visits to Jane are too lengthy to reproduce in their entirety here, sadly. As is true of most diarists, Debbie was not writing

for anyone else, and thus her style is straightforward and genuine and conveys an understated, accumulating drama that is quite hair-raising. With Debbie's permission, I have sent a complete copy of these records to the Yale archives, along with a copy of her immense, scholarly manuscript titled *Seth On Dreams* that she worked on for more than three years, completing it in 1995. This is a 500-plus page, fully indexed compilation of everything Seth had to say in published books up to that point about dreams and the dream state. A frustrating permissions snafu currently prevents its publication.

3. On the other hand, it could be noisy—as the following experience sent to me by David of Wooster, Ohio, might append. David never met Jane and knew her only through postcard replies to his letters. "She responded with encouragement to my poems, assured me that the poems were originals, and that I had made the Seth/Jane work my own," he wrote. "She encouraged me to continue writing and to believe in my own work." He goes on to relate the following:

> Now, a strange little tale. In August of 1984, I had a bicycle "accident"—collision—and was in the hospital for a few days. The whole thing was a time for new directions and a reassessment of my goals. During the collision I had an out-of-body and remembered little when I awoke but felt that friends in inner realities were helping me remember the goals I had set for myself this lifetime. During the trip to the hospital my blood pressure was near zero, while I willed myself to maintain my new-found focus. So while Jane was on her way out, I was becoming more and more in the here and now.
>
> Anyway—I believe this dramatic event and the focusing of my intent enabled me to catch Jane on her exit. I saw her rocketing off the planet towards dimensions unknown, but what was startling and exhilarating to watch was the *reckless glee* she showed soaring to new adventures. I felt she was feeling an effervescent joy that she couldn't contain if she tried.
>
> That's all I saw—Jane, like a comet rock and rolling to something new, but laughing and roaring, like lightning playing . . .

4. *Garden Madness: The Unpruned Truth About a Blooming Passion* (Golden, Colorado: Fulcrum, 1995).

Index

Other Books of Interest from Moment Point Press

Conversations with Seth
the story of Jane Roberts's
ESP class
Susan M. Watkins

Three Classics in Consciousness By
Jane Roberts
Adventures in Consciousness
Psychic Politics
The God of Jane

Consciously Creating Each Day
a 365 day perpetual calendar of
spirited thought
from voices past and present
Susan Ray, editor

Lessons from the Light
what we can learn from
the near-death experience
Kenneth Ring, Ph.D.

Mind into Matter
a new alchemy of
science and spirit
Fred Alan Wolf, Ph.D.